GREAT AMERICAN TRAVEL WRITINGS

GREAT AMERICAN TRAVEL WRITINGS

A JOURNEY AROUND AMERICA

MALLARD PRESS

An Imprint of BDD Promotional Book Company, Inc.
666 Fifth Avenue, New York, N.Y. 10103

This edition first published in the United States of America in 1990 by
The Mallard Press

By arrangement with The Octopus Group Limited

'Mallard Press and its accompanying design and logo are trademarks of BDD
Promotional Book Company, Inc.'

Copyright © 1990 Arrangement by The Octopus Group Limited

ISBN 0 792 45358 1

Contents

New England Vignettes

NATHANIEL HAWTHORNE

The following passages from Nathaniel Hawthorne's
American Notebook *(1841–1852) chronicle his thoughts*
and impressions of the town Augusta in Maine and Walden
Pond, New Hampshire.

THURSDAY, JULY 20TH.

A ride, yesterday afternoon, to a pond in the vicinity of Augusta, about nine miles off, to fish for white perch. Remarkables—the steering of the boat through the crooked, labyrinthine brook, into the open pond,— the man who acted as pilot, his talking with Bridge about politics, the bank, the iron money of a 'man who came in to reign, in Greece, over a city called Sparta' &c. his advice to Bridge to come amongst the laborers on the Mill-Dam, because it stimulated them to see a man 'grinning' amongst them. The man took hearty tugs at a bottle of Scotch and whiskey, as did Bridge also and all became pretty merry, especially the pilot. Fish caught—the yellow perch, which are not esteemed for eating; the white perch, a beautiful silvery, broad, round-backed fish, which bites eagerly, runs about with the line, while being pulled up, makes good sport, and an admirable dish—a great chub, and three horned pouts, which swallow the hook into their lowest entrails. Caught several dozen fish in an hour or two, and returned to the store where we had left our horse and wagon, the pilot making strange eccentricities in our rear. At the store we found five or six people, whom Bridge treated twice round with gin and brandy, we also drinking in all good fellowship. Scene, a small dingy store, dimly lighted by a single inch of candle, faintly disclosing various boxes, barrels standing on end, articles hanging from the cieling [sic]; the proprietor at the counter, whereon appears the said gin and brandy, respectively contained in a tin pint measure and an earthen-ware jug, with two or three tumblers beside them, out of which nearly all the party respectively drank. Some coming up to the counter frankly, others lingering in the back-ground, waiting to be pressed, two paying for their own liquor and withdrawing. Myself smoking a most vile American cigar; the pilot, after drinking his brandy, giving a history of our fishing expedition, and how many and how large fish we caught, and how we drank; Bridge making acquaintances and renewing them, and gaining great credit for liberality and free-heartedness; two or three boys looking on and listening to the talk;—the storekeeper smiling behind his counter, with the tarnished tin scales beside him; the inch of candle burned down almost to extinction. So we get into our wagon with the fish, and ride to Robinson's tavern, about five miles off, where we sup and pass the night. In the bar-room a fat old countryman on a journey, and a quack doctor of the vicinity, an Englishman, with a peculiar accent. Seeing Bridges jointed and brass-mounted fishing-pole, he took it for a theodolite and supposed that we had been on a surveying expedition. At supper (which consisted of bread, butter, cheese, cake, dough-nuts, gooseberry-pie &c) waited upon by a tall, very tall woman, young and maiden-looking, yet with a strongly outlined and determined face. Afterwards found her to be the wife of mine host. She poured out our tea, came in when we rang the table-bell, to refill our cups, and again retired. While at supper, the fat old traveller was ushered through the room into a contiguous bedroom. My own chamber, apparently the best in the house, its walls ornamented with a small gilt-framed, foot-square looking-glass, with a hair-brush hanging beneath it; a record of the deaths of the family, written on the blank tomb, in an engraving, where a father, mother, and child were represented in a grave-yard, weeping over said tomb; the mourners dressed in black, country-cut clothes; the engraving done in Vermont. A wood engraving of the declaration of Independence, with facsimiles of the autographs; a portrait of the Empress Josephine and another of Spring. In the two closets of the chamber were mine hostesse's cloak, best bonnet, and go-to-meeting apparel. A good bed, in which I slept tolerably well, and rising betimes, ate breakfast, consisting of some of our fish, and started for Augusta. The fat old traveller had gone off with the harness of our wagon, which the hostler had put on to his horse by mistake. The tavern keeper gave us his own harness, and started in pursuit of the old man, who was probably aware of the exchange, and well satisfied with it.

Our ride to Augusta, six or seven miles, was very pleasant; a heavy rain having fallen during the night, and laid the oppressive dust of the day before. Our road lay parallel with the Kennebec, of which we occasionally had near glimpses. The country swells back from the river in hills and ridges, without any interval of level ground; there were frequent woods, filling up the vallies [sic] or framing the summits; the land is good, the farms look neat, and the houses comfortable. The latter are generally of but one story, but with large barns; and it was a good sign, that while we saw no houses unfinished, or out of repair, one man, at least, had found it expedient to make an addition to his dwelling. At the distance of more than two miles, had a view of white Augusta, with its steeples, and the State-house at the farther end of the town. Observable matters along the road, the stage, all the dust of yesterday brushed off, and no new contracted; full of passengers inside and out; among them some gentlemanly people and pretty girls, all looking fresh, unsoiled, rosy, cheerful, and their curiosity as to the face of of [sic] the country, the faces of passing travellers, and the incidents of their journey, not yet damped, in the morning sunshine, by long miles of jolting over rough and hilly roads; to compare this with their appearance in mid-day, and as they drive into Bangor at dusk. Two women driving along in a wagon, and with a child—rattling pretty speedily down hill. People looking at us from their open doors and windows; the children, perhaps staring from the wayside; the mowers stopping, for a moment, the sway of their scythes; the matron of a family, indistinctly seen some distance within the house, her head and shoulders appearing through the window—perhaps drawing her handkerchief over her bosom, which had been uncovered to give the baby its breakfast;—the said baby, or its immediate predecessor, sitting at the door, turning round to crawl away on all fours. Yesterday, a man building a flat-bottomed boat by the roadside; he talked with Bridge about the boundary question, and swore fervently in favor of driving the British 'into Hell's kitchen' by main force.

Colonel Boardman, the engineer of the Mill-Dam, is now here, after about a fortnight's absence. A plain, country-squire looking [man?] with a figure but with rather a ponderous brow; a rough complexion; a gait, and general rigidity of manner, something like a schoolmaster. He originated in a country town, and is a self-educated man. As he walked down the gravel-walk, to-day after dinner, he took up a scythe, which one of the mowers had left in the sward, and began to mow, with quite a scientific swing. On the coming of the mower, he laid it down, perhaps a little ashamed of his amusement. I was interested in this—to see an eminent man, after twenty-five years of scientific occupation, thus trying whether his arms retained their strength and skill for the labors of his youth—mindful of the days when he wore striped trowsers and toiled and sweated in his shirt-sleeves—and now tasting again, for pastime, this toil beneath a fervid sun. He stood awhile looking at the mowers, and then went to oversee the laborers at the Mill-Dam.

OCTOBER 6TH. FRIDAY

Yesterday afternoon (leaving wifie with my sister Louisa, who has been with us two or three days) I took a solitary walk to Walden Pond. It was a cool, north-west windy day, with heavy clouds rolling and tumbling about the sky, but still a prevalence of genial autumn sunshine. The fields are still green, and the great masses of the woods have not yet assumed their many-colored garments; but here and there, are solitary oaks of a deep, substantial red, or maples of a more brilliant hue, or chesnuts[sic], either yellow or of a tenderer green than in summer. Some trees seem to return to their hue of May or early June, before they put on the brighter autumnal tints. In some places, along the borders of low and moist land, a whole range of trees were clothed in the perfect gorgeousness of autumn, of all shades of brilliant color, looking like the palette on which Nature was arranging the tints wherewith to paint a picture. These hues appeared to be thrown together without design; and yet there was perfect harmony among them, and a softness and delicacy made up of a thousand different brightnesses. There is not, I think, so much contrast among these colors as might at first appear; the more you consider them, the more they seem to have one element among them all—which is the reason that the most brilliant display of them soothes the observer, instead of of [*sic*] exciting him. And I know not whether it be a moral effect, or a physical one operating merely on the eye, but it is a pensive gaiety, which causes a sigh often, but never a smile. We never fancy, for instance, that these gaily-clad trees should be changed into young damsels in holiday attire, and betake themselves to dancing on the plain. If they were to undergo such a transformation, they would surely arrange themselves in a funeral procession, and go sadly along with their purple, and scarlet, and golden garments trailing over the withering grass. When the sunshine falls upon them, they seem to smile; but it is as if they were heartbroken. But it is in vain for me to attempt to describe these autumnal brilliances, or to convey the impression which they make on me. I have tried a thousand times, and always without the slightest self-satisfaction. Luckily, there is no need of such a record; for Nature renews the scene, year after year; and even when we shall have passed away from the world, we can spiritually create these scenes; so that we may dispense now and hereafter with all further efforts to put them into words.

Walden Pond was clear and beautiful, as usual. It tempted me to bathe; and though the water was thrillingly cold, it was like the thrill of a happy death. Never was there such transparent water as this. I threw sticks into it, and saw them float suspended on an almost invisible medium; it seemed as if the pure air was beneath them, as well as above. If I were to be baptized, it should be in this pond; but then one would not wish to pollute it by washing off his sins into it. None but angels should bathe there. It would be a fit bathing-place for my little wife; and sometimes or other, I hope, our blessed baby shall be dipt into its bosom.

In a small and secluded dell, that opens upon the most beautiful cove of the whole lake, there is a little hamlet of huts or shanties, inhabited by the Irish people who are at work upon the rail-road. There are three or four of these habitations, the very rudest, I should imagine, that civilized men ever made for themselves, constructed of rough boards, with protruding ends. Against some of them the earth is heaped up to the roof, or nearly so; and when the grass has had time to sprout upon them, they will look like small natural hillocks, or a species of ant-hill, or something in which Nature has a larger share than man. These huts are placed beneath the trees (oaks, walnuts, and white pines) wherever the trunks give them space to stand; and by thus adapting themselves to natural interstices instead of making new ones, they do not break or disturb the solitude and seclusion of the place. Voices are heard, and the shouts and laughter of children, who play about like the sunbeams that come down through the branches. Women are washing beneath the trees, and long lines of whitened clothes are extended from tree to tree, fluttering and gambolling in the breeze. A pig, in a stye [sic] even more extemporary than the shanties, is grunting, and poking his snout through the clefts of his habitation. The household pots and kettles are seen at the doors, and a glance within shows the rough benches that serve for chairs, and the bed upon the floor. The visiter's [sic] nose takes note of the fragrance of a pipe. And yet, with all these homely items, the repose and sanctity of the old wood do not seem to be destroyed or prophaned; she overshadows these poor people, and assimilates them, somehow or other, to the character of her natural inhabitants. Their presence did not shock me, any more than if I had merely discovered a squirrel's nest in a tree. To be sure, it is a torment to see the great, high, ugly embankment of the railroad, which is here protruding itself into the lake, or along its margin, in close vicinity to this picturesque little hamlet. I have seldom seen anything more beautiful than the cove, on the border of which the huts are situated; and the more I looked, the lovelier it grew. The trees overshadowed it deeply; but on one side there was some brilliant shrubbery which seemed to light up the whole picture with the effect of a sweet and melancholy smile. I felt as if spirits were there—or as if these shrubs had a spiritual life—in short, the impression was undefinable; and after gazing and musing a good while, I retraced my steps through the Irish hamlet, and plodded along a wood-path.

According to my invariable custom, I mistook my way, and emerging upon a road, I turned my back, instead of my face, towards Concord, and walked on very diligently, till a guide-board informed me of my mistake. I then turned about, and was shortly overtaken by an old yeoman in a chaise, who kindly offered me a ride, and shortly set me down in the village.

Cape Cod

HENRY DAVID THOREAU

Henry David Thoreau's perceptions of the natural wonders of Cape Cod are vividly recorded in this extract from his work on the area Cape Cod *(1865).*

WHAT ARE SPRINGS and waterfalls? Here is the spring of springs, the waterfall of waterfalls. A storm in the fall or winter is the time to visit it; a light-house or a fisherman's hut the true hotel. A man may stand there and put all America behind him.

Wishing to get a better view than I had yet of the ocean, which, we are told, covers more than two thirds of the globe, but of which a man who lives a few miles inland may never see any trace, more than of another world, I made a visit to Cape Cod in October, 1849, another the succeeding June, and another to Truro in July 1855; the first and last time with a single companion, the second time alone. I have spent, in all, about three weeks on the Cape; walked from Eastham to Province-town twice on the Atlantic side, and once on the Bay side also, excepting four or five miles, and crossed the Cape half a dozen times on my way; but having come so fresh to the sea, I have got but little salted. My readers must expect only so much saltness as the land breeze acquires from blowing over an arm of the sea, or is tasted on the windows and the bark of trees twenty miles inland, after September gales. I have been accustomed to make excursions to the ponds within ten miles of Concord, but latterly I have extended my excursions to the seashore.

I did not see why I might not make a book on Cape Cod, as well as my neighbor on 'Human Culture.' It is but another name for the same thing, and hardly a sandier phase of it. As for my title, I suppose that the word Cape is from the French cap; which is from the Latin caput, a head; which is, perhaps, from the verb capere, to take,—that being the part by which we take hold of a thing:—Take Time by the forelock. It is also the safest part to take a serpent by. And as for Cod, that was derived directly from that 'great store of codfish' which Captain Bartholomew Gosnold caught there in 1602; which fish appears to have been so called from the Saxon word codde, 'a case in which seeds are lodged' either from the form of the fish, or the quantity of spawn it contains; whence also, perhaps, codling ('pomum coctile'?) and coddle,—to cook like green peas. (V. Dic.)

Cape Cod is the bared and bended arm of Massachusetts: the shoulder is at Buzzard's Bay; the elbow, or crazy-bone, at Cape Mallebarre; the wrist at Truro; and the sandy fist at Provincetown,—behind which the State stands on her guard, with her back to the Green Mountains, and her feet planted on the floor of the ocean, like an athlete protecting her Bay,—boxing with northeast storms, and, ever and anon, heaving up her Atlantic adversary from the lap of earth,—ready to thrust forward her other fist, which keeps guard the while upon her breast at Cape Ann.

On studying the map, I saw that there must be an uninterrupted beach on the east or outside of the forearm of the Cape, more than thirty miles from the general line of the coast, which would afford a good sea view, but that, on account of an opening in the beach, forming the entrance to Nauset Harbor, in Orleans, I must strike it in Eastham, if I approached it by land, and probably I could walk thence straight to Race Point, about twenty-eight miles, and not meet with any obstruction ...

At length we reached the seemingly retreating boundary of the plain, and entered what had appeared at a distance an upland marsh, but proved to be dry sand covered with Beachgrass, the Bearberry, Bayberry, Shrub-oaks, and Beach-plum, slightly ascending as we approached the shore; then, crossing over a belt of sand on which nothing grew, though the roar of the sea sounded scarcely louder than before, and we were prepared to go half a mile farther, we suddenly stood on the edge of a bluff overlooking the Atlantic. Far below us was the beach, from half a dozen to a dozen rods in width, with a long line of breakers rushing to the strand. The sea was exceedingly dark and stormy, the sky completely overcast, the clouds still dropping rain, and the wind seemed to blow not so much as the exciting cause, as from sympathy with the already agitated ocean. The waves broke on the bars at some distance from the shore, and curving green or yellow as if over so many unseen dams, ten or twelve feet high, like a thousand waterfalls, rolled in foam to the sand. There was nothing but that savage ocean between us and Europe.

Having got down the bank, and as close to the water as we could, where the sand was the hardest, leaving the Nauset Lights behind us, we began to walk leisurely up the beach, in a northwest direction, toward Provincetown, which was about twenty-five miles distant, still sailing under our umbrellas with a strong aft wind, admiring in silence, as we walked, the great force of the ocean stream ... The white breakers were rushing to the shore; the foam ran up the sand, and then ran back as far as we could see (and we imagined how much farther along the Atlantic coast, before and behind us), as regularly, to compare great things with small, as the master of a choir beats time with his white wand; and ever and anon a higher wave caused us hastily to deviate from our path, and we looked back on our tracks filled with water and foam. The breakers looked like droves of a thousand wild horses of Neptune, rushing to the shore, with their white manes streaming far behind; and when, at length, the sun shone for a moment, their manes were rainbow-tinted. Also, the long kelp-weed was tossed up from time to time, like the tails of sea-cows sporting in the brine.

There was not a sail in sight, and we saw none that day,—for they had all sought harbors in the late storm, and had not been able to get out again; and the only human beings whom we saw on the surface we overlooked the greater part of the Cape. In short, we were traversing a desert, with the view of an autumnal landscape of extraordinary brilliancy, a sort of Promised Land, on the one hand, and the ocean on the other. Yet, though the prospect was so extensive, and the country for the most part destitute of trees, a house was rarely visible,—we never saw one from the beach,—and the solitude was that of the ocean and the desert combined. A thousand men could not have seriously interrupted it, but would have been lost in the vastness of the scenery as their footsteps in the sand.

The whole coast is so free from rocks, that we saw but one or two for more than twenty miles. The sand was soft like the beach, and trying to the eyes, when the sun shone. A few piles of drift-wood, which some wreckers had painfully brought up the bank and stacked up there to dry, being the only objects in the desert, looked indefinitely large and distant, even like wigwams, though, when we stood near them, they proved to be insignificant little 'jags' of wood.

For sixteen miles, commencing at the Nauset. Lights, the bank held its height, though farther north it was not so level as here, but interrupted by slight hollows, and the patches of Beach-grass and Bayberry frequently crept into the sand to its edge. There are some pages entitled 'A Description of the Eastern Coast of the County of Barnstable' printed in 1802, pointing out the spots on which the Trustees of the Humane Society have erected huts called Charity of Humane Houses, 'and other places where shipwrecked seamen may look for shelter.' Two thousand copies of this were dispersed, that every vessel which frequented this coast might be provided with one. I have read this Shipwrecked Seaman's Manual with a melancholy kind of interest,—for the sound of the surf, or, you might say, the moaning of the sea, is heard all through it, as if its author were the sole survivor of a shipwreck himself. Of this part of the coast he says: 'This highland approaches the ocean with steep and lofty banks, which it is extremely difficult to climb, especially in a storm. In violent tempests, during very high tides, the sea breaks against the foot of them, rendering it then unsafe to walk on the strand which lies between them and the ocean. Should the seaman succeed in his attempt to ascend them, he must forbear to penetrate into the country, as houses are generally so remote that they would escape his research during the night; he must pass on to the valleys by which the banks are intersected. These valleys, which the inhabitants call

Hollows, run at right angles with the shore, and in the middle or lowest part of them a road leads from the dwelling-houses to the sea.' By the word road must not always be understood a visible cart-track.

There were these two roads for us,—an upper and a lower one,—the bank and the beach; both stretching twenty-eight miles northwest, from Nauset Harbor to Race Point, without a single opening into the beach, and with hardly a serious interruption of the desert. If you were to ford the narrow and shallow inlet at Nauset Harbor, where there is not more than eight feet of water on the bar at full sea, you might walk ten or twelve miles farther, which would make a beach forty miles along,—and the bank and beach, on the east side of Nantucket, are but a continuation of these. I was comparatively satisfied. There I had got the Cape under me, as much as if I were riding it bare-backed. It was not as on the map, or seen from the stage-coach; but there I found it all out of doors, huge and real, Cape Cod! as it cannot be represented on a map, color it as you will; the thing itself, than which there is nothing more like it, no truer picture or account; which you cannot go farther and see. I cannot remember what I thought before that it was. They commonly celebrate those beaches only which have a hotel on them, not those which have a humane house alone. But I wished to see that seashore where man's works are wrecks; to put up at the true Atlantic House, where the ocean is land-lord as well as sea-lord, and comes ashore without a wharf for the landing; where the crumbling land is the only invalid, or at best is but dry land, and that is all you can say of it.

We walked on quite at our leisure, now on the beach, now on the bank,—sitting from time to time on some damp log, maple or yellow birch, which had long followed the seas, but had now at last settled on land; or under the lee of a sand-hill, on the bank, that we might gaze steadily on the ocean. The bank was so steep, that, where there was no danger of its caving, we sat on its edge as on a bench. It was difficult for us landsmen to look out over the ocean without imagining land in the horizon; yet the clouds appeared to hang low over it, and rest on the water as they never do on the land, perhaps on account of the great distance to which we saw. The sand was not without advantage, for, though it was 'heavy' walking in it, it was soft to the feet; and, notwithstanding that it had been raining nearly two days, when it held up for half an hour, the sides of the sand-hills, which were porous and sliding, afforded a dry seat. All the aspects of this desert are beautiful, whether you behold it in fair weather or foul, or when the sun is just breaking out after a storm, and shining on its moist surface in the distance, it is so white, and pure, and level, and each slight inequality and track is so distinctly revealed; and when your eyes slide off this, they fall on the ocean. In summer the mackerel gulls—which here have their nests among the neighbouring sand-hills—pursue the traveller anxiously, now and then diving close to his head with a squeak, and he may see them, like swallows, chase some crown which has been feeding on the beach, almost across the Cape.

Though for some time I have not spoken of the roaring of the breakers, and the ceaseless flux and reflux of the waves, yet they did not for a moment cease to dash and roar, with such a tumult that, if you had been there, you could scarcely have heard my voice the while; and they are dashing and roaring this very moment, though it may be with less din and violence, for there the sea never rests. We were wholly absorbed by this spectacle and tumult, and like Chryses, though in a different mood from him, we walked silent along the shore of the resounding sea . . .

The attention of those who frequent the camp-meetings at Eastham is said to be divided between the preaching of the Methodists and the preaching of the billows on the back side of the Cape, for they all stream over here in the course of their stay. I trust that in this case the loudest voice carries it. With what effect may we suppose the ocean to say, 'My hearers!' to the multitude on the bank! On that side some John N. Maffit; on this, the Reverend Poluphloisboios Thalassa.

There was but little weed cast up here, and that kelp chiefly, there being scarcely a rock for rockweed to adhere to. Who has not had a vision from some vessel's deck, when he had still his landlegs on, of this great brown apron, drifting half upright, and quite submerged through the green water, clasping a stone or a deep-sea mussel in its unearthly fingers? I have seen it carrying a stone half as large as my head. We sometimes watched a mass of this cable-like weed, as it was tossed up on the crest of a breaker, waiting with interest to see it come in, as if there was some treasure buoyed up by it; but we were always surprised and disappointed at the insignificance of the mass which had attracted us. As we looked out over the water, the smallest objects floating on it appeared indefinitely large, we were so impressed by the vastness of the ocean, and each one bore so large a proportion to the whole ocean, which we saw. We were so often disappointed in the size of such things as came ashore, the ridiculous bits of wood or weed, with which the ocean labored, that we began to doubt whether the Atlantic itself would bear a still closer inspection, and would not turn out to be but a small pond, if it should come ashore to us. This kelp, oar-weed, tangle, devil's-apron, sole-leather, or ribbon-weed,—as various species are called,—appeared to us a singularly marine and fabulous product, a fit invention for Neptune to adorn his car with, or a freak of Proteus. All that is told of the sea has a fabulous sound to an inhabitant of the land, and all its products have a certain fabulous quality, as if they belonged to another planet, from sea-weed to a sailor's yarn, or a fish-story. In this element the animal and vegetable kingdoms meet and are strangely mingled. One species of kelp, according to Bory St. Vincent, has a stem fifteen hundred feet long, and hence is the longest vegetable known, and a brig's crew spent two days to no purpose collecting the trunks of another kind cast ashore on the Falkland Islands, mistaking it for drift-wood. (See Harvey on Algae.) This species looked almost edible; at least, I thought that if I were starving I would try it. One sailor told me that the cows ate it. It cut like cheese; for I took the earliest opportunity to sit down and deliberately whittle up a fathom or two of it, that I might become more intimately acquainted with it, see how it cut, and if it were hollow all the way through. The blade looked like a broad belt, whose edges had been quilled, or as if stretched by hammering, and it was also twisted spirally. The extremity was generally worn and ragged from the lashing of the waves. A piece of the stem which I carried home shrunk to one quarter of its size a week afterward, and was completely covered with crystals of salt like frost. The reader will excuse my greenness,—though it is not sea-greenness, like his, perchance,—for I live by a river shore, where this weed does not wash up. When we consider in what meadows it grew, and how it was raked, and in what kind of hay weather got in or out, we may well be curious about it. One who is weather-wise has given the following account of the matter.

'When descends on the Atlantic
The gigantic
Storm-wind of the equinox,
Landward in his wrath he scourges
The toiling surges,
Laden with sea-weed from the rocks.

'From Bermuda's reefs, from edges
Of sunken ledges,
On some far-off bright Azore;
From Bahama and the dashing,
Silver-flashing
Surges of San Salvador;

'From the trembling surf that buries
The Orkneyan Skerries,
Answering the hoarse Hebrides;
And from wrecks and ships are drifting
Spars, uplifting
On the desolate rainy seas;

'Ever drifting, drifting, drifting
On the shifting
Currents of the restless main.'

But he was not thinking of this shore, when he added:—

'Till, in sheltered coves, and reaches
Of sandy beaches,
All have found repose again.'

These weeds were the symbols of those grotesque and fabulous
thoughts which have not yet got into the sheltered coves of literature.

'Ever drifting, drifting, drifting
On the shifting
Currents of the restless heart.'
And not yet 'in books recorded
They, like hoarded
Household words, no more depart.'

The beach was also strewn with beautiful sea-jellies, which the
wreckers called Sun-squall, one of the lowest forms of animal life, some
white, some wine-colored, and a foot in diameter. I at first thought
that they were a tender part of some marine monster, which the storm
or some other foe had mangled. What right has the sea to bear in its

bosom such tender things as sea-jellies and mosses, when it has such a boisterous shore, that the stoutest fabrics are wrecked against it? Strange that it should undertake to dandle such delicate children in its arm. I did not at first recognize these for the same which I had formerly seen in myriads in Boston Harbor, rising, with a waving motion, to the surface, as if to meet the sun, and discoloring the waters far and wide, so that I seemed to be sailing through a mere sun-fish soup. They say that when you endeavor to take one up, it will spill out the other side of your hand like quicksilver. Before the land rose out of the ocean, and became dry land, chaos reigned; and between high and low water mark, where she is partially disrobed and rising, a sort of chaos reigns still, which only anomalous creatures can inhabit. Mackerel-gulls were all the while flying over our heads and amid the breakers, sometimes two white ones pursuing a black one; quite at home in the storm, though they are as delicate organizations as sea-jellies and mosses; and we say that they were adapted to their circumstances rather by their spirits than their bodies. Theirs must be an essentially wilder, that is, less human, nature than that of larks and robins. Their note was like the sound of some vibrating metal, and harmonized well with the scenery and the roar of the surf, as if one had rudely touched the strings of the lyre, which ever lies on the shore; a ragged shred of ocean music tossed aloft on the spray. But if I were required to name a sound, the remembrance of which most perfectly revives the impression which the beach has made, it would be the dreary peep of the piping plover (Charadrius melodus) which haunts there. Their voices, too, are heard as a fugacious part in the dirge which is ever played along the shore for those mariners who have been lost in the deep since first it was created. But through all this dreariness we seemed to have a pure and unqualified strain of external melody, for always the same strain which is a dirge to one household is a morning song of rejoicing to another.

A remarkable method of catching gulls, derived from the Indians, was practised in Wellfleet in 1794. 'The Gull House' it is said, 'is built with crotchets, fixed in the ground on the beach, poles being stretched across for the top, and the sides made close with stakes and sea-weed. 'The poles on the top are covered with lean whale. The man being placed within, is not discovered by the fowls, and while they are contending for and eating the flesh, he draws them in, one by one, between the poles, until he has collected forty or fifty.' Hence, perchance, a man is said to be gulled, when he is taken in. We read that one 'sort of gulls is called by the Dutch mallemucke, i.e. the foolish fly, because they fall upon a whale as eagerly as a fly, and, indeed, all gulls are foolishly bold and easy to be shot. The Norwegians call this bird havhest, sea-horse (and the English translator says, it is probably what we call boobies). If they have eaten too much, they throw it up, and eat it again till they are tired. It is this habit in the gulls of parting with their property (disgorging the contents of their stomachs to the skuas), which has given rise to the terms gull, fuller, and gulling, among men.' We also read that they used to kill small birds which roosted on the beach at night, by making a fire with hog's lard in a frying pan. The Indians probably used pine torches; the birds flocked to the light, and were knocked down with a stick. We noticed holes dug near the edge of the bank, where gunners conceal themselves to shoot the large gulls which coast up and down a-fishing, for these are considered good to eat.

We found some large clams, of the species Mactra solidissima, which the storm had torn up from the bottom, and cast ashore. I selected one of the largest, about six inches in length, and carried it along, thinking to try an experiment on it. We soon after met a wrecker, with a grapple and a rope, who said that he was looking for tow cloth, which had made part of the cargo of the ship Franklin, which was wrecked here in the spring, at which time nine or ten lives were lost. The reader may remember this wreck, from the circumstance that a letter was found in the captain's valise, which washed ashore, directing him to wreck the vessel before he got to America, and from the trail which took place in consequence. The wrecker said that tow cloth was still cast up in such storms as this. He also told us that the clam which I had was the sea-clam, or hen, and was good to eat. We took our nooning under a sand-hill, covered with beach-grass, in a dreary little hollow, on the top of the bank, while it alternately rained and shined. There, having reduced some damp drift-wood, which I had picked up on the shore, to shavings with my knife, I kindled a fire with a match and some paper, and cooked my clam on the embers for my dinner; for breakfast was commonly the only meal which I took in a house on this excursion. When the clam was done, one valve held the meat and the other the liquor. Though it was very tough, I found it sweet and savory, and ate the whole with a relish. Indeed, with the addition of a cracker or two, it would have been a beautiful dinner . . .

Nantucket

HERMAN MELVILLE

In this chapter from his novel Moby Dick (1851), *Herman Melville's young hero Ishmael describes the island of Nantucket.*

NOTHING MORE HAPPENED on the passage worthy the mentioning; so, after a fine run, we safely arrived in Nantucket.

Nantucket! Take out your map and look at it. See what a real corner of the world it occupies; how it stands there, away off shore, more lonely than the Eddystone lighthouse. Look at it—a mere hillock, and elbow of sand; all beach, without a background. There is more sand there than you would use in twenty years as a substitute for blotting paper. Some gamesome wights will tell you that they have to plant weeds there, they don't grow naturally; that they import Canada thistles; that they have to send beyond seas for a spile to stop a leak in an oil cask; that pieces of wood in Nantucket are carried about like bits of the true cross in Rome; that people there plant toadstools before their houses, to get under the shade in summer time; that one blade of grass makes an oasis, three blades in a day's walk a prairie; that they wear quicksand shoes, something like Laplander snowshoes; that they are so shut up, belted about, every way inclosed, surrounded, and made an utter island of by the ocean, that to their very chairs and tables small clams will sometimes be found adhering, as to the backs of sea turtles. But these extravaganzas only show that Nantucket is no Illinois.

Look now at the wondrous traditional story of how this island was settled by the red-men. Thus goes the legend. In olden times an eagle swooped down upon the New England coast, and carried off an infant Indian in his talons. With loud lament the parents saw their child borne out of sight over the wide waters. They resolved to follow in the same direction. Setting out in their canoes, after a perilous passage, they discovered the island, and there they found an empty casket,—the poor little Indian's skeleton.

What wonder, then, that these Nantucketers, born on a beach, should take to the sea for a livelihood! They first caught crabs and quohogs in the sand; grown bolder, they waded out with nets for mackerel; more experienced they pushed off in boats and captured cod; and at last, launching a navy of great ships on the sea, explored this watery world; put an incessant belt of circumnavigation round it; peeped in at Bhering's Straits; and in all seasons and all oceans declared everlasting war with the mightiest animated mass that has survived the flood; most monstrous and most mountainous! That Himmalehan, salt-sea Mastodon, clothed with such portentousness of unconscious power, that his very panics are more to be dreaded than his most fearless and malicious assaults!

And thus have these naked Nantucketers, these sea-hermits, issuing from their ant-hill in the sea, overrun and conquered the watery world like so many Alexanders; parcelling out among them the Atlantic, Pacific, and Indian oceans, as the three pirate powers did Poland. Let America add Mexico to Texas, and pile Cuba upon Canada; let the English overswarm all India, and hang out their blazing banner from the sun; two thirds of this terraqueous globe are the Nantucketer's. For the sea is his; he owns it, as Emperors own empires; other seamen having but a right of way through it. Merchant ships are but extension bridges; armed ones but floating forts; even pirates and privateers, though following the sea as highwaymen the road, they but plunder other ships, other fragments of the land like themselves, without seeking to draw their living from the bottomless deep itself. The Nantucketer, he alone resides and riots on the sea; he alone, in Bible language, goes down to it in ships; to and fro ploughing it as his own special plantation. *There* is his home; *there* lies his business, which a Noah's flood would not interrupt, though it overwhelmed all the millions in China. He lives on the sea, as prairie cocks in the prairie; he hides among the waves, he climbs them as chamois hunters climb the Alps. For years he knows not the land; so that when he comes to it at last, it smells like another world, more strangely than the moon would to an Earthsman. With the landless gull, that at sunset folds her wings and is rocked to sleep between billows; so at nightfall, the Nantucketer, out of sight of land, furls his sails, and lays him to his rest, while under his very pillow rush herds of walruses and whales.

New York

HENRY JAMES

In this extract from his collection of travel writing The American
Scene (1907), *Henry James records his impressions of New York
City on his return there after an absence of some 25 years.*

THE SINGLE IMPRESSION or particular vision most answering to the greatness of the subject would have been, I think, a certain hour of large
circumnavigation that I found prescribed, in the fulness of the spring,
as the almost immediate crown of a return from the Far West. I had
arrived at one of the transpontine stations of the Pennsylvania Railroad;
the question was of proceeding to Boston, for the occasion, without
pushing through the terrible town—why 'terrible' to my sense, in many
ways, I shall presently explain—and the easy and agreeable attainment
of this great advantage was to embark on one of the mightiest (as

appeared to me) of train-bearing barges and descending the western waters, pass round the bottom of the city and remount the other current to Harlem; all without 'losing touch' of the Pullman that had brought me from Washington. This absence of the need of losing touch, this breadth of effect, as to the whole process, involved in the prompt floating of the huge concatenated cars not only without arrest or confusion, but as for positive prodigal beguilement of the artless traveller, had doubtless much to say to the ensuing state of mind, the happily-excited and amused view of the great face of New York. The extent, the ease, the energy, the quantity and number, all notes scattered about as if, in the whole business and in the splendid light, nature and science were joyously romping together, might have been taking on again, for their symbol, some collective presence of great circling and plunging, hovering and perching seabirds, white winged images of the spirit, of the restless freedom of the Bay. The Bay had always, on other opportunities, seemed to blow its immense character straight into one's face—coming 'at' you, so to speak, bearing down on you, with the full force of a thousand prows of steamers seen exactly on the line of their longitudinal axis; but I had never before been so conscious of its boundless cool assurance or seemed to see its genius so grandly at play. This was presumably indeed because I had never before enjoyed the remarkable adventure of taking in so much of the vast bristling promontory from the water, of ascending the East River, in especial, to its upper diminishing expanses.

Something of the air of the occasion and the mood of the moment caused the whole picture to speak with its largest suggestion; which suggestion is irresistible when once it is sounded clear. It is all, absolutely, an expression of things lately and currently *done*, done on a large impersonal stage and on the basis of inordinate gain—it is not an expression of any other matters whatever; and yet the sense of the scene (which had at several previous junctures, as well, put forth to my imagination its power) was commanding and thrilling, was in certain lights almost charming. So it befell, exactly, that an element of mystery and wonder entered into the impression—the interest of trying to make out, in the absence of features of the sort usually supposed indispensable, the reason of the beauty and the joy. It is indubitably a 'great' bay, a great harbour, but no one item of the romantic, or even the picturesque, as commonly understood, contributes to its effect. The shores are low and for the most part depressingly furnished and prosaically peopled; the islands, though numerous, have not a grace to exhibit, and one thinks of the other, the real flowers of geography in this order, of Naples, of Capetown, of Sydney, of Seattle, of San Francisco, of Rio, asking how if *they* justify a reputation, New York should seem to justify one. Then, after all, we remember that there are reputations and reputations; we remember above all that the imaginative response to the conditions here presented may just happen to proceed from the intellectual extravagance of the given observer. When this personage is open to corruption by almost any large view of an intensity of life, his vibrations tend to become a matter difficult even for *him* to explain. He may have to confess that the group of evident facts fails to account by itself for the complacency of his appreciation. Therefore it is that I find myself rather backward with a perceived sanction, of an at all proportionate kind, for the fine exhilaration with which, in this free wayfaring relation to them, the wide waters of New York inspire me. There is the beauty of light and air, the great scale of space, and, as seen far away to the west, the open gates of the Hudson, majestic in their degree, even at a distance, and announcing still nobler things. But the real appeal, unmistakably, is in the note of vehemence in the local life of which I have spoken, for it is the appeal of a particular type of dauntless power.

The aspect the power wears then is indescribable; it is the power of the most extravagant of cities, rejoicing, as with the voice of the morning, in its might, its fortune, its unsurpassable conditions, and imparting to every object and element, to the motion and expression of every floating, hurrying, panting thing, to the throb of ferries and tugs, to the splash of the waves and the play of winds and the glint of lights and the shrill of whistles and the quality and authority of breeze-born cries—all, practically, a diffused, wasted clamour of *detonations*—something of its sharp free accent and, above all, of its sovereign sense of being 'backed' and able to back. The universal *applied* passion struck me as shining unprecedentedly out of the composition; in the bigness and bravery and insolence, especially, of everything that rushed and shrieked; in the air as of a great intricate frenzied dance, half merry, half desperate, or at least half defiant, performed on the huge water floor. This appearance of the bold lacing-together, across the waters, of the scattered members of the monstrous organism—lacing as by the ceaseless play of an enormous system of steam shuttles or electric bobbins (I scarce know what to call them), commensurate in form with their infinite work—does perhaps more than anything else to give the pitch of the vision of energy. One has the sense that the monster grows and grows, flinging abroad its loose limbs even as some unmannered young giant at his 'larks' and that the binding stitches must for ever fly further and faster and draw harder; the future complexity of the web, all under the sky and over the sea, becoming thus that of some colossal set of clockworks, some steel-souled machine-room of brandished arms and hammering fists and opening and closing jaws. The immeasurable bridges are but as the horizontal sheaths of pistons working at high pressure, day and night, and subject, one apprehends with perhaps inconsistent gloom, to certain, to fantastic, to merciless multiplication. In the light of this apprehension indeed the breezy brightness of the Bay puts on the semblance of the vast white page that awaits beyond any other perhaps the black overscoring of science.

Let me hasten to add that its present whiteness is precisely its charming note, the frankest of the signs you recognize and remember it by. This is the distinction I was just feeling my way to name as the main ground of its doing so well, for effect, without technical scenery. There are great imposing ports—Glasgow and Liverpool and London—that have already their page blackened almost beyond redemption from any such light of the picturesque as can hope to irradiate fog and grime, and there are others, Marseilles and Constantinople say, or, for all I know to the contrary, New Orleans, that contrive to abound before everything else in colour, and so to make a rich and instant and obvious show. But memory and the actual impression keep investing New York with the tone, predominantly, of summer dawns and winter frost, of sea-foam, of bleached sails and stretched awnings, of blanched hulls, of scoured decks, of new ropes, of polished brasses, of streamers clear in the blue air; and it is by this harmony, doubtless, that the projection of the individual character of the place, of the candour of its avidity and the freshness of its audacity, is most conveyed. The 'tall buildings' which have so promptly usurped a glory that affects you as rather surprised, as yet, at itself, the multitudinous sky-scrapers standing up to the view, from the water, like extravagant pins in a cushion already overplanted, and stuck in as in the dark, anywhere and anyhow, have at least the felicity of carrying out the fairness of tone, of taking the sun and the shade in the manner of towers of marble. They are not all of marble, I believe, by any means, even if some may be, but they are impudently new and still more impudently 'novel'—this in common with so many other terrible things in America—and they are triumphant payers of dividends;

all of which uncontested and unabashed pride, with flash of innumerable windows and flicker of subordinate gilt attributions, is like the flare, up and down their long, narrow faces, of the lamps of some general permanent 'celebration.'

You see the pin-cushion profile, so to speak, on passing between Jersey City and Twenty-third Street, but you get it broadside on, this loose nosegay of architectural flowers, if you skirt the Battery, well out, and embrace the whole plantation. Then the 'American beauty' the rose of interminable stem, becomes the token of the cluster at large—to that degree that, positively, this is all that is wanted for emphasis of your final impression. Such growths, you feel, have confessedly arisen but to be 'picked' in time, with a shears; nipped short off, by waiting fate, as soon as 'science' applied to gain, has put upon the table, from far up its sleeve, some more winning card. Crowned not only with no history, but with no credible possibility of time for history, and consecrated by no uses save the commercial at any cost, they are simply the most piercing notes in that concert of the expensively provisional into which your supreme sense of New York resolves itself. They never begin to speak to you, in the manner of the builded majesties of the world as we have heretofore known such—towers or temples or fortresses or palaces—with the authority of things of permanence or even of things of long duration. One story is good only till another is told, and skyscrapers are the last word in economic ingenuity only till another word be written. This shall be possibly a word of still uglier meaning, but the vocabulary of thrift at any price shows boundless resources, and the consciousness of that truth the consciousness of the finite, the menaced, the essentially *invented* state, twinkles ever, to my perception, in the thousand glassy eyes of these giants of the mere market. Such a structure as the comparatively windowless bell-tower of Giotto, in Florence, looks supremely serene in its beauty. You don't feel it to have risen by the breath of an interested passion that, restless beyond all passions, is for ever seeking more pliable forms. Beauty has been the object of its creator's idea, and, having found beauty, it has found the form in which it splendidly rests.

Beauty indeed was the aim of the creator of the spire of Trinity Church, so cruelly overtopped and so barely distinguishable, from your train-bearing barge, as you stand off, in its abject helpless humility; and it may of course be asked how much of this superstition finds voice in the actual shrunken presence of that laudable effort. Where, for the eye, is the felicity of simplified Gothic, of noble pre-eminence, that once made of this highly-pleasing edifice the pride of the town and the feature of Broadway? The answer is, as obviously, that these charming elements are still there, just where they ever were, but that they have been mercilessly deprived of their visibility. It aches and throbs, this smothered visibility, we easily feel, in its caged and dishonoured condition, supported only by the consciousness that the dishonour is no fault of its own. We commune with it, in tenderness and pity, through the encumbered air; our eyes, made, however unwillingly, at home in strange vertiginous upper atmospheres, look down on it as on a poor ineffectual thing, an architectural object addressed, even in its prime aspiration to the patient pedestrian sense and permitting thereby a relation of intimacy. It was to speak to me audibly enough on two or three other occasions—even through the thick of that frenzy of Broadway just where Broadway receives from Wall Street the fiercest application of the maddening lash; it was to put its tragic case there with irresistible lucidity. 'Yes, the wretched figure I am making is as little as you see my fault—it is the fault of the buildings whose very first care is to deprive churches of their visibility. There are but two or three—two or three outward and visible churches—left in New York ''anyway,'' as you must have noticed, and even they are hideously threatened: a fact at which no one, indeed, appears to be shocked, from which no one draws the least of the inferences that stick straight out of it, which every one seems in short to take for granted either with remarkable stupidity or with remarkable cynicism.' So, at any rate, they may still effectively communicate, ruddy-brown (where not browny-black) old Trinity and any pausing, any attending survivor of the clearer age—that there is yet more of the bitterness of history to be tasted in such a tacit passage, as I shall presently show.

Was it not the bitterness of history, meanwhile, that on that day of circumnavigation, that day of highest intensity of impression, of which I began by speaking, the ancient rotunda of Castle Garden, viewed from just opposite, should have lurked there as a vague nonentity? One had known it from far, far back and with the indelibility of the childish vision—from the time when it was the commodious concert-hall of New York, the firmament of long-extinguished stars; in spite of which extinction there outlives for me the image of the infant phenomenon Adelina Patti, whom (another large-eyed infant) I had been benevolently taken to hear: Adelina Patti, in a fan-like little white frock and 'pantalettes' and a hussar-like red jacket, mounted on an armchair, its back supporting her, wheeled to the front of the stage and warbling like a tiny thrush even in the nest. Shabby, shrunken, barely discernible today, the ancient rotunda, adjusted to other uses, had afterwards, for many decades, carried on a conspicuous life—and it was the present remoteness, the repudiated barbarism of all this, foreshortened by one's own experience, that dropped the acid into the cup. The sky-scrapers and the league-long bridges, present and to come, marked the point where the age—the age of which Castle Garden could have been, in its day, a 'value'—had come out. That in itself was nothing—ages do come out, as a matter of course, so far from where they have gone in. But it had done so, the latter half of the nineteenth century, in one's own more or less immediate presence; the difference, from pole to pole, was so vivid and concrete that no single shade of any one of its aspects was lost. This impact of the whole condensed past at once produced a horrible, hateful sense of personal antiquity.

Yet was it after all that those monsters of the mere market, as I have called them, had more to say, on the question of 'effect,' than I had at first allowed?—since they are the element that looms largest for me through a particular impression, with remembered parts and pieces melting together rather richly now, of 'down-town' seen and felt from the inside. 'Felt'—I use that word, I dare say, all presumptuously, for a relation to matters of magnitude and mystery that I could begin neither to measure nor to penetrate, hovering about them only in magnanimous wonder, staring at them as at a world of immovably-closed doors behind which immense 'material' lurked, material for the artist, the painter of life, as we say, who shouldn't have begun so early and so fatally to fall away from possible initiations. This sense of a baffled curiosity, an intellectual adventure forever renounced, was surely enough a state of feeling, and indeed in presence of the different half-hours, as memory presents them, at which I gave myself up both to the thrill of Wall Street (by which I mean that of the whole wide edge of the whirlpool), and the too accepted, too irredeemable ignorance, I am at a loss to see what intensity of response was wanting. The imagination might have responded more if there had been a slightly less settled inability to understand what every one, what any one, was really doing; but the picture, as it comes back to me, is, for all this foolish subjective poverty, so crowded with its features that I rejoice, I confess, in not having more of them to handle. No open apprehension, even if it be as open as a public vehicle plying for hire, can carry more than a certain amount of life, of a kind; and there was nothing at play in the outer air, at least, of the scene, during these glimpses, that didn't scramble for admission into mine very much as I had seen the mob seeking entrance to an up-town or a down-town electric car fight for life at one of the apertures. If it had been the final function of the Bay to make one feel one's age, so, assuredly, the mouth of Wall Street proclaimed it, for one's private ear, distinctly enough; the breath of existence being taken, wherever one turned, as that of youth on the run and with the prize of the race in sight, and the new landmarks crushing the old quite as violent children stamp on snails and caterpillars.

The hour I first recall was a morning of winter drizzle and mist, of dense fog in the Bay, one of the strangest sights of which I was on my way to enjoy; and I had stopped in the heart of the business quarter to pick up a friend who was to be my companion. The weather, such as it was, worked wonders for the upper reaches of the buildings, round which it drifted and hung very much as about the flanks and summits of emergent mountain-masses—for, to be just all round, there *was* some evidence of their having a message for the eyes. Let me parenthesize, once for all, that there are other glimpses of this message, up and down the city, frequently to be caught; lights and shades of winter and summer air, of the literally 'finishing' afternoon in particular, when refinement of modelling descends from the skies and lends the towers, all new and crude and commercial and over-windowed as they are, a fleeting distinction. The morning I speak of offered me my first chance of seeing one of them from the inside—which was an opportunity I sought again, repeatedly, in respect to others; and I became conscious of the force with which this vision of their prodigious working, and of the multitudinous life, as if each were a swarming city in itself, that they are capable of housing, may beget, on the part of the free observer, in other words of the restless analysts, the impulse to describe and present the facts and express the sense of them. Each of these huge constructed and compressed communities, throbbing, through its myriad arteries and pores, with a single passion, even as a complicated watch throbs with the one purpose of telling you the hour and the minute, testified overwhelmingly to the *character* of New York—and the passion of the restless analyst, on his side, is for the extraction of character. But there would be too much to say, just here, were this incurable eccentric to let himself go; the impression in question, fed by however brief an experience, kept overflowing the cup and spreading in a wide waste of speculation. I must dip into these depths, if it prove possible, later on; let me content myself for the moment with remembering how from the first, on all such ground, my thought went straight to poor great wonder-working Émile Zola and *his* love of the human aggregation, the artificial microcosm, which had to spend itself on great shops, great businesses, great 'apartment-houses' of inferior, of mere Parisian scale. His image, it seemed to me, really asked for compassion—in the presence of this material that his energy of evocation, his alone, would have been of a stature to meddle with. What if *Le Ventre de Paris*, what if *Au Bonheur des Dames*, what if *Pot-Bouille* and *L'Argent*, could but have come into being under the New York inspiration?

The answer to that, however, for the hour, was that, in all probability, New York was not going (as it turns such remarks) to produce both the maximum of 'business' spectacle and the maximum of ironic reflection of it. Zola's huge reflector got itself formed, after all, in a far other air; it had hung there, in essence, awaiting the scene that was to play over it, long before the scene really approached it in scale. The reflecting surfaces, of the ironic, of the epic order, suspended in the New York atmosphere, have yet to show symptoms of shining out, and the monstrous phenomena themselves, meanwhile, strike me as having, with their immense momentum, got the start, got ahead of, in proper parlance, any possibility of poetic, of dramatic capture. That conviction came to me most perhaps while I gazed across at the special sky-scraper that overhangs poor old Trinity to the north—a south face as high and wide as the mountain-wall that drops the Alpine avalanche, from time to time, upon the village, and the village spire at its foot; the interest of this case being above all, as I learned, to my stupefaction, in the fact that the very creators of the extinguisher are the churchwardens themselves, or at least the trustees of the church property. What was the case but magnificent for pitiless ferocity?—that inexorable law of the growing invisibility of churches, their everywhere reduced or abolished *presence*, which is nine-tenths of their virtue, receiving thus, at such hands, its supreme consecration. This consecration was positively the greater that just then, as I have said, the vast money-making structure quite horribly, quite romantically justified itself, looming through the weather with an insolent cliff-like sublimity. The weather, for all that experience, mixes intimately with the fulness of my impression; speaking not least, for instance, of the way 'the state of the streets' and the assault of the turbid air seemed all one with the look, the tramp, the whole quality and *allure*, the consummate monotonous commonness, of the pushing male crowd, moving in its dense mass—with the confusion carried to chaos for any intelligence, any perception; a welter of objects and sounds in which relief, detachment, dignity, meaning, perished utterly and lost all rights. It appeared, the muddy medium, all one with every other element and note as well, all the signs of the heaped industrial battlefield, all the sounds and silences, grim, pushing, trudging silences too, of the universal will to move—to move, move, move, as an end in itself, an appetite at any price.

In the Bay, the rest of the morning, the dense raw fog that delayed the big boat, allowing sight but of the immediate ice-masses through which it thumped its way, was not less of the essence. Anything blander, as a medium, would have seemed a mockery of the facts of the terrible little Ellis Island, the first harbour of refuge and stage of patience for the million or so of immigrants annually knocking at our official door. Before this door, which opens to them there only with a hundred forms and ceremonies, grindings and grumblings of the key, they stand appealing and waiting, marshalled, herded, divided, subdivided, sorted, sifted, searched, fumigated, for longer or shorter periods—the effect of all which prodigious process, an intendedly 'scientific' feeding of the mill, is again to give the earnest observer a thousand more things to think of than he can pretend to retail. The impression of Ellis Island, in fine, would be—as I was to find throughout that so many of my impressions would be—a chapter by itself; and with a particular page for recognition of the degree in which the liberal hospitality of the eminent Commissioner of this wonderful service, to whom I had been introduced, helped to make the interest of the whole watched drama poignant and unforgettable. It is a drama that goes on, without a pause, day by day and year by year, this visible act of ingurgitation on the part of our body politic and social, and constituting really an appeal to amazement beyond that of any sword-swallowing or fire-swallowing of the circus. The wonder that one couldn't keep down was the thought that these two or three hours of one's own chance vision of the business were but as a tick or two of the mighty clock, the clock that never, never stops—least of all when it strikes, for a sign of so much winding-up, some louder hour of our national fate than usual. I think indeed that the simplest account of the action of Ellis Island on the spirit of any sensitive citizen who may have happened to 'look-in' is that he comes back from his visit not at all the same person that he went. He has eaten of the tree of knowledge, and the taste will be for ever in his mouth. He had thought he knew before, though he had the sense of the degree in which it is his American fate to share the sanctity of his American consciousness, the intimacy of his American patriotism, with the inconceivable alien; but the truth had never come home to him with any such force. In the lurid light projected upon it by those courts of dismay it shakes him—or I like at least to imagine it shakes him—to the depths of his being; I like to think of him, I positively *have* to think of him, as going about ever afterwards with a new look, for those who can see it, in his face, the outward sign of the new chill in his heart. So is stamped, for detection, the questionably privileged person who has had an apparition, seen a ghost in his supposedly safe old house. Let not the unwary, therefore visit Ellis Island.

The after-sense of that acute experience, however, I myself found, was by no means to be brushed away; I felt it grow and grow on the contrary, wherever I turned: other impressions might come and go, but this affirmed claim of the alien, however immeasurably alien, to share in one's supreme relation was everywhere the fixed element, the reminder not to be dodged. One's supreme relation, as one had always put it, was one's relation to one's country—a conception made up so largely of one's countrymen and one's countrywomen. Thus it was as if, all the while, with such a fond tradition of what these products predominantly were, the idea of the country itself underwent something of that profane overhauling through which it appears to suffer the indignity of change. Is not our instinct in this matter, in general, essentially the safe one—that of keeping the idea simple and strong and continuous, so that it shall be perfectly sound? To touch it overmuch, to pull it about, is to put it in peril of weakening; yet on this free assault upon it, this readjustment of it in *their* monstrous, presumptuous interest, the aliens, in New York, seemed perpetually to insist. The combination there of their quantity and their quality—that loud primary stage of alienism which New York most offers to sight—operates, for the native, as their note of settled possession, something they have nobody to thank for; so that *un*settled possession is what we, on our side, seem reduced to—the implication of which, in its turn, is that, to recover confidence and regain lost ground, we, not they, must make the surrender and accept the orientation. We must go, in other words, *more* than half-way to meet them; which is all the difference, for us, between possession and dispossession. This sense of dispossession, to be brief about it, haunted me so, I was to feel, in the New York streets, just as one tumbles back into the streets in appalled reaction from *them*, that the art of beguiling or duping it became an art to be cultivated—though the fond alternative vision was never long to be obscured, the imagination, exasperated to envy, of the ideal, in the order in question; of the luxury of some such close and sweet and *whole* national consciousness as that of the Switzer and the Scot.

II

My recovery of impressions, after a short interval, yet with their flush a little faded, may have been judged to involve itself with excursions of memory—memory directed to the antecedent time—reckless almost to extravagance. But I recall them today, none the less, for that value in them which ministered, at happy moments, to an artful evasion of the actual. There was no escape from the ubiquitous alien into the future, or even into the present; there was an escape but into the past. I count as quite a triumph in this interest as unbroken ease of frequentation of that ancient end of Fifth Avenue to the whole neighbourhood of which one's earlier vibrations, a very far-away matter now, were attuned. The precious stretch of space between Washington Square and Fourteenth Street had a value, had even a charm, for the revisiting spirit—a mild and melancholy glamour which I am conscious of the difficulty of 'rendering' for new and heedless generations. Here again the assault of suggestion is too great; too large, I mean the number of hares started, before the pursuing imagination, the quickened memory, by this fact of the felt moral and social value of this comparatively unimpaired morsel of the Fifth Avenue heritage. Its reference to a pleasanter, easier, hazier past is absolutely comparative, just as the past in question itself enjoys as such the merest courtesy-title. It is all recent history enough, by the measure of the whole, and there are flaws and defacements enough, surely, even in its appearance of decency of duration. The tall building, grossly tall and grossly ugly, has failed of an admirable chance of distinguished consideration for it, and the dignity of many of its peaceful fronts has succumbed to the presence of those industries whose foremost need is to make 'a good thing' of them. The good thing is doubtless being made, and yet this lower end of the once agreeable street still just escapes being a wholly bad thing. What held the fancy in thrall, however, as I say, was the admonition, proceeding from all the facts, that values of this romantic order are at best, anywhere, strangely relative. It was an extraordinary statement on the subject of New York that the space between Fourteenth Street and Washington Square *should* count for 'tone' figure as the old ivory of an overscored tablet.

True wisdom, I found, was to let it, to make it, so count and figure as much as it would, and charming assistance came for this, I also found, from the young good-nature of May and June. There had been neither assistance nor good-nature during the grim weeks of mid-winter; there had been but the meagre fact of a discomfort and an ugliness less formidable here than elsewhere. When toward the top of the town, circulation, alimentation, recreation, every art of existence, gave way before the full onset of winter, when the upper avenues had become as so many congested bottle-necks, through which the wine of life simply refused to be decanted, getting back to these latitudes resembled really a return from the North Pole to the Temperate Zone: it was as if the wine of life had been poured for you, in advance, into some pleasant old punch-bowl that would support you through the temporary stress. Your condition was not reduced to the endless vista of a clogged tube, of a thoroughfare occupied as to the narrow central ridge with trolley-cars stuffed to suffocation, and as to the mere margin, on either side, with snow-banks resulting from the cleared rails and offering themselves as a field for all remaining action. Free existence and good manners, in New York, are too much brought down to a bare rigour of marginal relation to the endless electric coil, the monstrous chain that winds round the general neck and body, the general middle and legs, very much as the boa-constrictor winds round the group of the Laocoon. It struck me that when these folds are tightened in the terrible stricture of the snow-smothered months of the year, the New York predicament leaves far behind the anguish represented in the Vatican figures. To come and go where East Eleventh Street, where West Tenth, opened their kind short arms was at least to keep clear of the awful hug of the serpent. And this was a grace that grew large, as I have hinted, with the approach of summer, and that made the afternoons of May and the first half of June, above all, an insidious appeal. There, I repeat, was the delicacy, there the mystery, there the wonder, in especial, of the unquenchable intensity of the impressions received in childhood. They are made then once for all, be their intrinsic beauty, interest, importance, small or great; the stamp is indelible and never wholly fades. This in fact gives it an importance when a lifetime has intervened. I found myself intimately recognizing every house my officious tenth year had, in the way of imagined adventure, introduced to me—incomparable master of ceremonies after all; the privilege had been offered since to millions of other objects that had made nothing of it, that had gone as they came; so that here were Fifth Avenue corners with which one's connection was fairly exquisite. The lowered light of the days' ends of early summer became them, moreover, exceedingly, and they fell, for the quiet northward perspective, into a dozen delicacies of composition and tone.

One could talk of 'quietness' now, for the shrinkage of life so marked, in the higher latitudes of the town, after Easter, the visible early flight of that 'society' which, by the old custom, used never to budge before June or July, had almost the effect of clearing some of the streets, and indeed of suggesting that a truly clear New York might have an unsuspected charm or two to put forth. An approach to peace and harmony might have been, in a manner promised, and the sense of other days took advantage of it to steal abroad with a ghostly treat. It kept meeting, half the time, to its discomfiture, the lamentable little Arch of Triumph which bestrides these beginnings of Washington Square—lamentable because of its poor and lonely and unsupported and unaffiliated state. With this melancholy monument it could make no terms at all, but turned its back to the strange sight as often possible, helping itself thereby, moreover, to do a little of the pretending required, no doubt, by the fond theory that nothing hereabouts was changed. Nothing *was*, it could occasionally appear to me—there was no new note in the picture, not one, for instance, when I paused before a low house in a small row on the south side of Waverley Place and lived again into the queer medieval costume (preserved by the daguerreotypist's art) of the very little boy for whom the scene had once embodied the pangs and pleasures of a dame's small school. The dame must have been Irish, by her name, and the Irish tradition, only intensified and coarsened, seemed still to possess the place, the fact of the survival, the sturdy sameness, of which arrested me, again and again, to fascination. The shabby red house, with its mere two storeys, its lowly 'stoop' its dislocated ironwork of the forties, the early fifties, the record, in its face of blistering summers and of the long stages of the loss of self-respect, made it as consummate a morsel of the liquor-scented, heated-looking city, the city of no pavements, but of such a plenty of politics, as I could have desired. And neighbouring Sixth Avenue, overstraddled though it might be with feats of engineering unknown to the primitive age that otherwise so persisted, wanted only, to carry off the illusion, the warm smell of the bakery on the corner of Eighth Street, a blessed repository of doughnuts, cookies, cream-cakes and pies, the slow passing by which, on returns from school, must have had much in common with the experience of the shipment of old who came, in long voyages, while they tacked and hung back, upon those belts of ocean that are haunted with the balm and spice of tropic islands.

These were the felicities of the backward reach, which, however, had also its melancholy checks and snubs; nowhere quite so sharp as in presence, so to speak, of the rudely, the ruthlessly suppressed birthhouse on the other side of the Square. That was where the pretence that nearly nothing was changed had most to come in; for a high, square, impersonal structure, proclaiming its lack of interest with a crudity all its own, so blocks, at the right moment for its own success, the view of the past, that the effect for me, in Washington Place, was of having been amputated of half my history. The grey and more or less 'hallowed' University building—wasn't it somehow, with a desperate bravery, both castellated and gabled?—has vanished from the earth, and vanished with it the two or three adjacent houses, of which the birthplace was one. This was the snub, for the complacency of retrospect, that, whereas the inner sense had positively erected there for its private contemplation a commemorative mural tablet, the very wall that should have borne this inscription had been smashed as for demonstration that tablets, in New York, are unthinkable. And I have had indeed to permit myself this free fantasy of the hypothetic rescued identity of a given house— taking the vanished numbers in Washington Place as most pertinent—in order to invite the reader to gasp properly with me before the fact that we not only fail to remember, in the whole length of the city, one of these frontal records of birth, sojourn, or death, under a celebrated name, but that we have only to reflect an instant to see any such form of civic piety inevitably and for ever absent. The form is cultivated, to the greatly quickened interest of street-scenery, in many of the cities of Europe;

and is it not verily bitter, for those who feel a poetry in the noted passage, longer or shorter, here and there, of great lost spirits, that the institution, the profit, the glory of any such association is denied in advance to communities tending as the phrase is, to 'run' preponderantly to the sky-scraper? Where, in fact, is the point of inserting a mural tablet, at any legible height, in a building certain to be destroyed to make room for a sky-scraper? And from where, on the other hand, in a facade of fifty floors, does one 'see' the pious plate recording the honour attached to one of the apartments look down on a responsive people? We have but to ask the question to recognize our necessary failure to answer it as a supremely characteristic local note—a note in the light of which the great city is projected into its future as, practically, a huge, continuous fifty-floored conspiracy against the very idea of the ancient graces, those that strike us as having flourished just in proportion as the parts of life and the signs of character have *not* been lumped together, not been indistinguishably sunk in the common fund of mere economic convenience. So interesting, as object-lessons, may the developments of the American gregarious ideal become; so traceable, at every turn, to the restless analyst at least, are the heavy footprints, in the finer texture of life of a great commercial democracy seeking to abound supremely in its own sense and having none to gainsay it.

Let me not, however, forget, amid such contemplations, what may serve here as a much more relevant instance of the operation of values, the price of the as yet undiminished dignity of the two most southward of the Fifth Avenue churches. Half the charm of the prospect, at that extremity, is in their still being there, and being as they are; this charm, this serenity of escape and survival positively works as a blind on the side of the question of their architectural importance. The last shade of pedantry or priggishness drops from your view of that element; they illustrate again supremely your grasped truth of the comparative character, in such conditions, of beauty and of interest. The special standard they may or may not square with signifies, you feel, not a jot: all you know, and want to know, is that they are probably menaced—some horrible voice of the air has murmured it—and that with them will go, if fate overtakes them, the last cases worth mentioning (with a single exception), of the modest felicity that sometimes used to be. Remarkable certainly the state of things in which mere exemption from the 'squashed' condition can shed such a glamour; but we may accept the state of things if only we can keep the glamour undispelled. It reached its maximum for me, I hasten to add, on my penetrating into Ascension, at chosen noon, and standing for the first time in presence of that noble work of John La Farge, the representation, on the west wall, in the grand manner of the theological event from which the church takes its title. Wonderful enough, in New York, to find one's self in a charming and considerably dim 'old' church, hushed to admiration before a great religious picture; the sensation, for the moment, upset so all the facts. The hot light, outside, might have been that of an Italian *piazetta*; the cool shade, within, with the important work of art shining through it, seemed part of some other-world pilgrimage—all the more that the important work of art itself, a thing of the highest distinction, spoke, as soon as one had taken it in, with that authority which makes the difference, ever afterwards between the remembered and the forgotten quest. A rich note of interference came, I admit, through the splendid window-glass, the finest of which, unsurpassably fine, to my sense, is the work of the same artist; so that the church, as it stands, is very nearly as commemorative a monument as a great reputation need wish. The deeply pictorial windows, in which clearness of picture and fulness of expression consort so successfully with a tone as of magnified gems, did not strike one as looking into a yellow little square of the south—they put forth a different implication; but the flaw in the harmony was, more than anything else, that sinister voice of the air of which I have spoken, the fact that one *could* stand there, vibrating to such impressions, only to remember the suspended danger, the possibility of the doom. Here was the loveliest cluster of images, begotten on the spot, that the preoccupied city had ever taken thought to offer itself; and here, to match them, like some black shadow they had been condemned to cast, was this particular prepared honour of 'removal' that appeared to hover about them.

One's fear, I repeat, was perhaps misplaced—but what an air to live in, the shuddering pilgrim mused, the air in which such fears are not misplaced only when we are conscious of very special reassurances! The vision of the doom that does descend, that had descended all round, was at all events, for the half-hour, all that was wanted to charge with the last tenderness one's memory of the transfigured interior. Afterwards, outside, again and again, the powers of removal struck me as looming, awfully, in the newest mass of multiplied floors and windows visible at this point. *They*, ranged in this terrible recent erection, were going to bring in money—and was not money the only thing a self-respecting structure could be thought of as bringing in? Hadn't one heard, just before, in Boston, that the security, that the sweet serenity of the Park Street Church, charmingest, there, of aboriginal notes, the very light, with its perfect position and its dear old delightful Wren-like spire, of the starved city's eyes, had been artfully practised against, and that the question of saving it might become, in the near future, acute? Nothing, fortunately, I think, is so much the 'making' of New York, at its central point, for the visual, almost for the romantic, sense, as the Park Street Church is the making, by its happy coming-in, of Boston; and, therefore if it were thinkable that the peculiar rectitude of Boston might be laid in the dust, what mightn't easily come about for the reputedly less austere conscience of New York? Once such questions had obtained lodgment, to take one's walks was verily to look at almost everything in their light; and to commune with the sky-scraper under this influence was really to feel worsted, more and more, in any magnanimous attempt to adopt the aesthetic view of it. I may appear to make too much of these invidious presences, but it must be remembered that they represent, for our time, the only claim to any consideration other than merely statistical established by the resounding growth of New York. The attempt to take the aesthetic view is invariably blighted sooner or later by their most salient characteristic, *the* feature that speaks loudest for the economic idea. Window upon window, at any cost, is a condition never to be reconciled with any grace of building, and the logic of the matter here happens to put on a particularly fatal front. If quiet interspaces, always half the architectural battle, exist no more in such a structural scheme than quiet tones, blest breathing-spaces, occur, for the most part, in New York conversation, so the reason is, demonstrably, that the building can't afford them. (It is by very much the same law, one supposes, that New York conversation cannot afford stops.) The building can only afford lights, each light having a superlative value as an aid to the transaction of business and the conclusion of sharp bargains. Doesn't it take in fact acres of window-glass to help even an expert New Yorker to get the better of another expert one, or to see that the other expert one doesn't get the better of *him*? It is easy to conceive that, after all, with this origin and nature stamped upon their foreheads, the last word of the mercenary monsters should not be their address to our sense of formal beauty.

Still, as I have already hinted, there was always the case of the one other rescued identity and preserved felicity, the happy accident of the elder day still ungrudged and finally legitimated. When I say ungrudged, indeed, I seem to remember how I had heard that the divine little City Hall had *been* grudged, at a critical moment, to within an inch of its life; had but just escaped, in the event, the extremity of grudging. It lives on securely, by the mercy of fate—lives on in the delicacy of its beauty, speaking volumes again (more volumes, distinctly, than are anywhere else spoken) for the exquisite truth of the *conferred* value of interesting objects, the value derived from the social, the civilizing function for which they have happened to find their opportunity. It is the opportunity that gives them their price, and the luck of there being, round about them, nothing greater than themselves to steal it away from them. They strike thus, virtually, the supreme note, and—such is the mysterious play of our finer sensibility!—one takes this note, one is glad to work it, as the phrase goes, for all it is worth. I so work the note of the City Hall, no doubt, in speaking of the spectacle there constituted as 'divine'; but I do it precisely by reason of the spectacle taken *with* the delightful small facts of the building: largely by reason, in other words, of the elegant, gallant little structure's situation and history, the way it has played, artistically, ornamentally, its part, has held out for the good cause, the very centre of that assault of vulgarity of which the innumerable mementos rise within view of it and tower, at a certain distance, over it; and it has never parted with a square inch of its character, it has forced them, in a manner, to stand off. I hasten to add that in expressing thus its uncompromised state I speak of its outward, its aesthetic character only. So, at all events, it has discharged the civilizing function I just named as inherent in such cases—that of representing, to the community possessed of it, all the Style the community is likely to get, and of making itself responsible for the same.

The consistency of this effort, under difficulties, has been the story that brings tears to the eyes of the hovering kindly critic, and it is through his tears, no doubt, that such a personage reads the best passages of the tale and makes out the proportions of the object. Mine I recognize, didn't prevent my seeing that the pale yellow marble (or whatever it may be) of the City Hall has lost, by some late excoriation, the remembered charm of its old surface, the pleasant promiscuous patina of time; but the perfect taste and finish, the reduced yet ample scale, the harmony of parts, the just proportions, the modest classic grace, the living look of the type aimed at, these things, with gaiety of detail undiminished and 'quaintness' of effect augmented, are all there; and I see them, as I write, in that glow of appreciation which made it necessary, of a fine June morning, that I should somehow pay the whole place my respects. The simplest, in fact the only way, was, obviously, to pass under the charming portico and brave the consequences: this impunity of such audacities being, in America, one of the last of the lessons the repatriated absentee finds himself learning. The crushed spirit he brings back from European discipline never quite rises to the height of the native argument, the brave sense that the public, the civic building is his very own, for any honest use, so that he may treat even its most expensive pavements and staircases (and very expensive, for the American citizen, these have lately become,) without a question asked. This further and further unchallenged penetration begets in the perverted person I speak of a really romantic thrill: it is like some assault of the dim seraglio, with the guards bribed, the eunuchs drugged and one's life carried in one's hand. The only drawback to such freedom is that penetralia it is so easy to penetrate fail a little of a due impressiveness, and that if stationed sentinels are bad for the temper of the freeman they are good for the 'prestige' of the building.

Never, in any case, it seemed to me, had any freeman made so free with the majesty of things as I was to make on this occasion with the mysteries of the City Hall—even to the point of coming out into the presence of the Representative of the highest office with which City Halls are associated, and whose thoroughly gracious condonation of my act set the seal of success upon the whole adventure. Its dizziest intensity in fact sprang precisely from the unexpected view opened into the old official, the old so thick-peopled local, municipal world: upper chambers of council and state, delightfully of their nineteenth-century time, as to design and ornament, in spite of rank restoration; but replete, above all, with portraits of past worthies, past celebrities and city fathers, Mayors, Bosses, Presidents, Governors, Statesmen at large, Generals and Commodores at large, florid ghosts, looking so unsophisticated now, of years not remarkable, municipally, for the absence of sophistication. Here were types, running mainly to ugliness and all bristling with the taste of their day and the quite touching provincialism of their conditions, as to many of which nothing would be more interesting than a study of New York annals in the light of their personal look, their very noses and mouths and complexions and heads of hair—to say nothing of their waistcoats and neckties; with such colour, such sound and movement would the thick stream of local history then be interfused.

Wouldn't its thickness fairly become transparent? since to walk through the collection was not only to see and feel so much that had happened, but to understand, with the truth again and again inimitably pointed, why nothing could have happened otherwise; the whole array thus presenting itself as an unsurpassed demonstration of the real reasons of things. The florid ghosts look out from the exceedingly gilded frames—all that *that* can do is bravely done for them—with the frankest responsibility for everything; their collective presence becomes a kind of copious telltale document signed with a hundred names. There are few of these that at this hour, I think, we particularly desire to repeat; but the place where they may be read is, all the way from river to river and from the Battery to Harlem, the place in which there is most of the terrible town.

III

If the Bay had seemed to me, as I have noted, most to help the fond observer of New York aspects to a sense, through the eyes, of embracing possession, so the part played there for the outward view found its match for the inward in the portentous impression of one of the great caravansaries administered to me of a winter afternoon. I say with intention 'administered': on so assiduous a guide, through the endless labyrinth of the Waldorf-Astoria was I happily to chance after turning out of the early dusk and the January sleet and slosh into permitted, into enlightened contemplation of a pandemonium not less admirably ordered, to all appearance, than rarely intermitted. The seer of great cities is liable to easy error, I know, when he finds this, that or the other caught glimpse the supremely significant one—and I am willing to preface with that remark my confession that New York told me more of her story at once, then and there, than she was again and elsewhere to tell. With this apprehension that she was in fact fairly shrieking it into one's ears came a curiosity, corresponding, as to its kind and its degree of interest; so that there was nought to do, as we picked our tortuous way, but to stare with all our eyes and miss as little as possible for the revelation. That harshness of the essential conditions, the outward, which almost any large attempt at the amenities, in New York, has to take account of and make the best of, has at least the effect of projecting the visitor with force upon the spectacle prepared for him at this particular point and of marking the more its sudden high pitch, the character of violence which all its warmth, its colour and glitter so completely muffle. There is violence outside, mitigating sadly the frontal majesty of the monument, leaving it exposed to the vulgar assault of the street by the operation of those dire facts of absence of margin, of meagreness of site, of the brevity of the block, of the inveteracy of the near thoroughfare, which leave 'style', in construction, at the mercy of the impertinent cross-streets, make problem, preclude without pity any element of court or garden, and open to the builder in quest of distinction the one alternative, and the great adventure, of seeking his reward in the sky.

Of their licence to pursue it there to any extent whatever New Yorkers are, I think, a trifle too assertively proud; no court of approach, no interspace worth mention, ever forming meanwhile apart of the ground-plan or helping to receive the force of the breaking public wave. New York pays at this rate the penalty of her primal topographic curse, her old inconceivably bourgeois scheme of composition and distribution, the uncorrected labour of minds with no imagination of the future and blind before the opportunity given them by their two magnificent water-fronts. This original sin of the longitudinal avenues perpetually, yet meanly intersected, and of the organized sacrifice of the indicated alter-native, the great perspectives from East to West, might still have earned forgiveness by some occasional departure from its pettifogging consist-ency. But, thanks to this consistency, the city is, of all cities, the least endowed with any blest item of stately square or goodly garden, with any happy accident or surprise, any fortunate nook or casual corner, any deviation, in fine, into the liberal or the charming. That way, how-ever, for the regenerate filial mind, madness may be said to lie—the way of imagining what might have been and putting it all together in the light of what so helplessly is. One of the things that helplessly are, for instance, is just this assault of the street, as I have called it, upon any direct dealings with our caravansary. The electric cars, with their double track, are everywhere almost as tight a fit in the narrow channel of the roadway as the projectile in the bore of a gun; so that the Waldorf-Astoria, sitting by this absent margin for life with her open lap and arms, is reduced to confessing with a strained smile, across the traffic and the danger, how little, outside her mere swing-door, she can do for you. She seems to admit that the attempt to get at her may cost you your safety, but reminds you at the same time that any good American, and even any good inquiring stranger, is supposed willing to risk that boon for her. '*Un bon mouvement*, therefore: you must make a dash for it, but you'll see I'm worth it.' If such a claim as this last be ever justified, it would indubitably be justified here; the survivor scrambling out of the current and up the bank finds in the amplitude of the entertainment awaiting him an instant sense as of applied restoratives. The amazing hotel-world quickly closes round him; with the process of transition reduced to its minimum he is transported to conditions of extraordinary complexity and brilliancy, operating—and with proportionate perfection—by laws of their own and expressing after their fashion a complete scheme of life. The air swarms, to intensity, with the *characteristic*, the characteristic condensed and accumulated as he rarely elsewhere has had the luck to find it. It jumps out to meet his every glance, and this unanimity of its spring, of all its aspects and voices, is what I just now referred to as the essence of the loud New York story. That effect of violence in the whole communication, at which I thus hint, results from the inordinate mass, the quantity of presence, as it were, of the testimony heaped together for emphasis of the wondrous moral.

The moral in question, the high interest of the tale, is that you are in presence of a revelation of the possibilities of the hotel—for which the American spirit has found so unprecedented a use and a value; leading it on to express so a social, indeed positively an aesthetic ideal, and making it so, at this supreme pitch, a synonym for civilization, for the capture of conceived manners themselves, that one is verily tempted to ask if the hotel-spirit may not just *be* the American spirit most seeking and most finding itself. That truth—the truth that the present is more and more the day of the hotel—had not waited to burst on the mind at the view of this particular establishment; we have all more or less been educated to it, the world over, by the fruit-bearing action of the American example: in consequence of which it has been opened to us to see still other societies moved by the same irresistible spring and trying, with whatever grace and ease they may bring to the business, to unlearn as many as possible of their old social canons, and in especial their old discrimination in favour of the private life. The business for them—for communities to which the American ease in such matters is not native—goes much less of itself and produces as yet a scantier show; the great difference with the American show being that in the United States every one is, for the lubrication of the general machinery, practically in everything, whereas in Europe, mostly, it is only certain people who are in anything; so that the machinery, so much less generalized, works in a smaller, stiffer way. This one cara- vansary makes the American case vivid, gives it, you feel, that quantity of illustration which renders the place a new thing under the sun. It is an expression of the gregarious state breaking down every barrier but two—one of which, the barrier consisting of the high pecuniary tax, is the immediately obvious. The other, the rather more subtle, is the condition, for any member of the flock, that he or she—in other words especially she—be presumably 'respectable,' be, that is, not discoverably anything else. The rigour with which any appearance of pursued or desired adventure is kept down—adventure in the florid sense of the word, the sense in which it remains an euphemism—is not the least interesting note of the whole immense promiscuity. Protected at those two points the promiscuity carries, through the rest of the range, every- thing before it.

It sat there, it walked and talked, and ate and drank, and listened and danced to music, and otherwise revelled and roamed, and bought and sold, and came and went there, all on its own splendid terms and with an encompassing material splendour, a wealth and variety of consti- tuted picture and background, that might well feed it with the finest illusions about itself. It paraded through halls and saloons in which art and history, in masquerading dress, muffled almost to suffocation as in the gold brocade of their pretended majesties and their conciliatory graces, stood smirking on its passage with the last cynicism of hypocrisy. The exhibition is wonderful for that, for the suggested sense of a promis- cuity which manages to be at the same time an inordinate untempered monotony; manages to be so, on such ground as this, by an extraordinary trick of its own, wherever one finds it. The combination forms, I think, largely, the very interest, such as it is, of these phases of the human scene in the United States—if only for the pleasant puzzle of our wonder- ing how, when types, aspects, conditions, have so much in common, they should seem at all to make up a conscious miscellany. That question, however, the question of the play and range, the practical elasticity, of the social sameness, in America, will meet us elsewhere on our path, and I confess that all questions gave way, in my mind, to a single irresistible obsession. This was just the ache of envy of the spirit of a society which had found there, in its prodigious public setting, so exactly what it wanted. One was in presence, as never before, of a realized ideal and of that childlike rush of surrender to it and clutch at it which one was so repeatedly to recognize, in America, as the note of the supremely gregarious state. It made the whole vision unforgettable, and I am now carried back to it, I confess, in musing hours, as to one of my few glimpses of perfect human felicity. It had the admirable sign that it was, precisely, so comprehensively collective—that it made so vividly, in the old phrase, for the greatest happiness of the greatest number. Its rare beauty, one felt with instant clarity of perception, was that it was, for a 'mixed' social manifestation, blissfully exempt from any principle or possibility of discord with itself. It was absolutely a fit to its conditions, those conditions which were both its earth and its heaven, and every part of the picture, every item of the immense sum, every wheel of the wondrous complexity, was on the best terms with all the rest.

The sense of these things became for the hour as the golden glow in which one's envy burned, and through which, while the sleet and the slosh, and the clangorous charge of cars, and the hustling, hustled crowds held the outer world, one carried one's charmed attention from one chamber of the temple to another. For that is how the place speaks, as great constructed and achieved harmonies mostly speak—as a temple builded, with clustering chapels and shrines, to an idea. The hundreds and hundreds of people in circulation, the innumerable huge-hatted ladies in especial, with their air of finding in the gilded and storied labyrinth the very firesides and pathways of home, became thus the serene faithful, whose rites one would no more have sceptically brushed than one would doff one's disguise in a Mohammedan mosque. The question of who they all might be, seated under palms and by fountains, or communing, in some inimitable New York tune, with the shade of Marie Antoinette in the queer recaptured actuality of an easy Versailles or an intimate Trianon—such questions as that, interesting in other societies and at other times, insisted on yielding here to the mere eloquence of the general truth. Here was a social order in positively stable equilibrium. Here was a world whose relation to its form and medium was practically imperturbable; here was a conception of publicity *as* the vital medium organized with the authority with which the American genius for organization, put on its mettle, alone could organize it. The whole thing remains for me, however, I repeat, a gorgeous golden blur, a paradise peopled with unmistakable American shapes, yet in which, the general and the particular, the organized and the extemporized, the element of ingenuous joy below and of consummate management above, melted together and left one uncertain which of them one was, at a given turn of the maze, most admiring. When I reflect indeed that without my clue I should not have even known the maze—should not have known, at the given turn, whether I was engulfed, for instance, in the *vente de charité* of the theatrical profession and the onset of persuasive peddling actresses, or in the annual tea-party of German lady-patronesses (of I know not what) filling with their Oriental opulence and their strange idiom a playhouse of the richest rococo, where some other expensive anniversary, the ball of a guild or the carouse of a club, was to tread on their heels and instantly mobilize away their paraphernalia—when I so reflect I see the sharpest dazzle of the eyes as precisely the play of the genius for organization.

There are a thousand forms of this ubiquitous American force, the most ubiquitous of all, that I was in no position to measure; but there was often no resisting a vivid view of the form it may take, on occasion, under pressure of the native conception of the hotel. Encountered embodiments of the gift, in this connection, master-spirits of management whose influence was as the very air, the very expensive air, one breathed, abide with me as the intensest examples of a type which has even on the American ground, doubtless, not said its last word, but which has at least treated itself there to a luxury of development. It gives the impression, when at all directly met, of having at its service something of that fine flame that makes up personal greatness; so that, again and again, as I found, one would have liked to see it more intimately at work. Such failures of opportunity and of penetration, however, are but the daily bread of the visionary tourist. Whenever I dip back, in fond memory, none the less, into the vision I have here attempted once more to call up, I see the whole thing overswept as by the colossal extended arms, waving the magical bâton, of some high-stationed orchestral leader, the absolute presiding power, conscious of every note of every instrument, controlling and commanding the whole volume of sound, keeping the whole effect together and making it what it is. What may one say of such a spirit if not that he understands, so to speak, the forces he sways, understands his boundless American material and plays with it like a master indeed? One sees it thus, in its crude plasticity, almost in the likeness of an army of puppets whose strings the wealth of his technical imagination teaches him innumerable ways of pulling, and yet whose innocent, whose always ingenuous agitation of their members he has found means to make them think of themselves as delightfully free and easy. Such was my impression of the perfection of the concert that, for fear of its being spoiled by some chance false note, I never went into the place again.

It might meanwhile seem no great adventure merely to walk the streets; but (beside the fact that there is, in general, never a better way of taking in life), this pursuit irresistibly solicited, on the least pretext, the observer whose impressions I note—accustomed as he had even been conscientiously to yield to it: more particularly with the relenting year, when the breath of spring, mildness being really installed, appeared the one vague and disinterested presence in the place, the one presence not vociferous and clamorous. Any definite presence that doesn't bellow and bang takes on in New York by that simple fact a distinction practically exquisite; so that one goes forth to meet it as a guest of honour, and that, for my own experience, I remember certain aimless strolls as snatches of intimate communion with the spirit of May and June—as abounding, almost to enchantment, in the comparatively *still* condition. Two secrets, at this time, seemed to profit by that influence to tremble out; one of these to the effect that New York would really have been 'meant' to be charming, and the other to the effect that the restless analyst, willing at the lightest persuasion to let so much of its ugliness edge away unscathed from his analysts, must have had for it, from far back, one of those loyalties that are beyond any reason.

'It's all very well' the voice of the air seemed to say, if I may so take it up; 'it's all very well to "criticize" but you distinctly take an interest and are the victim of your interest, be the grounds of your perversity what they will. You can't escape from it, and don't you see that this, precisely, is what *makes* an adventure for you (an adventure, I admit, as with some strident, battered, questionable beauty, truly some "bold bad" charmer), of almost any odd stroll, or waste half-hour, or other promiscuous passage, that results for you in an impression? There is always your bad habit of receiving through almost any accident of vision more impressions than you know what to do with; but that, for common convenience, is your eternal handicap and may not be allowed to plead here against your special responsibility. You *care* for the terrible town, yea even for the "horrible" as I have overheard you call it, or at least think it, when you supposed no one would know; and you see now

how, if you fly such fancies as that it was conceivably meant to be charming, you are tangled by that weakness in some underhand imagination
of its possibly, one of these days, as a riper fruit of time becoming so.
To do that, you indeed sneakingly provide, it must get away from itself;
but you are ready to follow its hypothetic dance even to the mainland
and to the very end of its tether. What makes the general relation of
your adventure with it is that, at bottom, you are all the while wondering,
in presence of the aspects of its genius and its shame, what elements
or parts, if any, would be worth its saving, worth carrying off for the
fresh embodiment and the better life, and which of them would have,
on the other hand, to face the notoriety of going *first* by the board.
I have literally heard you qualify the monster as ''shameless''—though
that was wrung from you, I admit, by the worst of the winter conditions,
when circulation, in any fashion consistent with personal decency or
dignity, was merely mocked at, when the stony-hearted ''trolleys'' cars
of Juggernaut in their power to squash, triumphed all along the line,
when the February blasts became as cyclones in the darkened gorges
of masonry (which down-town, in particular, put on, at their mouths,
the semblance of black rat-holes, holes of gigantic rats, inhabited by
whirlwinds;) when all the pretences and impunities and infirmities, in
fine, had massed themselves to be hurled at you in the fury of the elements, in the character of the traffic, in the unadapted state of the place
to almost *any* dense movement, and, beyond everything, in that pitch
of all the noises which acted on your nerves as so much wanton provoca-
tion, so much conscious cynicism. The fury of sound took the form
of derision of the rest of your woe, and thus it *might*, I admit, have
struck you as brazen that the horrible place should, in such confessed
collapse, still be swaggering and shouting. It might have struck you
that great cities, with the eyes of the world on them, as the phrase
is, should be capable either of a proper form or (failing this) of a proper
compunction; which tributes to propriety were, on the part of New York,
equally wanting. This made you remark, precisely, that nothing was
wanting, on the other hand, to that analogy with the character of the
bad bold beauty, the creature the most blatant of whose pretensions
is that she is one of those to whom everything is always forgiven. On
what ground ''forgiven''? of course you ask; but note that you ask it
while you're in the very act of forgiving. Oh yes, you are; you've as
much as said so yourself. So there it all is; arrange it as you can. Poor
dead bad bold beauty; there must indeed be something about her—!'

Let me grant then, to get on, that there *was* doubtless, in the better time, something about her; there was enough about her, at all events, to conduce to that distinct cultivation of her company for which the contemplative stroll, when there was time for it, was but another name. The analogy was in truth complete; since the repetition of such walks, and the admission of the beguiled state contained in them, resembled nothing so much as the visits so often still incorrigibly made to com-promised charmers. I defy even a master of morbid observation to peram-bulate New York unless he be interested; so that in a case of memories so gathered the interest must be taken as a final act. Let me figure it, to this end, as lively in every connection—and so indeed no more lively at one mild crisis than at another. The crisis—even of observation at the morbid pitch—is inevitably mild in cities intensely new; and it was with the quite peculiarly insistent newness of the upper reaches of the town that the spirit of romantic inquiry had always, at the best, to reckon. There are new cities enough about the world, goodness knows, and there are new parts enough of old cities—for examples of which we need go no farther than London, Paris and Rome, all of late so mercilessly renovated. But the newness of New York—unlike even that of Boston, I seemed to discern—had this mark of its very own, that it affects one, in every case, as having treated itself as still more provisional, if possible, than any poor dear little interest of antiquity it may have annihilated. The very sign of its energy is that it doesn't believe in itself; it fails to succeed, even at a cost of millions, in persuading you that it does. Its mission would appear to be, exactly, to gild the temporary, with its gold, as many inches thick as may be, and then, with a fresh shrug, a shrug of its splendid cynicism for its freshly detected inability to con-vince, give up its actual work, however exorbitant, as the merest of stop-gaps. The difficulty with the compromised charmer is just this con-stant inability to convince; to convince ever, I mean, that she is serious, serious about any form whatever, or about anything but that perpetual passionate pecuniary purpose which plays with all forms, which derides and devours them, though it may pile up the cost of them in order to rest a while, spent and haggard, in the illusion of their finality.

The perception of this truth grows for you by your simply walking up Fifth Avenue and pausing a little in presence of certain forms, certain exorbitant structures, in other words, the elegant domiciliary, as to which the illusion of finality was within one's memory magnificent and com-plete, but as to which one feels today that their life wouldn't be, as against any whisper of a higher interest, worth an hour's purchase. They sit there in the florid majesty of the taste of their time—a light now, alas, generally clouded; and I pretend of course to speak, in alluding to them, of no individual case of danger or doom. It is only a question of that unintending and unconvincing expression of New York everywhere, as yet, on the matter of the *maintenance* of a given effect—which comes back to the general insincerity of effects, and truly even (as I have already noted) to the insincerity of the effect of the sky-scrapers themselves. There results from all this—and as much where the place most smells of its millions as elsewhere—that unmistakable New York admission of unattempted, impossible maturity. The new Paris and the new Rome do at least propose, I think, to be old—one of these days; the new London even, erect as she is on leaseholds destitute of dignity, yet does, for the period, appear to believe in herself. The vice I glance at is, however, when showing, in our flagrant example, on the forehead of its victims, much more a cause for pitying than for decrying them. Again and again, in the upper reaches, you pause with that pity; you learn, on the occasion of a kindly glance up and down a quiet cross-street (there being objects and aspects in many of them appealing to kindness), that such and such a house, or a row, is 'coming down'; and you gasp, in presence of the elements involved, at the strangeness of the moral so pointed. It rings out like the crack of that lash in the sky, the play of some mighty teamster's whip, which ends by affecting you as the poor New Yorker's one association with the idea of 'powers above.' 'No'—this is the tune to which the whip seems flourished—'there's no step at which you shall rest, no form, as I'm constantly showing you, to which, consistently with my interests, you *can*. I build you up but to tear you down, for if I were to let sentiment and sincerity once take root, were to let any tenderness of association once accumulate, or any "love of the old" once pass unsnubbed, what would become of *us*, who have our hands on the whipstock, please? Fortunately we've learned the secret for keeping association at bay. We've learned that the great thing is not to suffer it to so much as begin. Wherever it does begin we find we're lost; but as that takes you some time we get in ahead. It's the reason, if you must know, why you shall "run" all, without exception, to the fifty floors. We defy you even to aspire to venerate shapes so grossly constructed as the arrangement in fifty floors. You may have a feeling for keeping on with an old staircase, consecrated by the tread of generations—especially when it's "good" and old staircases are often so lovely, how can you have a feeling for keeping on with an old elevator, how can you have it any more than for keeping on with an old omnibus? You'd be ashamed to venerate the arrangement in fifty floors, accordingly, even if you could; whereby, saving you any moral trouble or struggle, they are conceived and constructed—and you must do us the justice of this care for your sensibility—in a manner to put the thing out of the question. In such a manner, moreover, as that there shall be immeasurably more of them, in quantity, to tear down than of the actual past that we are now sweeping away. Wherefore we shall be kept in precious practice. The word will perhaps be then— who knows?—for building from the earth-surface downwards; in which case it will be a question of tearing, so to speak, ''up.'' It little matters, so long as we blight the superstition of rest.'

Yet even in the midst of this vision of eternal waste, of conscious, sentient-looking houses and rows, full sections of streets, to which the rich taste of history is forbidden even while their fresh young lips are just touching the cup, something charmingly done, here and there, some bid for the ampler permanence, seems to say to you that the particular place only asks, as a human home, to lead the life it has begun, only asks to enfold generations and gather in traditions, to show itself capable of growing up to character and authority. Houses of the best taste are like clothes of the best tailors—it takes their age to show us how good they are; and I frequently recognized, in the region of the upper reaches, this direct appeal of the individual case of happy construction indescribably precipitate and elaborate—the latter face about it always so oddly hand in hand with the former; and we should exceed in saying that felicity is always its mark. But some highly liberal, some extravagant intention almost always is, and we meet here even that happy accident, already encountered and acclaimed, in its few examples, down-town, of the object shining almost absurdly in the light of its merely comparative distinction. All but lost in the welter of instances of sham refinement, the shy little case of real refinement detaches itself ridiculously, as being (like the saved City Hall, or like the pleasant old garden-walled houses on the north-west corner of Washington Square and Fifth Avenue) of so beneficent an admonition as to show, relatively speaking, for priceless. These things, which I may not take time to pick out, are the salt that saves, and it is enough to say for their delicacy that they are the direct counterpart of those other dreadful presences, looming round them, which embody the imagination of new kinds and new clustered, emphasized quantities of vulgarity. To recall these fine notes and these loud ones, the whole play of wealth and energy and untutored liberty, of the movement of a breathless civilization reflected, as brick and stone and marble may reflect, through all the contrasts of prodigious flight and portentous stumble, is to acknowledge, positively, that one's rambles were delightful, and that the district abutting on the east side of the Park, in particular, never engaged my attention without, by the same stroke, making the social question dance before it in a hundred interesting forms.

The social question quite fills the air, in New York, for any spectator whose impressions at all follow themselves up; it wears, at any rate, in what I have called the upper reaches, the perpetual strange appearance as of Property perched high aloft and yet itself looking about, all ruefully, in the wonder of what it is exactly doing there. We see it perched, assuredly, in other and older cities, other and older social orders; but it strikes us in those situations as knowing a little more where it is. It strikes us as knowing how it has got up and why it must, infallibly, stay up; it has not the frightened look, measuring the spaces around, of a small child set on a mantelshelf and about to cry out. If old societies are interesting, however, I am far from thinking that young ones may not be more so—with their collective countenance so much more presented, precisely, to observation, as by their artless need to get themselves explained. The American world produces almost everywhere the impression of appealing to any attested interest for the world, the *fin mot*, of what it may mean; but I somehow see those parts of it most at a loss that are already explained not a little by the ample possession of money. This is the amiable side there of the large developments of private ease in general—the amiable side of those numerous groups that are rich enough and, in the happy vulgar phrase, bloated enough, to be candidates for the classic imputation of haughtiness. The amiability proceeds from an essential vagueness; whereas real haughtiness is never vague about itself—it is only vague about others. That is the human note in the huge American rattle of gold—so far as the 'social' field is the scene of the rattle. The 'business' field is a different matter—as to which the determination of the audibility in it of the human note (so interesting to try for if one had but the warrant) is a line of research closed to me, alas, by my fatally uninitiated state. My point is, at all events, that you cannot be 'hard' really, with any society that affects you as ready to learn from you, and from this resource for it of your detachment combining with your proximity, what in the name of all its possessions and all its destitutions it would honestly be 'at.'

Chicago

CHARLES DUDLEY WARNER

In this essay from Studies in the South and West *(1890),
Charles Dudley Warner describes his views on the city of
Chicago and its people, gathered over the years he spent
there while practicing law.*

THE COUNTRY GETS its impression of Chicago largely from the Chicago
newspapers. In my observation, the impression is wrong. The press
is able, vigorous, voluminous, full of enterprise, alert, spirited; its news
columns are marvellous in quantity, if not in quality; nowhere are important events, public meetings, and demonstrations more fully, graphically,
and satisfactorily reported; it has keen and competent writers in several
departments of criticism—theatrical, musical, and occasionally literary;
independence, with less of personal bias than in some other cities; the

editorial pages of most of the newspapers are bright, sparkling, witty, not seldom spiced with knowing drollery, and strong, vivid, well-informed and well-written, in the discussion of public questions, with an allowance always to be made for the 'personal equation' in dealing with particular men and measures—as little provincial in this respect as any press in the country.

But it lacks tone, elevation of purpose; it represents to the world the inferior elements of a great city rather than the better, under a mistaken notion in the press and the public, not confined to Chicago, as to what is 'news.' It cannot escape the charge of being highly sensational; that is, the elevation into notoriety of mean persons and mean events by every rhetorical and pictorial device. Day after day the leading news, the most displayed and most conspicuous, will be of vulgar men and women, and all the more expanded if it have in it a spice of scandal. This sort of reading creates a diseased appetite, which requires a stronger dose daily to satisfy; and people who read it lose their relish for the higher, more decent, if less piquant, news of the world. Of course the Chicago newspapers are not by any means alone in this course; it is a disease of the time. Even New York has recently imitated successfully this feature of what is called Western journalism.

But it is largely from the Chicago newspapers that the impression has gone abroad that the city is pre-eminent in divorces, pre-eminent in scandals, that its society is fast, that it is vulgar and pretentious, that its tone is 'shoddy,' and its culture a sham. The laws of Illinois in regard to divorces are not more lax than in some Eastern States, and divorces are not more numerous there of residents (according to population) than in some Eastern towns; but while the press of the latter give merely an official line to the court separations, the Chicago papers parade all the details, and illustrate them with pictures. Many people go there to get divorces, because they avoid scandal at their homes, and because the Chicago courts offer unusual facilities in being open every month in the year. Chicago has a young, mobile population, an immense foreign brutal element. I watched for some weeks the daily reports of divorces and scandals. Almost without exception they related to the lower, not to say the more vulgar, portions of social life. In several years the city has had, I believe, only two *causes célèbres* in what is called good society—a remarkable record for a city of its size. Of course a city of this magnitude and mobility is not free from vice and immorality and fast living; but I am compelled to record the deliberate opinion, formed on a good deal of observation and inquiry, that the moral tone in Chicago society, in all the well-to-do industrious classes which give the town its distinctive character, is purer and higher than in any other city of its size with which I am acquainted, and purer than in many much smaller. The tone is not so fast, public opinion is more restrictive, and women take, and are disposed to take, less latitude in conduct. This was not my impression from the newspapers. But it is true not only that social life holds itself to great propriety, but that the moral atmosphere is uncommonly pure and wholesome. At the same time, the city does not lack gayety of movement, and it would not be called prudish, nor in some respects conventional.

It is curious, also, that the newspapers, or some of them, take pleasure in mocking at the culture of the town. Outside papers catch this spirit, and the 'culture' of Chicago is the butt of the paragraphers. It is a singular attitude for newspapers to take regarding their own city. Not long ago Mr McClurg published a very neat volume, in vellum, of the fragments of Sappho, with translations. If the volume had appeared in Boston it would have been welcomed and most respectfully received in Chicago. But instead of regarding it as an evidence of the growing literary taste of the new town, the humorists saw occasion in it for exquisite mockery in the juxtaposition of Sappho with the modern ability to kill seven pigs a minute, and in the cleverest and most humorous manner set all the country in a roar over the incongruity. It goes without saying that the business men of Chicago were not sitting up nights to study the Greek poets in the original; but the fact was that there was enough literary taste in the city to make the volume a profitable venture, and that its appearance was an evidence of intellectual activity and scholarly inclination that would be creditable to any city in the land. It was not at all my intention to intrude my impressions of a newspaper press so very able and with such magnificent opportunities as that of Chicago, but it was unavoidable to mention one of the causes of the misapprehension of the social and moral condition of the city.

The business statistics of Chicago, and the story of its growth, and the social movement, which have been touched on in a previous paper, give only a half-picture of the life of the town. The prophecy for its great and more hopeful future is in other exhibitions of its incessant activity. My limits permit only a reference to its churches, extensive charities (which alone would make a remarkable and most creditable chapter), hospitals, medical schools, and conservatories of music. Club life is attaining metropolitan proportions. There is on the south side the Chicago, the Union League, the University, the Calumet, and on the north side the Union—all vigorous, and most of them housed in superb buildings of their own. The Women's Exchange is a most useful organization, and the Ladies' Fortnightly ranks with the best intellectual associations in the country. The Commercial Club, composed of sixty representative business men in all departments, is a most vital element in the prosperity of the city. I cannot dwell upon these. But at least a word must be said about the charities, and some space must be given to the schools.

The number of solicitors for far West churches and colleges who pass by Chicago and come to New York and New England for money have created the impression that Chicago is not a good place to go for this purpose. Whatever may be the truth of this, the city does give royally for private charities, and liberally for mission work beyond her borders. It is estimated by those familiar with the subject that Chicago contributes for charitable and religious purposes, exclusive of the public charities of the city and country, not less that five millions of dollars annually. I have not room to give even the partial list of the benevolent societies that lies before me, but beginning with the Chicago Relief and Aid, and the Armour Mission, and going down to lesser organizations, the sum annually given by them is considerably over half a million dollars. The amount raised by the churches of various denominations for religious purposes is not less than four millions yearly. These figures prove the liberality, and I am able to add that the charities are most sympathetically and intelligently administered.

Inviting, by its opportunities for labor and its facilities for business, comers from all the world, a large proportion of whom are aliens to the language and institutions of America, Chicago is making a noble fight to assimilate this material into good citizenship. The popular schools are liberally sustained, intelligently directed, practise the most advanced and inspiring methods, and exhibit excellent results. I have not the statistics of 1887; but in 1886, when the population was only 703,000, there were 129,000 between the ages of six and sixteen, of whom 83,000 were enrolled as pupils, and the average daily attendance in schools was over 65,000. Besides these there were about 43,000 in private schools. The census of 1886 reports only 34 children between the ages of six and twenty-one who could neither read nor write. There were 91 school buildings owned by the city, and two rented. Of these, three are high-schools, one in each division, the newest, on the west side, having 1000 students. The school attendance increases by a large per cent each year. The principals of the high-schools were men; of the grammar and primary schools, 35 men and 42 women. The total of teachers was 1440, of whom 56 were men. By the census of 1886 there were 106,929 children in the city under six years of age. No kindergartens are attached to the public schools, but the question of attaching them is agitated. In the lower grades, however, the instruction is by object lessons, drawing, writing, modelling and exercises that train the eye to observe, the tongue to describe, and that awaken attention without weariness. The alertness of the scholars and the enthusiasm of the teachers were marked. It should be added that German is extensively taught in the grammar schools, and that the number enrolled in the German classes in 1886 was over 28,000. There is some public sentiment for throwing out German from the public schools, and generally for restricting studies in the higher branches. The argument against this is that very few of the children, and the majority of those girls, enter the high-schools; the boys are taken out early for business, and get no education afterwards. In 1885 were organized public elementary evening schools (which had, in 1886, 6709 pupils), and an evening high-school, in which book-keeping, stenography, mechanical drawing, and advanced mathematics were taught. The School Committee also have in charge day schools for the education of deaf and dumb children.

The total expenditure for 1886 was $2,060,803; this includes $1,023,394 paid to superintendents and teachers, and large sums for new buildings. apparatus, and repairs. The total cash receipts for school purposes were $2,091,951. Of this was from the school tax fund $1,758,053 (the total city tax for all purposes was $5,368,409), and the rest from State dividend and school fund bonds and miscellaneous sources. These figures show that education is not neglected.

Of the quality and efficacy of this education there cannot be two opinions, as seen in the schools which I visited. The high-school on the west side is a model of its kind; but perhaps as interesting an example of popular education as any is the Franklin grammar and primary school on the north side, in a district of laboring people. Here were 1700 pupils, all children of working people, mostly Swedes and Germans, from the age of six years upwards. Here were found some of the children of the late anarchists, and nowhere else can one see a more interesting attempt to manufacture intelligent American citizens. The instruction rises through the several grades from object lessons, drawing, writing and reading (and writing and reading well), to elementary physiology, political and constitutional history, and physical geography. Here is taught to young children what they cannot learn at home, and might never clearly comprehend otherwise; not only something of the geography and history of the country, but the distinctive principles of our government, its constitutional ideas, the growth, creeds, and relations of political parties, and the personality of the great men who have represented them. That the pupils comprehend these subjects fairly well I had evidence in recitations that were as pleasing as surprising. In this way Chicago is teaching its alien population American ideas, and it is fair to presume that the rising generation will have some notion of the nature and value of our institutions that will save them from the inclination to destroy them.

The public mind is agitated a good deal on the question of the introduction of manual training into the public schools. The idea of some people is that manual training should only be used as an aid to mental training, in order to give definiteness and accuracy to thought; others would like actual trades taught; and others think that it is outside the function of the State to teach anything but elementary mental studies. The subject would require an essay by itself, and I only allude to it to say that Chicago is quite alive to the problems and the most advanced educational ideas. If one would like to study the philosophy and the practical working of what may be called physico-mental training, I know no better place in the country to do so than the Cook County Normal School, near Englewood, under the charge of Colonel F. W. Parker, the originator of what is known as the Quincy (Massachusetts) System. This is a training school for about 100 teachers, in a building where they have practice on about 500 children in all stages of education, from the kindergarten up to the eighth grade. This may be called a thorough manual training school, but not to teach trades, work being done in drawing, modelling in clay, making raised maps, and wood-carving. The Quincy System, which is sometimes described as the development of character by developing mind and body, has a literature to itself. This remarkable school, which draws teachers for training from all over the country, is a notable instance of the hospitality of the West to new and advanced ideas. It does not neglect the literary side in education. Here and in some of the grammar schools of Chicago the experiment is successfully tried of interesting young children in the best literature by reading to them from the works of the best authors, ancient and modern, and giving them a taste for what is excellent, instead of the trash that is likely to fall into their hands—the cultivation of sustained and consecutive interest in narratives, essays, and descriptions in good literature, in place of the scrappy selections and reading-books written down to the childish level. The written comments and criticisms of the children on what they acquire in this way are a perfect vindication of the experiment. It is to be said also that this sort of education, coupled with the manual training, and the inculcated love for order and neatness, is beginning to tell on the homes of these children. The parents are actually being educated and civilized through the public schools.

An opportunity for superior technical education is given in the Chicago Manual Training School, founded and sustained by the Commercial Club. It has a handsome and commodious building on the corner of Michigan Avenue and Twelfth Street, which accommodates over two hundred pupils, under the direction of Dr Henry H. Belfield, assisted by an able corps of teachers and practical mechanics. It has only been in operation since 1884, but has fully demonstrated its usefulness in the training of young men for places of responsibility and profit. Some of the pupils are from the city schools, but it is open to all boys of good character and promise. The course is three years, in which the tuition is $80, $100, and $120 a year; but the club provides for the payment of the tuition of a limited number of deserving boys whose parents lack the means to give them this sort of education. The course includes the higher mathematics, English, and French or Latin, physics, chemistry—in short, a high-school course—with drawing, and all sorts of technical training in work in wood and iron, the use and making of tools, and the building of machinery, up to the construction of steam-engines, stationary and locomotive. Throughout the course one hour each day is given to drawing, two hours to shop-work, and the remainder of the school day to study and recitation. The shops—the wood-work rooms, the foundery, the forge-room, the machine-shop—are exceedingly well equipped and well managed. The visitor cannot but be pleased by the tone of the school and the intelligent enthusiasm of the pupils. It is an institution likely to grow, and perhaps become the nucleus of a great technical school, which the West much needs. It is worthy of notice also as an illustration of the public spirit, sagacity, and liberality of the Chicago business men. They probably see that if the city is greatly to increase its importance as a manufacturing centre, it must train a considerable proportion of its population to the highest skilled labor, and that splendidly equipped and ably taught technical schools would do for Chicago what similar institutions in Zurich have done for Switzerland. Chicago is ready for a really comprehensive technical and industrial college, and probably no other investment would now add more to the solid prosperity and wealth of the town.

Such an institution would not hinder, but rather help, the higher education, without which the best technical education tends to materialize life. Chicago must before long recognize the value of the intellectual side by beginning the foundation of a college of pure learning. For in nothing is the Western society of to-day more in danger than in the superficial half-education which is called 'practical', and in the lack of logic and philosophy. The tendency to the literary side—awakening a love for good books—in the public schools is very hopeful. The existence of some well-chosen private libraries shows the same tendency. In art and archaeology there is also much promise. The Art Institution is a very fine building, with a vigorous school in drawing and painting, and its occasional loan exhibitions show that the city contains a good many fine pictures, though scarcely proportioned to its wealth. The Historical Society, which has had the irreparable misfortune twice to lose its entire collections by fire, is beginning anew with vigor, and will shortly erect a building from its own funds. Among the private collections which have a historical value is that relating to the Indian history of the West made by Mr Edward Ayer, and a large library of rare and scarce books, mostly of the English Shakespeare period, by the Rev Frank M. Bristoll. These, together with the remarkable collection of Mr C. F. Gunther (of which further mention will be made), are prophecies of a great literary and archaeological museum.

The city has reason to be proud of its Free Public Library, organized under the general library law of Illinois, which permits the support of a free library in every incorporated city, town, and township by taxation. This library is sustained by a tax of one half-mill on the assessed value of all the city property. This brings it in now about £80,000 a year, which makes its income for 1888, together with its fund and fines, about £90,000. It is at present housed in the City Hall, but will soon have a building of its own (on Dearborn Park), towards the erection of which it has a considerable fund. It has about 130,000 volumes, including a fair reference library and many expensive art books. The institution has been well managed hitherto, notwithstanding its connection with politics in the appointment of the trustees by the mayor, and its dependence upon the city councils. The reading-rooms are thronged daily; the average daily circulation has increased yearly; it was 2263 in 1887—a gain of eleven per cent over the preceding year. This is stimulated by the establishment of eight delivering stations in different parts of the city. The cosmopolitan character of the users of the library is indicated by the uncommon number of German, French, Dutch, Bohemian, Polish and Scandinavian books. Of the books issued at the delivery stations in 1887 twelve per cent were in the Bohemian language. The encouraging thing about this free library is that it is not only freely used, but that it is as freely sustained by the voting population.

Another institution, which promises to have still more influence on the city, and indeed on the whole North-west, is the Newberry Library, now organizing under an able board of trustees, who have chosen Mr W. F. Poole as librarian. The munificent fund of the donor is now reckoned at about $2,500,000, but the value of the property will be very much more than this in a few years. A temporary building for the library, which is slowly forming, will be erected at once, but the library, which is to occupy a square on the north side, will not be erected until the plans are fully matured. It is to be a library of reference and study solely, and it is in contemplation to have the books distributed in separate rooms for each department, with ample facilities for reading and study in each room. If the library is built and the collections are made in accordance with the ample means at command, and in the spirit of its projectors, it will powerfully tend to make Chicago not only the money but the intellectual centre of the North-west, and attract to it hosts of students from all quarters. One can hardly over-estimate the influence that such a library as this may be will have upon the character and the attractiveness of the city.

I hope that it will have ample space for, and that it will receive, certain literary collections, such as are the glory and the attraction, both to students and sight-seers, of the great libraries of the world. And this leads me to speak of the treasures of Mr Gunther, the most remarkable private collection I have ever seen, and already worthy to rank with some of the most famous on public exhibition. Mr Gunther is a candy manufacturer, who has an archaeological and 'curio' taste, and for many years has devoted an amount of money to the purchase of historical relics that if known would probably astonish the public. Only specimens of what he has can be displayed in the large apartment set apart for the purpose over his shop. The collection is miscellaneous, forming a varied and most interesting museum. It contains relics—many of them unique, and most of them having a historical value—from many lands and all periods since the Middle Ages, and is strong in relics and documents relating to our own history, from the colonial period down to the close of our civil war. But the distinction of the collection is in its original letters and manuscripts, and rare books. It is hardly possible to mention a name famous since America was discovered that is not here represented by an autograph letter or some personal relics. We may pass by such mementos as the Appomattox table, a sampler worked by Queen Elizabeth, a prayer-book of Mary, Queen of Scots, personal belongings of Washington, Lincoln, and hundreds of other historical characters, but we must give a little space to the books and manuscripts, in order that it may be seen that all the wealth of Chicago is not in grain and meat.

It is only possible here to name a few of the original letters, manuscripts, and historical papers in this wonderful collection of over seventeen thousand. Most of the great names in the literature of our era are represented. There is an autograph letter of Molière, the only one known outside of France, except one in the British Museum; there are letters of Voltaire, Victor Hugo, Madame Roland, and other French writers. It is understood that this is not a collection of mere autographs, but of letters or original manuscripts of those named. In Germany, nearly all the great poets and writers—Goethe, Schiller, Uhland, Lessing, etc.; in England, Milton, Pope, Shelley, Keats, Wordsworth, Coleridge, Cowper, Hunt, Gray, etc.; the manuscript of Byron's 'Prometheus,' the 'Auld Lang Syne' of Burns, and his 'Journal in the Highlands;' 'Sweet Home' in the author's hand; a poem by Thackeray; manuscript stories of Scott and Dickens. Among the Italians, Tasso. In America, the known authors, almost without exception. There are letters from nearly all the prominent reformers—Calvin, Melanchthon, Zwingle, Erasmus, Savonarola; a letter of Luther in regard to the Pope's bull; letters of prominent leaders—William the Silent, John the Steadfast, Gustavus Adolphus, Wallenstein. There is a curious collection of letters of the saints—St Francis de Sales, St Vincent de Paul, St Borromeo; letters of the Popes for three centuries and a half, and of many of the great cardinals.

I must set down a few more of the noted names, and that without much order. There is a manuscript of Charlotte Corday (probably the only one in this country), John Bunyan, Izaak Walton, John Cotton,

Michael Angelo, Galileo, Lorenzo the Magnificent; letters of Queen Elizabeth, Mary, Queen of Scots, Mary of England, Anne, several of Victoria (one at the age of twelve), Catherine de' Medici, Marie Antoinette, Josephine, Marie Louise; letters of all the Napoleons, of Frederick the Great, Marat, Robespierre, St Just; a letter of Hernando Cortez to Charles the Fifth; a letter of Alverez; letters of kings of all European nations, and statesmen and generals without number.

The collection is rich in colonial and Revolutionary material; original letters from Plymouth Colony, 1621, 1622, 1623—I believe the only ones known; manuscript sermons of the early American ministers; letters of the first bishops, White and Seabury; letters of John André, Nathen Hale, Kosciusko, Pulaski, De Kalb, Steuben, and of great numbers of the general and subordinate officers of the French and Revolutionary wars; William Tudor's manuscript account of the battle of Bunker Hill; a letter of Aide-de-camp Robert Orhm to the Governor of Pennsylvania relating Braddock's defeat; the original of Washington's first Thanksgiving proclamation; the report of the committee of the Continental Congress on its visit to Valley Forge on the distress of the army; the original proceedings of the Commissioners of the Colonies at Cambridge for the organization of the Continental army; original returns of the Hessians captured at Princeton; orderly books of the Continental army; manuscripts and surveys of the early explorers; letters of Lafitte, the pirate, Paul Jones, Captain Lawrence, Bainbridge, and so on. Documents relating to the Washington family are very remarkable: the original will of Lawrence Washington bequeathing Mount Vernon to George; will of John Custis to his family; letters of Martha, of Mary, the mother of George, of Betty Lewis, his sister, of all his step and grand children of the Custis family.

In music there are the original manuscript compositions of all the leading musicians in our modern world, and there is a large collection of the choral books from ancient monasteries and churches. There are exquisite illuminated missals on parchment of all periods from the eighth century. Of the large array of Bibles and other early printed books it is impossible to speak, except in a general way. There is a copy of the first English Bible, Coverdale's, also of the very rare second Matthews, and of most of the other editions of the English Bible; the first Scotch, Irish, French, Welsh, and German Luther Bibles; the first Eliot's Indian Bible, of 1662, and the second, of 1685; the first American Bibles; the first American primers, almanacs, newspapers, and the first patent, issued in 1794; the first book printed in Boston; the first printed accounts of New York, Pennsylvania, New Jersey, Virginia, South Carolina, Georgia; the first picture of New York City, an original plan of the city in 1700, and one of it in 1765; early surveys of Boston, Philadelphia, and New York; the earliest maps of America, including the first, second, and third map of the world in which America appears.

Returning to England, there are the Shakespeare folio editions of 1632 and 1685; the first of his printed 'Poems' and the 'Rape of Lucrece;' an early quarto of 'Othello;' the first edition of Ben Jonson, 1616, in which Shakespeare's name appears in the cast for a play; and letters from the Earl of Southampton, Shakespeare's friend, and Sir Walter Raleigh, Francis Bacon, and Essex. There is also a letter written by Oliver Cromwell while he was engaged in the conquest of Ireland.

The relics, documents, and letters illustrating our civil war are constantly being added to. There are many old engravings, caricatures, and broadsides. Of oil-portraits there are three originals of Washington, one by Stuart, one by Peals, one by Polk, and I think I remember one or two miniatures. There is also a portrait in oil of Shakespeare which may become important. The original canvas has been remounted, and there are indubitable signs of its age, although the picture can be traced back only about one hundred and fifty years. The owner hopes to be able to prove that it is a contemporary work. The interesting fact about it is that while it is not remarkable as a work of art, it is recognizable at once as a likeness of what we suppose from other portraits and the busts to be the face and head of Shakespeare, and yet it is different from all other pictures we know, so that it does not suggest itself as a copy.

The most important of Mr Gunther's collection is an autograph of Shakespeare; if it prove to be genuine, it will be one of the four in the world, and a great possession for America. This autograph is pasted on the fly-leaf of a folio of 1632, which was the property of one John Ward. In 1839 there was published in London, from manuscripts in possession of the medical Society, extracts from the diary of John Ward (1648-1679), who was vicar and doctor at Stratford-on-Avon. It is to this diary that we owe certain facts theretofore unknown about Shakespeare. The editor, Mr Stevens, had this volume in his hands while he was compiling his book, and refers to it in his preface. He supposed it to have belonged to the John Ward, Vicar, who kept the diary. It turns out, however, to have been the property of John Ward the actor, who was in Stratford in 1740, was an enthusiast in the revival of Shakespeare, and played Hamlet there in order to raise money to repair the bust of the poet in the church. This folio has the appearance of being much used. On the fly-leaf is writing by Ward and his signature; there are marginal notes and directions in his hand, and several of the pages from which parts were torn off have been repaired by manuscript text neatly joined.

The Shakespeare signature is pasted on the leaf above Ward's name. The paper on which it is written is unlike that of the book in texture. The slip was pasted on when the leaf was not as brown as it is now, as can be seen at one end where it is lifted. The signature is written out fairly and in full, *William Shakespeare*, like the one to the will, and differs from the two others, which are hasty scrawls, as if the writer were cramped for room, or finished off the last syllable with a flourish, indifferent to the formation of the letters. I had the opportunity to compare it with a careful tracing of the signature to the will sent over by Mr Hallowell-Phillips. At first sight the two signatures appear to be identical; but on examination they are not; there is just that difference in the strokes, spaces, and formation of the letters that always appears in two signatures by the same hand. One is not a copy of the other, and the one in the folio had to me the unmistakable stamp of genuineness. The experts in handwriting and the microscopists in this country who have examined ink and paper as to antiquity, I understand, regard it as genuine.

There seems to be all along the line no reason to suspect forgery. What more natural than that John Ward, the owner of the book, and a Shakespeare enthusiast, should have enriched his beloved volume with an autograph which he found somewhere in Stratford. And in 1740 there was no craze or controversy about Shakespeare to make the forgery of his autograph an object. And there is no suspicion that the book has been doctored for a market. It never was sold for a price. It was found in Utah, whither it had drifted from England in the possession of an emigrant, and he readily gave it in exchange for a new and fresh edition of Shakespeare's works.

I have dwelt upon this collection at some length, first because of its intrinsic value, second because of its importance to Chicago as a nucleus for what (I hope in connection with the Newberry Library) will become one of the most interesting museums in the country, and lastly as an illustration of what a Western business man may do with his money.

New York is the first and Chicago the second base of operations on this continent—the second in point of departure, I will not say for another civilization, but for a great civilizing and conquering movement, at once a reservoir and distributing point of energy, power, and money. And precisely here is to be fought out and settled some of the most important problems concerning labor, supply, and transportation. Striking as are the operations of merchants, manufacturers, and traders, nothing in the city makes a greater appeal to the imagination than the railways that centre there, whether we consider their fifty thousand miles of track, the enormous investment in them, or their competition for the carrying trade of the vast regions they pierce and apparently compel to be tributary to the central city. The story of their building would read like a romance, and a simple statement of their organization, management, and business rivals the affairs of an empire. The present development of a belt road round the city, to serve as a track of freight exchange for all the lines, like the transfer grounds between St Paul and Minneapolis, is found to be an affair of great magnitude, as must needs be to accommodate lines of traffic that represent an investment in stock and bonds of $1,305,000,000.

As it is not my purpose to describe the railway systems of the West, but only to speak of some of the problems involved in them, it will suffice to mention two of the leading corporations. Passing by the great eastern lines, and those like the Illinois Central, and the Chicago, Alton, and St Louis, and the Atchison, Topeka, and Santa Fé, which are operating mainly to the south and south-west, and the Chicago, Milwaukee, and St Paul, one of the greatest corporations, with a mileage which had reached 4921 December 1, 1885, and has increased since, we may name the Chicago and North-western, and the Chicago, Burlington, and Quincy. Each of these great systems, which has grown by accretion and extension and consolidations of small roads, operates over four thousand miles of road, leaving out from the North-western's mileage that of the Omaha system, which it controls. Looked at on the map, each of these systems completely occupies a vast territory, the one mainly to the north of the other, but they interlace to some extent and parallel each other in very important competitions.

The North-western system, which includes, besides the lines that have its name, the St. Paul, Minneapolis, and Omaha, the Fremont, Elkhorn, and Missouri Valley, and several minor roads, occupies northern Illinois and southern Wisconsin, sends a line along Lake Michigan to Lake

Superior, with branches, a line to St Paul, with branches tapping Lake Superior again at Bayfield and Duluth, sends another trunk line, with branches, into the far fields of Dakota, drops down a tangle of lines through Iowa and into Nebraska, sends another great line through northern Nebraska into Wyoming, with a divergence into the Black Hills, and runs all these feeders into Chicago by another trunk line from Omaha. By the report of 1887 the gross earnings of this system (in round numbers) were over twenty-six millions, expenses over twenty millions, leaving a net income of over six million dollars. In these items the receipts for freight were over nineteen millions, and from passengers less than six millions. Not to enter into confusing details, the magnitude of the system is shown in the general balance-sheet for May, 1887, when the cost of road (4101 miles), the sinking funds, the general assets, and the operating assets foot up $176,048,000. Over 3500 miles of this road are laid with steel rails; the equipment required 735 engines and over 23,000 cars of all sorts. It is worthy of note that a table makes the net earnings of 4000 miles of road, 1887, only a little more than those of 3000 miles of road in 1882—a greater gain evidently to the public than to the railroad.

In speaking of this system territorially, I have included the Chicago, St Paul, Minneapolis, and Omaha, but not in the above figures. The two systems have the same president, but different general managers and other officials, and the reports are separate. To the over 4000 miles of the other North-western lines, therefore, are to be added the 1360 miles of the Omaha system (report of December, 1886, since considerably increased). The balance-sheet of the Omaha system (December, 1886) shows a cost of over fifty-seven millions. Its total net earnings over operating expenses and taxes were about $2,304,000. It then required an equipment of 194 locomotives and about 6000 cars. These figures are not, of course, given for specific railroad information, but merely to give a general idea of the magnitude of operations. This may be illustrated by another item. During the year for which the above figures have been given the entire North-western system ran on the average 415 passenger and 732 freight trains each day through the year. It may also be an interesting comparison to say that all the railways in Connecticut, including those that run into other States, have 416 locomotives, 668 passenger cars, and 11,502 other cars, and that their total mileage in the State is 1405 miles.

The Chicago, Burlington, and Quincy (report of December, 1886) was operating 4036 miles of road. Its only eccentric development was the recent Burlington and Northern, up the Mississippi River to St Paul. Its main stem from Chicago branches out over northern and western Illinois, runs down to St Louis, from thence to Kansas City by way of Hannibal, has a trunk line to Omaha, criss-crosses northern Missouri and southern Iowa, skirts and pierces Kansas, and fairly occupies three-quarters of Nebraska with a network of tracks, sending out lines north of the Platte, and one to Cheyenne and one to Denver. The whole amount of stock and bonds, December, 1886 were over twenty-six millions (over nineteen of which was for freight and over five for passengers), operating expenses over fourteen millions, leaving over twelve millions net earnings. The system that year paid eight per cent dividends (as it had done for a long series of years), leaving over fixed charges and dividends about a million and a half to be carried to surplus or construction overlays. The equipment for the year required 619 engines and over 24,000 cars. These figures do not give the exact present condition of the road, but only indicate the magnitude of its affairs.

Both these great systems have been well managed, and both have been, and continue to be, great agents in developing the West. Both have been profitable to investors. The comparatively small cost of building roads in the West and the profit hitherto have invited capital, and stimulated the construction of roads not absolutely needed. There are too many miles of road for capitalists. Are there too many for the accommodation of the public? What locality would be willing to surrender its road?

It is difficult to understand the attitude of the Western Granger and the Western Legislatures towards the railways, or it would be if we didn't understand pretty well the nature of demagogues the world over. The people are everywhere crazy for roads, for more and more roads. The whole West we are considering is made by railways. Without them the larger part of it would be uninhabitable, the lands of small value, produce useless for want of a market. No railways, no civilization. Year by year settlements have increased in all regions touched by railways, land has risen in price, and freight charges have diminished. And yet no sooner do the people get the railways near them than they become hostile to the companies; hostility to railway corporations seems to be the dominant sentiment in the Western mind, and the one most naturally invoked by any political demagogue who wants to climb up higher in elective office. The roads are denounced as 'monopolies'—a word getting to be applied to any private persons who are successful in business—and their consolidation is regarded as a standing menace to society.

Of course it goes without saying that great corporations with exceptional privileges are apt to be arrogant, unjust, and grasping, and especially when, as in the case of railways, they unite private interests and public functions, they need the restraint of law and careful limitations of powers. But the Western situation is nevertheless a very curious one. Naturally when capital takes great risks it is entitled to proportionate profits; but profits always encourage competition, and the great Western lines are already in a war for existence that does not need much unfriendly legislation to make fatal. In fact, the lowering of rates in railway wars has gone on so rapidly of late years that the most active Granger Legislature cannot frame hostile bills fast enough to keep pace with it. Consolidation is objected to. Yet this consideration must not be lost sight of: the West is cut up by local roads that could not be maintained; they would not pay running expenses if they had not been made parts of a great system. Whatever may be the danger of the consolidation system, the country has doubtless benefited by it.

The present tendency of legislation, pushed to its logical conclusion, is towards a practical confiscation of railway property; that is, its tendency is to so interfere with management, so restrict freedom of arrangement, so reduce rates, that the companies will with difficulty continue operations. The first effect of this will be, necessarily, poorer service and deteriorated equipments and tracks. Roads that do not prosper cannot keep up safe lines. Experienced travellers usually shun those that are in the hands of a receiver. The Western roads of which I speak have been noted for their excellent service and the liberality towards the public in accommodations, especially in fine cars and matters pertaining to the comfort of passengers. Some dining cars on the Omaha system were maintained last year at a cost to the company of ten thousand dollars over receipts. The Western Legislatures assume that because a railway which is thickly strung with cities can carry passengers for two cents a mile, a railway running over an almost unsettled plain can carry for the same price. They assume also that because railway companies in a foolish fight for business cut rates, the lowest rate they touch is a living one for them. The same logic that induces Legislatures to fix rates of transportation, directly or by means of a commission, would lead it to set a price on meat, wheat and groceries. Legislative restriction is one thing; legislative destruction is another. There is a craze of prohibition and interference. Iowa has an attack of it. In Nebraska, not only the Legislature but the courts have been so hostile to railway enterprise that one hundred and fifty miles of new road graded last year, which was to receive its rails this spring, will not be railed, because it is not safe for the company to make further investments in that State. Between the Grangers on the one side and the labor unions on the other, the railways are in a tight place. Whatever restrictions great corporations may need, the sort of attack now made on them in the West is altogether irrational. Is it always made from public motives? The legislators of one Western State had been accustomed to receive from the various lines that centred at the capital trip passes, in addition to their personal annual passes. Trip passes are passes that the members can send to their relations, friends, and political allies who want to visit the capital. One year the several roads agreed that they would not issue trip passes. When the members asked the agent for them they were told that they were not ready. As days passed and no trip passes were ready, hostile and annoying bills began to be introduced into the Legislature. In six weeks there was a shower of them. The roads yielded, and began to give out the passes. After that, nothing more was heard of the bills.

What the public have a right to complain of is the manipulation of railways in Wall Street gambling. But this does not account for the hostility to the corporations which are developing the West by an extraordinary outlay of money, and cutting their own throats by a war of rates. The vast interests at stake, and the ignorance of the relation of legislation to the laws of business, make the railway problem to a spectator in Chicago one of absorbing interest.

In a thorough discussion of all interests it must be admitted that the railways have brought many of their troubles upon themselves by their greedy wars with each other, and perhaps in some cases by teaching Legislatures that have bettered their instructions, and that tyrannies in management and unjust discriminations (such as the Inter-State Commerce Law was meant to stop) have much to do in provoking hostility that survives many of its causes.

I cannot leave Chicago without a word concerning the town of Pullman, although it has already been fully studied in the pages of HARPER'S MONTHLY. It is one of the most interesting experiments in the world. As it is only a little over seven years old, it would be idle to prophesy about it, and I can only say that thus far many of the predictions as to the effect of 'paternalism' have not come true. If it shall turn out that its only valuable result is an 'object lesson' in decent and orderly living, the experiment will not have been in vain. It is to be remembered that it is not a philanthropic scheme, but a purely business operation, conducted on the idea that comfort, cleanliness, and agreeable surroundings conduce more to the prosperity of labor and of capital than the opposites.

Pullman is the only city in existence built from the foundation on scientific and sanitary principles, and not more or less the result of accident and variety of purpose and incapacity. Before anything else was done on the flat prairie, perfect drainage, sewerage, and water supply were provided. The shops, the houses, the public buildings, the parks, the streets, the recreation grounds, then followed in intelligent creation. Its public buildings are fine, and the grouping of them about the open flower-planted spaces is very effective. It is a handsome city, with the single drawback of monotony in the well-built houses. Pullman is within the limits of the village of Hyde Park, but it is not included in the annexation of the latter to Chicago.

It is certainly a pleasing industrial city. The workshops are spacious, light, and well ventilated, perfectly systematized; for instance, timber goes into one end of the long car-shop and, without turning back, comes out a freight car at the other, the capacity of the shop being one freight car every fifteen minutes of the working hours. There are a variety of industries, which employ about 4500 workmen. Of these about 500 live outside the city, and there are about 1000 workmen who live in the city and work elsewhere. The company keeps in order the streets, parks, lawns, and shade trees, but nothing else except the schools is free. The schools are excellent, and there are over 1300 children enrolled in them. The Company has a well-selected library of over 6000 volumes, containing many scientific and art books, which is open to all residents on payment of an annual subscription of three dollars. Its use increases yearly, and study classes are formed in connection with it. The company rents shops to dealers, but it carries on none of its own. Wages are paid to employees without deduction, except as to rent, and the women appreciate a provision that secures them a home beyond peradventure. The competition among dealers brings prices to the Chicago rates, or lower, and then the great city is easily accessible for shopping. House rent is a little higher for ordinary workmen than in Chicago, but not higher in proportion to accommodations, and living is reckoned a little cheaper. The reports show that the earnings of operatives exceed those of other working communities, averaging per capita (exclusive of the higher pay of the general management) $590 a year. I noticed that piece-wages were generally paid, and always when possible. The town is a hive of busy workers; employment is furnished to all classes except the school-children, and the fine moral and physical appearance of the young women in the upholstery and other work rooms would please a philanthropist.

Both the health and the *morale* of the town are exceptional; and the moral tone of the workmen has constantly improved under the agreeable surroundings. Those who prefer the kind of independence that gives them filthy homes and demoralizing associations seem to like to live elsewhere. Pullman has a population of 10,000. I do not know another city of 10,000 that has not a place where liquor is sold, nor a house nor a professional woman of ill repute. With the restrictions as to decent living, the community is free in its political action, its church and other societies, and in all healthful social activity. It has several ministers; it seems to require the services of only one or two policemen; it supports four doctors and one lawyer.

I know that any control, any interference with individual responsibility, is un-American. Our theory is that every person knows what is best for himself. It is not true, but it may be safer, in working out all the social problems, than any lessening of responsibility either in the home or in civil affairs. When I contrast the dirty tenements, with contiguous seductions to vice and idleness, in some parts of Chicago, with the homes of Pullman, I am glad that this experiment has been made. It may be worth some sacrifice to teach people that it is better for them, morally and pecuniarily, to live cleanly and under educational influences that increase their self-respect. No doubt it is best that people should own their homes, and that they should assume all the responsibilities of citizenship. But let us wait the full evolution of the Pullman idea. The town could not have been built as an object lesson in any other way than it was built. The hope is that laboring people will voluntarily do hereafter what they have here been induced to accept. The model city stands there as a lesson, the wonderful creation of less than eight years. The company is now preparing to sell lots on the west side of the railway-tracks, and we shall see what influence this nucleus of order, cleanliness, and system will have upon the larger community rapidly gathering about it. Of course people should be free to go up or go down. Will they be injured by the opportunity of seeing how much pleasanter it is to go up than to go down?

Washington

HENRY JAMES

*Following an absence of almost 25 years, Henry James made
a pilgrimage across America, rediscovering the towns, cities
and countryside of his homeland. These are his impressions
of Washington taken from* The American Scene *(1907).*

I WAS TWICE in Washington, the first time for a winter visit, the second
to meet the wonderful advance of summer, to which, in that climate
of many charms, the first days of May open wide the gates. This latter
impression was perforce much the more briefly taken; yet, though I had
gathered also from other past occasions, far-away years now, something
of the sense of the place at the earlier season, I find everything washed
over, at the mention of the name, by the rare light, half green, half golden,
of the lovely leafy moment. I see all the rest, till I make the effort to
break the spell, through that voluminous veil; which operates, for

memory, quite as the explosion of spring works, even to the near vision, in respect to the American scene at large—dressing it up as if for company, preparing it for social, for human intercourse, making it in fine publicly presentable, with an energy of renewal and an effect of redemption not often to be noted, I imagine, on other continents. Nowhere, truly, can summer have such work cut out for it as here—nowhere has it to take upon itself to repaint the picture so completely. In the 'European' land-scape, in general, some, at least, of the elements and objects remain upon the canvas; here, on the other hand, one seems to see intending Nature, the great artist of the season, decline to touch that surface unless it be first swept clean—decline, at any rate, to deal with it save by ignoring all its perceived pretensions. Vernal Nature, in England, in France, in Italy, has still a use, often a charmed or amused indulgence, for the material in hand, the furniture of the foreground, the near and middle distances, the heterogeneous human features of the face of the land. She looks at her subject much as the portrait-painter looks at the personal properties, this or that household object, the official uniform, the badges and ornaments, the favourite dress, of his sitter—with an 'Oh, yes, I can bring them in; they're just what I want, and I see how they will help me out.' But I try in vain to recall a case in which, either during the New England May and June, or during those of the Middle States (since these groups of weeks have in the two regions a differing identity and value), the genius in question struck me as adopting with any frank-ness, as doing more than passively, helplessly accept, the supplied para-phernalia, the signs of existing life. The business is clearly to get rid of them as far as may be, to cover and smother them; dissimulating with the biggest, freest brush their impertinence and their ugliness.

I must ask myself, I meanwhile recognize, none the less, why I should have found Mount Vernon exquisite, the first of May, if the interest had all to be accounted for in the light of nature. The light of nature was there, splendid and serene; the Potomac opened out in its grandest manner; the bluff above the river, before the sweep of its horizon, raised its head for the historic crown. But it was not for a moment to be said that this was the whole story; the human interest and the human charm lay in wait and held one fast—so that, if one had been making light, elsewhere, of their suggestion and office, one had at least this case ser-iously to reckon with. I speak straightway, thus, of Mount Vernon, though it be but an outlying feature of Washington, and at the best a minor impression; the image of the particular occasion is seated so softly in my path. There was a glamour, in fine, for the excursion—that of an extraordinary gracious hospitality; and the glamour would still have been great even if I had not, on my return to the shadow of the Capitol, found the whole place transfigured. The season was over, the President away, the two Houses up, the shutters closed, the visitor rare; and one lost one's way in the great green vistas of the avenues quite as one might have lost it in a 'sylvan solitude'—that is in the empty alleys of a park. The emptiness was qualified at the most, here and there, by some encounter with a stray diplomatic agent, wreathed for the most part in sincerer smiles than we are wont to attribute to his class. 'This'—it was the meaning of these inflections—'was the *real* Washington, a place of enchantment; so that if the enchantment were never less who could ever bring himself to go away?' The enchantment had been so much less in January—one could easily understand; yet the recognition seemed truly the voice of the hour, and one picked it up with a patriotic flutter not diminished by the fact that the speaker would probably be going away, and with delight, on the morrow.

The memory of some of the smiles and inflections comes back in that light; Washington being the one place in America, I think, where those qualities are the values and vehicles, the medium of exchange. No small part of the interest of the social scene there consists, inevitably, for any restless analyst, in wonder about the 'real' sentiments of appointed foreign participants, the delegates of Powers and pledged alike to penetration and to discretion, before phenomena which, whatever they may be, differ more from the phenomena of other capitals and other societies than they resemble them. This interest is susceptible, on occasion, of becoming intense; all the more that curiosity must, for the most part, pursue its object (that of truly looking over the alien shoulder and of seeing, judging, building, fearing, reporting with the alien sense) by subtle and tortuous ways. This represents, first and last, even for a watcher abjectly irresponsible, a good deal of speculative tension; so that one's case is refreshing in presence of the clear candour of such a proposition as that the national capital *is* charming in proportion as you don't see it. For that is what it came to, in the bowery condition; the as yet unsurmounted bourgeois character of the whole was screened and disguised; the dressing-up, in other words, was complete, and the great park-aspect gained, and became nobly artificial, by the very complexity of the plan of the place— the perpetual perspectives, the converging, radiating avenues, the frequent circles and crossways, where all that was wanted for full illusion was that the bronze generals and admirals, on their named pedestals, should have been great garden-gods, mossy mythological marble. This would have been the perfect note; the long vistas yearned for it, and the golden chequers scattered through the gaps of the high arches waited for some bending nymph or some armless Hermes to pick them up. The power of the scene to evoke such visions sufficiently shows, I think, what had become, under the mercy of nature, of the hard facts, as one must everywhere call them; and yet though I could, diplomatically, patrioti-cally pretend, at the right moment, that such a Washington *was* the 'real' one, my assent had all the while a still finer meaning for myself.

I am hanging back, however, as with sacred terror, from Mount Ver-non, where indeed I may not much linger, or only enough to appear not to have shirked the responsibility incurred at the opening of these remarks. There, in ample possession, was masking, dissimulating sum-mer, the envelope and disguise to which I have hinted that the American picture owes, on its human side, *all* its best presentability; and at the same time, unmistakable, there was the spell, as quite a distinct matter, of the hard little facts in themselves. How came it that if they could throw a spell they were yet so abject and no negligible? How came it that if they had no intrinsic sweetness, no visible dignity, they could yet play their part in so unforgettable an impression? The answer to this can only be, I think, that we happen here to 'strike', as they say, one of the rarest of cases, a spot on which all sorts of sensibilities are touched and on which a lively emotion, and one yet other than the aesthetic, makes us its prey. The old high-placed house, unquestionably, is charming, and the felicity of the whole scene, on such a day as that of my impression, scarce to be uttered. The little hard facts, facts of form, of substance, of scale, facts of essential humility and exiguity, none the less, look us straight in the face, present themselves literally to be counted over—and reduce us thereby to the recognition of our supreme example of the rich interference of association. Association does, at Mount Vernon, simply what it likes with us—it is of so beautiful and noble a sort; and to this end it begins by making us unfit to say whether or no we would in its absence have noticed the house for any material grace at all. We scarce care more for its being proved pictur-esque, the house, than for its being proved plain; its architectural interest and architectural nullity become one and the same thing for us. If asked what we would think of it if it hadn't been, or if we hadn't known it for, Washington's, we retort that the inquiry is inane, since it is not the possessive case, but the straight, serene nominative, that we are dealing with. The whole thing *is* Washington—not his invention and his property, but his presence and his person; with discriminations (as distinguished from enthusiasms) as invidious and unthinkable as if they were addressed to his very ears.

The great soft fact, as opposed to the little hard ones, is the beauty of the site itself; that is definitely, if ever so delicately, sublime, but it fails to rank among the artificial items that I began by speaking of, those of so generally compromising an effect in the American picture. Everything else is *communicated* importance, and the magic so wrought for the American sensibility—by which I mean the degree of the importance and the sustained high pitch of the charm—place it, doubtless, the world over, among the few supreme triumphs of such communications. The beauty of the site, meanwhile, as we stand there, becomes but the final aspect of the man; under which everything conduces to a single great representative image, under which every feature of the scene, every object in the house, however trivial, borrows from it and profits by it. The image is the largest, clearest possible of the resting, as distinguished from the restless, consciousness of public service consummately rendered. The terms we commonly use for that condition—peace with honour, well-earned repose, enjoyment of homage, recognition of facts—render but dimly the luminous stillness in which, on its commanding eminence, we see our image bathed. It hangs together with the whole bright immensity of air and view. It becomes truly the great white, decent page on which the whole sense of the place is written. It does more things even besides; attends us while we move about and goes with us from room to room; mounts with us the narrow stairs, to stand with us in these small chambers and look out of the low windows; takes up for us, to turn them over with spiritual hands, the objects from which we respectfully forbear, and places an accent in short, through the rambling old phrase, wherever an accent is required. Thus we arrive at the full meaning, as it were—thus we know, at least, why we are so moved.

It is for the same reason for which we are always inordinately moved, on American ground, I think, when the unconscious minor scale of the little old demonstrations to which we owe everything is made visible to us, when their disproportionate modesty is proved upon them. The reason worked at Mount Vernon, for the restless analyst, quite as it had worked a few months before, on the small and simple scene of Concord Fight: the slight, pale, bleeding Past, in a patched homespun suit, stands there taking the thanks of the bloated Present—having woundedly rescued from thieves and brought to his door the fat, locked pocket-book of which that personage appears the owner. The pocket-book contains, 'unbeknown' to the honest youth, bank-notes of incredible figure, and what breaks our heart, if we be cursed with the historic imagination, is the grateful, wan smile with which the great guerdon of sixpence is received. I risk, floridly, the assertion that half the intensity of the impression of Mount Vernon, for many a visitor, will ever be in this vision there of Washington *only* (so far as consciously) so rewarded. Such fantastications, I indeed admit, are refinements of response to any impression, but the ground had been cleared for them, and it ministered to luxury of thought, for instance, that we were a small party at our ease there, with no other circulation—with the prowling ghosts of fellow-pilgrims, too harshly present on my previous occasion, all conveniently laid. This alone represented privilege and power, and they in turn, with their pomp and circumstance of a charming Government launch, under official attendance, at the Navy-Yard steps, amid those large, clean, protecting and protected properties of the State which always make one think much of the State, whatever its actual infirmities—these things, to say nothing of other rich enhancements, above all those that I may least specify, flung over the day I scarce know what iridescent reflection of the star-spangled banner itself, in the folds of which I had never come so near the sense of being positively wrapped. That consciousness, so unfamiliar, was, under the test, irresistible; it pressed the spring, absolutely, of intellectual exaltation—with the consequent loud resonance that my account of my impressions doubtless sufficiently translates.

II

Washington itself meanwhile—the Washington always, I premise, of the rank outsider—had struck me from the first as presenting two distinct faces; the more obvious of which was the public and official, the monumental, with features all more or less majestically playing the great administrative, or, as we nowadays put it, Imperial part. This clustered, yet at the same time oddly scattered, city, a general impression of high granite steps, of light grey corniced colonnades, rather harmoniously low, contending for effect with slaty mansard roofs and masses of iron excrescence, a general impression of somewhat vague, empty, sketchy, fundamentals, however expectant, however spacious, overweighted by a single Dome and overaccented by a single shaft—this loose congregation of values seemed, strangely, a matter disconnected and remote, though remaining in its way portentous and bristling all incoherently at the back of the scene. The back of the scene, indeed, to one's quite primary sense, might have been but an immense painted, yet unfinished cloth, hung there to a confessedly provisional end and marked with the queerness, among many queernesses, of looking always the same; painted once for all in clear, bright, fresh tones, but never emerging from its flatness, after the fashion of other capitals, into the truly, the variously, modelled and rounded state. (It appeared provisional therefore because looking as if it might have been unhooked and removed as a whole; because any one object in it so treated would have made the rest also come off.) The foreground was a different thing, a thing that, ever so quaintly, seemed to represent the force really in possession; though consisting but of a small company of people engaged perpetually in conversation and (always, I repeat, for the rank outsider) singularly destitute of conspicuous marks or badges. This little society easily became for the detached visitor, *the* national capital and the greater part of the story; and that, ever, in spite of the comparatively scant intensity of its political permeation. The political echo was of course to be heard in it, and the public character, in his higher forms, to be encountered— though only in 'single spies' not in battalions; but there was something that made it much more individual than any mere predominance of political or administrative colour would have made it; leaving it in that case to do no more than resemble the best society in London, or that in best possession of the field in Paris.

Two sharp signs my remoter remembrance had shown me the then Washington world, and the first met, as putting forth; one of these the fact of its being extraordinarily easy and pleasant, and the other that of one's appearing to make out in it not more than half-a-dozen members of the Lower House and not more than a dozen of the Upper. This kept down the political permeation, and was bewildering, if one was able to compare, in the light of the different London condition, the fact of the social ubiquity there of the acceptable M.P. and that of the social frequency even of his more equivocal hereditary colleague. A London nesting under the towers of Westminster, yet practically void of members of the House of Commons, and with the note of official life far from exclusively sounding, that might have been in those days the odd image of Washington, had not the picture been stamped with other variations still. These were a whole cluster, not instantly to be made out, but constituting the unity of the place as soon as perceived; representing that finer extract or essence which the self-respecting observer is never easy till he be able to shake up and down in bottled form. The charming company of the foreground then, which referred itself so little to the sketchy back-scene, the monstrous Dome and Shaft, figments of the upper air, the pale colonnades and mere myriad-windowed Buildings, was the second of the two faces, and the more one lived with it the more, up to a certain point, one lived away from the first. In time, and after perceiving *how* it was what it so agreeably was, came the recognition of common ground; the recognition that, in spite of strange passages of the national life, liable possibly to recur, during which the President himself was scarce thought to be in society, the particular precious character that one had apprehended could never have ripened without a general consensus. One had put one's finger on it when one had seen disengage itself from many anomalies, from not a few drolleries, the superior, the quite majestic fact of the City of Conversation pure and simple, and positively by the only specimen, of any such intensity, in the world.

That had remained for me, from the other time, the properest name of Washington, and nothing could so interest me, on a renewal of acquaintance, too long postponed and then too woefully brief, as to find my description wholly justified. If the emphasis added by 'pure and simple' be invariably retained, the description will continue, I think, to embrace and exhaust the spectacle, while yet leaving it every inch of its value. Clearly quite immeasurable on American ground, the value of such an assertion of a town-type directly opposed to the unvarying American, and quite unique, on any ground, so organized a social indifference to the vulgar vociferous Market. Washington may of course *know* more than she confesses—no community could perhaps really be as ignorant as Washington used at any rate to look, and to like to look, of this particular thing, of 'goods' and shares and rises and falls and all such sordidities; but she knows assuredly still the very least she can get off with, and nothing even yet pleases her more than to forget what she does know. She unlearns, she turns her back, while London, Paris, Berlin, Rome, in their character of political centres, strike us as, on the contrary, feverishly learning, trying more and more to do the exact opposite. (I speak, naturally, as to Washington, of knowing actively and interestedly, in the spirit of gain—not merely of the enjoyed lights of political and administrative science, doubtless as abundant there as anywhere else.) It might fairly have been, I used to think, that the charming place—charming in the particular connection I speak of—had on its conscience to make one forget for an hour the colossal greed of New York. Nothing, in fact, added more to its charm than its appearing virtually to invite one to impute to it some such vicarious compunction.

If I be reminded indeed, that the distinction I here glance at is negative, and be asked what then (if she knew nothing of the great American interest) Washington did socially know, my answer, I recognize, has at once to narrow itself, and become perhaps truly the least bit difficult to utter. It none the less remains distinct enough that, the City of Conservation being only in question, and a general subject of all the conversation having thereby to be predicated, our responsibility is met as soon as we are able to say what Washington mainly talks, and appears always to go mainly talking, about. Washington talks about herself, and about almost nothing else; falling superficially indeed, on that ground, but into line with the other capitals. London, Paris, Berlin, Rome, goodness knows, talk about themselves: that is each member of this sisterhood talks, sufficiently or inordinately, of the great number of divided and differing selves that form together her controlling identity. London, for instance, talks of everything in the world without thereby for a moment, as it were, ceasing to be egotistical. It has taken everything in the world to make London up, so that she is in consequence simply doomed never to get away from herself. Her conversation is largely, I think, the very effort to do that; but she inevitably figures in it but as some big buzzing insect which keeps bumping against a treacherous mirror. It is in positive quest of an identity of some sort, much rather—an identity other than merely functional and technical—that Washington goes forth, encumbered with no ideal of avoidance or escape: it is about herself *as* the City of Conversation precisely that she incessantly converses; adorning the topic, moreover, with endless ingenuity and humour. But that, absolutely, remains the case; which thus becomes one of the most thorough, even if probably one of the most natural and of the happiest, cases of collective self-consciousness that one knows. The spectacle, as it at first met my senses, was that of a numerous community in ardent pursuit of some workable conception of its social self, and trying meanwhile intelligently to talk itself, and even this very embarrassment, into a *subject* for conversation. Such a picture might not seem purely pleasing, on the side of variety of appeal, and I admit one may have had one's reserves about it; reserves sometimes reflected, for example, in dim inward speculation—one of the effects of the Washington air I have already glanced at—as to the amount of response it might evoke in the diplomatic body. It may have been on my part a morbid obsession, but the diplomatic body was liable to strike one there as more characteristically 'abysmal' than elsewhere, more impenetrably bland and inscrutably blank; and it was obvious, certainly, that their concern to help the place intellectually to find itself was not to be expected to approach in intensity the concern even of a repatriated absentee. You were concerned only if you had, by your sensibility, a stake in the game; which was the last thing a foreign representative would wish to confess to, this being directly opposed to all his enjoined duties. It is no part of the office of such personages to assist the societies to which they are accredited to find themselves—it is much more their mission to leave all such vaguely and, so far as may be, grotesquely groping; so apt are societies, in finding themselves, to find other things too. This detachment from the whole mild convulsion of effort, the considerate pretence of not being too aware of it, combined with latent probabilities of alarm about it no less than of amusement, represented, to the unquiet fancy, much more the spirit of the old-time Legations.

What *was*, at all events, better fun, of the finer sort, than having one's self a stake in the outcome?—what helped the time (so much of it as there was!) more to pass than just to join in the so fresh experiment of constitutive, creative talk? The boon, it should always be mentioned, meanwhile went on not in the least in the tone of solemnity. That would have been fatal, because probably irritating, and it was where the good star of Washington intervened. The tone was, so to speak, of *conscious* self-consciousness, and the highest genius for conversation doubtless dwelt in the fact that the ironic spirit was ready always to give its very self away, fifty times over, for the love, or for any quickening, of the theme. The foundation for the whole happy predicament remained, moreover, of the firmest, and the essence of the case was to be as easily stated as the great social fact is, in America, whether through exceptions or aggravations, everywhere to be stated. Nobody was in 'business'—

that was the sum and substance of it; and for the one large human assemblage on the continent of which this was true the difference made was huge. Nothing could strike one more than that it was the only way in which, over the land, a difference *could* be made, and than how, in our vast commercial democracy, almost any difference—by which I mean almost any exception—promptly acquires prodigious relief. The value here was at once that the place could offer to view a society, the only one in the country, in which Men existed, and that the rich little fact became the key to everything. Superficially taken, I recognize, the circumstance fails to look portentous; but it looms large immediately, gains the widest bearing, in the light of any direct or extended acquaintance with American conditions. From the moment it is adequately borne in mind that the business-man, the size of the field he so abdicates is measured, as well as the fact of the other care to which his abdication hands it over. It lies there waiting, pleading from all its pores, to be occupied—the lonely waste, the boundless gaping void of 'society'; which is but a rough name for all the *other* so numerous relations with the world he lives in that are imputable to the civilized being. Here it is then that the world he lives in accepts its doom and becomes, by his default, subject and plastic to his mate; his default having made, all around him, the unexampled opportunity of the woman—which she would have been an incredible fool not to pounce upon. It needs little contact with American life to perceive how she *has* pounced, and how, outside business, she has made it over in her image. She has been, up to now, on the vast residual tract, in peerless possession, and is occupied in developing and extending her wonderful conquest, which she appreciates to the last inch of its extent.

III

She has meanwhile probably her hours of amazement at the size of her windfall; she cannot quite live without wonder at the oddity of her so 'sleeping' partner, the strange creature, by her side, with his values and his voids, but who is best known to her as having yielded what she would have clutched to the death. Yet these are mere mystic,

inscrutable possibilities—dreams, for us, of her hushed, shrouded hours:
the face she shows, on all the facts, is that of mere unwinking tribute
to the matter of course. The effect of these high signs of assurance in
her has been—and it is really her master-stroke—to represent the situation as perfectly normal. Her companion's attitude, totally destitute of
high signs, does everything it can to further this feat; so that, as disposed
together in the American picture, they testify, extraordinarily, to the
successful rupture of a universal law, the sight is at first, for observation,
most mystifying. Then the impunity of the whole thing gains upon us;
the equilibrium strikes us, however strangely, as at least provisionally
stable; we see that a society in many respects workable would seem
to have been arrived at, and that we shall in any case have time to
study it. The phenomenon may easily become, for a spectator, the sen-
tence written largest in the American sky: when he is in search of the
characteristic, what else so plays the part? The woman is two-thirds
of the apparent life—which means that she is absolutely all of the social;
and, as this is nowhere else the case, the occasion is unique for seeing
what such a situation may make of her. The result elsewhere, in Europe
generally, of conditions in which men have actively participated and
to which, throughout, they personally contribute, she has only the old
story to tell, and keeps telling it after her fashion. The woman produced
by a women-made society alone has obviously quite a new story—to
which it is not for a moment to be gainsaid that the world at large
has, for the last thirty years in particular, found itself lending an atten-
tive, at times even a charmed, ear. The extent and variety of this attention
have been the specious measure of the personal success of the type
in question, and are always referred to when its value happens to be
challenged. 'The American woman?—why, she has beguiled, she has
conquered, the globe: look at her fortune everywhere and fail to accept
her if you can.'

She has been, accordingly, about the globe, beyond all doubt, a huge
success of curiosity; she has at her best—and far beyond any consciousness and intention of her own, lovely as these for the most part usually
are—infinitely amused the nations. It has been found among them that,
for more reasons than we can now go into, her manner of embodying
and representing her sex has fairly made of her a new human convenience, not unlike fifty of the others, of a slightly different order, the
ingenious mechanical appliances, stoves, refrigerators, sewing-
machines, type-writers, cash-registers, that have done so much, in the

household and the place of business, for the American name. By which I am of course far from meaning that the revelation has been of her utility as a domestic drudge; it has been much rather in the fact that the advantages attached to her being a woman at all have been so happily combined with the absence of the drawbacks, for persons intimately dealing with her, traditionally suggested by that condition. The corresponding advantages, in the light of almost any old order, have always seemed inevitably paid for by the drawbacks; but here, unmistakably, was a case in which—as at first appeared, certainly—they were to be enjoyed very nearly for nothing. What it came to, evidently, was that she had been grown in an air in which a hundred of the 'European' complications and dangers didn't exist, and in which also she had had to take upon herself a certain training for freedom. It was not that she had had, in the vulgar sense, to 'look out' for herself, inasmuch as it was of the very essence of her position not to be threatened or waylaid; but that she could develop her audacity on the basis of her security, just as she could develop her 'powers' in a medium from which criticism was consistently absent. Thus she arrived, full-blown, on the general scene, the least criticized object, in proportion to her importance, that had ever adorned it. It would take long to say why her situation, under this retrospect, may affect the inner fibre of the critic himself as one of the most touching on record; he may merely note his perception that she was to have been after all but the sport of fate. For why need she originally, he wonders, have embraced so confidently, so gleefully, yet so unguardedly, the terms offered her to an end practically so perfidious? Why need she, unless in the interest of her eventual discipline, have turned away with so light a heart after watching the Man, the deep American man, retire into his tent and let down the flap? She had her 'paper' from him, their agreement signed and sealed; but would she not, in some other air and under some other sky, have been visited by a saving instinct? Would she not have said 'No, this is too unnatural; there must be a trap in it somewhere—it's addressed really, in the long run, to making a fool of me?' It is impossible, of course, to tell; and her case, as it stands for us, at any rate, is that she showed no doubts. It is not on the American scene and in the presence of mere American phenomena that she is even yet to be observed as showing them; but does not my digression find itself meanwhile justified by the almost clear certainty that the first symptoms of the revulsion—of the *convulsion*, I am tempted to say—must break out in Washington?

For here—and it is what I have been so long in coming to—here alone in the American world, do we catch the other sex not observing the agreement. I have described this anomaly, at Washington, as that of Man's socially 'existing'; since we have seen that his fidelity to his compact throughout the country in general has involved his not doing so. What has happened, obviously, has been that his reasons, at a stroke, have dropped, and that he finds himself, without them, a different creature. He has discovered that he *can* exist in other connections than that of the Market, and that all he has therefore to settle is the question of whether he may. The most delicate interest of Washington is the fact that it is quite practically being settled there—in the practical way which is yet also the dramatic. *Solvitur ambulando*; it is being settled—that is the charm—as it goes, settled without discussion. It would be awkward and gross to say that Man has dealt any conscious blow at the monopoly of his companion, or that her prestige, as mistress of the situation, has suffered in any manner a noted abatement. Yet none the less, as he has there, in a degree, socially found himself and, allured by the new sense, is evidently destined to seek much further still, the sensible effect, the change of impression on one's coming from other places, is of the most marked. Man is solidly, vividly present, and the presence of Woman has consequently, for the proposed intensity, to reckon with it. The omens on behalf of the former appearance are just now strikingly enhanced, as happens, by the accident of the rare quality, as it were, of the particular male presence supremely presiding there; and it would certainly be strange that this idea of the re-committal to masculine hands of some share at least in the interests of civilization, some part of the social property and social office, should not, from so high an example, have received a new impulse and a new consecration. Easily enough, if we had space here to consider it, might come up the whole picture of the new indications thus afforded, the question of the degree in which a sex capable, in the American air, of having so despoiled itself may really be capable of retracing its steps and repairing its mistake. It would appear inevitable to ask whether such a mistake on such a scale *can* prove effectively reparable—whether ground so lost can be effectively recovered. Has not the American woman, with such a start, gained such an irreducible advance, on the whole high plane of the amenities, that her companion will never catch up with her? This last is an inquiry that I must, alas, brush aside, though feeling it, as I have already noted, *the* most oddly interesting that the American spectacle proposes to us;

only saying, provisionally, that the aspect of manners through the nation at large offers no warrant whatever for any prompt 'No' to it.

It is not, however, of the nation at large I here speak; the case is of the extremely small, though important and significant, fraction of the whole represented by the Washington group—which thus shows us the Expropriated Half in the very act of itself pondering that issue. Is the man 'up to it' up to the major heritage, the man who *could*, originally, so inconceivably, and for a mere mess of pottage if there ever was one, let it go? 'Are we up to it, really, at this time of day, and what on earth will awfully become of us if the question, once put to the test, shall have to be decided against us?' I think it not merely fanciful to say that some dim, distressful interrogative sound of that sort frequently reached, in the Washington air, the restless analyst—though not to any quickening of his own fear. With a perfect consciousness that it was still early to say, that the data are as yet insufficient and that the missing quantity must absolutely be found before it can be weighed and valued, he was none the less struck with the felicity of many symptoms and would fairly have been able to believe at moments that the character hitherto so effaced has but to show the confidence of taking itself for granted. That act of itself reveals, restores, reinstates and completes this character. Is it not, for that matter, essentially implied in our recognition of the place as the City of Conversation? The victim of effacement, the outcast at the door, has, all the while we have been talking of him, *talked himself* back; and if anything could add to this happy portent it would be another that had scarcely less bearing. Nowhere more than in Washington, positively, were the women to have struck me as naturally and harmoniously in the social picture—as happily, soothingly, proportionately, and no more than proportionately, participant and ministrant. Hence the irresistible conclusion that with the way really shown them they would only ask to take it; the way being their assent to the truth that the abdication of the Man proves even (after the first flush of their triumph) as bad really for their function as for his. Hence, in fine, the appearance that, with the proportions re-established, they will come to recognize their past world as a fools' paradise, and their present, and still more their future, as much more made to endure. They could not, one reasoned, have been in general, so perfectly agreeable unless they had been pleased, and they could not have been pleased without the prospect of gaining, by the readjusted relation, more, on the whole, than they were to lose; without the prospect even again perhaps of truly and insidiously gaining more than the other beneficiary. That *would* be, I think, the feminine conception of a readministered justice. Washington, at such a rate, in any case, might become to them as good as 'Europe' and a Europe of their own would obviously be better than a Europe of other people's. There are, after all, other women on the other continents.

IV

One might have been sure in advance that the character of a democracy would nowhere more sharply mark itself than in the democratic substitute for a court city, and Washington is cast in the mould that expresses most the absence of salient social landmarks and constituted features. Here it is that conversation, as the only invoked presence, betrays a little in its adequacy to the furnishing forth, all by itself, of an outward view. It tells us it must be there, since in all the wide empty vistas nothing else is, and the general elimination *can* but have left it. A pleading, touching effect, indeed, lurks in this sense of it as seated, at receipt of custom, by any decent door of any decent domicile and watching the vacancy for reminder and appeal. It is left to conversation alone to people the scene with accents; putting aside two or three objects to be specified, there is *never* an accent in it, up and down, far and wide, save such as fall rather on the ear of the mind: those projected by the social spirit starved for the sense of an occasional emphasis. The White House is an accent—one of the lightest, sharpest possible; and the Capitol, of course, immensely, another; though the latter falls on the exclusively political page, as to which I have been waiting to say a word. It should meanwhile be mentioned that we are promised these enhancements, these illustrations, of the great general text, on the most magnificent scale; a splendid projected and announced Washington of the future, with approaches even now grandly outlined and massively marked; in face of which one should perhaps confess to the futility of any current estimate. If I speak thus of the Capitol, however, let me not merely brush past the White House to get to it—any more than feel free to pass into it without some preliminary stare at that wondrous Library of Congress which glitters in fresh and almost unmannerly emulation, almost frivolous irrelevance of form, in the neighbourhood of the greater building. About the ingenuities and splendours of this last costly structure, a riot of rare material and rich ornament, there would doubtless be much to say—did not one everywhere, on all such ground, meet the open eye of criticism simply to establish with it a private intelligence, simply to respond to it by a deprecating wink. The guardian of the altar, I think, is but too willing, on such a hint, to let one pass without the sacrifice.

It is a case again here, as on fifty other occasions, of the tribute instantly paid by the revisiting spirit; but paid, all without question, to the general *kind* of presence for which the noisy air, over the land, feels so sensibly an inward ache—the presence that corresponds there, no matter how loosely, to that of the housing and harbouring European Church in the ages of great disorder. The Universities and the greater Libraries (the smaller, for a hundred good democratic reasons, are another question), repeat, in their manner, to the imagination, East and West, the note of the old thick-walled convents and quiet cloisters: they are large and charitable, they are sturdy, often proud and often rich, and they have the incalculable value that they represent the only intermission to inordinate rapacious traffic that the scene offers to view. With this suggestion of sacred ground they play even upon the most restless of analysts as they will, making him face about, with ecstasy, any way they seem to point; so that he feels it his business much less to count over their shortcomings than to proclaim them places of enchantment. They are better at their worst than anything else at its best, and the comparatively sweet sounds that stir their theoretic stillness are for him as echoes of the lyre of Apollo. The Congressional Library is magnificent, and would become thus a supreme sanctuary even were it ten times more so; there would seem to be nothing then but to pronounce it a delight and have done with it—or let the appalled imagination, in other words, slink into it and stay there. But here is pressed precisely, with particular force, the spring of the question that takes but a touch to sound: is the case of this remarkable creation, by exception, a case in which the violent waving of the pecuniary wand *has* incontinently produced interest? The answer can only be, I feel, a shy assent—though shy indeed only till the logic of the matter is apparent. This logic is that, though money alone can gather in on such a scale the treasures of knowledge, these treasures, in the form of books and documents, themselves organize and furnish their world. They appoint and settle the proportions, they thicken the air, they people the space, they create and consecrate all their relations, and no one shall say that, where they scatter life, which they themselves in fact *are*, history does not promptly attend. Emphatically yes, therefore, the great domed and tiered, galleried and statued central hall of the Congressional, the last word of current constructional science and artistic resource, already crowns itself with that grace.

The graceful thing in Washington beyond any other, none the less, is the so happily placed and featured White House, the late excellent extensions and embellishments of which have of course represented expenditure—but only of the refined sort imposed by some mature portionless gentlewoman on relatives who have accepted the principle of making her, at a time of life, more honourably comfortable. The whole ample precinct and margin formed by the virtual continuity of its grounds with those expanses in which the effect of the fine Washington Obelisk rather spends or wastes itself (not a little as if some loud monosyllable had been uttered, in a preoccupied company, without a due production of sympathy or sense)—the fortunate isolation of the White House, I say, intensifies its power to appeal to that musing and mooning visitor whose perceptions alone, in all the conditions, I hold worthy of account. Hereabouts, beyond doubt, history had from of old seemed to me insistently seated, and I remember a short spring-time of years ago when Lafayette Square itself, contiguous to the Executive Mansion, could create a rich sense of the past by the use of scarce other witchcraft than its command of that pleasant perspective and its possession of the most prodigious of all Presidential effigies, Andrew Jackson, as archaic as a Ninevite king, prancing and rocking through the ages. If that atmosphere, moreover, in the fragrance of the Washington April, was even a quarter of a century since as a liquor of bitter-sweet taste, overflowing its cup, what was the ineffable mixture, now, with all the elements further distilled, all the life further sacrificed, to make it potent? One circled about the place as for meeting the ghosts, and one paused, under the same impulse, before the high palings of the White House drive, as if wondering at haunted ground. There the ghosts stood in their public array, spectral enough and clarified; yet scarce making it easier to 'place' the strange, incongruous blood-drops, as one looked through the rails, on that revised and freshened page. But one fortunately has one's choice, in all these connections, as one turns away; the mixture, as I have called it, is really here so fine. General Jackson, in the centre of the Square, still rocks his hobby and the earth; but the fruit of the interval, to my actual eyes, hangs nowhere brighter than in the brilliant memorials lately erected to Lafayette and to Rochambeau. Artful, genial, expressive, the tribute of French talent, these happy images supply, on the spot, the note without which even the most fantasticating sense of our national past would feel itself rub forever against mere brown homespun. Everything else gives way, for me, I confess, as I again stand before them; everything, whether as historic fact, or present *agrément*, or future possibility, yields to this one high luxury of our old friendship with France.

The 'artistic' Federal city already announced spreads itself then before us, in plans elaborated even to the finer details, a city of palaces and monuments and gardens, symmetries and circles and far radiations, with the big Potomac for water-power and water-effect and the recurrent Maryland spring, so prompt and so full-handed, for a perpetual benediction. This imagery has, above all, the value, for the considering mind, that it presents itself as under the wide-spread wings of the general Government, which fairly make it figure to the rapt vision as the object caught up in eagle claws and lifted into fields of air that even the high brows of the municipal boss fail to sweep. The wide-spread wings affect us, in the prospect, as great fans that, by their mere tremor, will blow the work, at all steps and stages, clean and clear, disinfect it quite ideally of any germ of the job, and prepare thereby for the American voter, on the spot and in the pride of possession, quite a new kind of civic consciousness. The scheme looms largest, surely, as a demonstration of the possibilities of that service to him, and nothing about it will be more interesting than to measure—though this may take time—the nature and degree of his alleviation. Will the new pride I speak of sufficiently inflame him? Will the taste of the new consciousness, finding him so fresh to it, prove the right medicine? One can only regret that we must still rather indefinitely wait to see—and regret it all the more that there is always, in America, yet another lively source of interest involved in the execution of such designs, and closely involved just in proportion as the high intention, the formal majesty, of the thing seems assured. It comes back to what we constantly feel, throughout the country, to what the American scene everywhere depends on for half its appeal or its effect; to the fact that the social conditions, the material, pressing and pervasive, make the particular experiment or demonstration, whatever it may pretend to, practically a new and incalculable thing. This general Americanism is often the one tag of character attaching to the case after every other appears to have abandoned it. The thing is happening, or will have to happen, in the American way—that American way which is more different from all other native ways, taking country with country, than any of these latter are different from each other; and the question is of how, each time, the American way will see it through.

The element of suspense—beguilement, ever, of the sincere observer—is provided for by the fact that, though this American way never fails to come up, he has to recognize as by no means equally true that it never fails to succeed. It is inveterately applied, but with consequences bewilderingly various; which means, however, for our present moral, but that the certainty of the *determined* American effect is an element to attend quite especially such a case as the employment of the arts of design, on an unprecedented scale, for public uses, the adoption on this scale of the whole aesthetic law. Encountered in America, phenomena of this order strike us mostly as occurring in the historic void, as having to present themselves in the hard light of that desert, and as needing to extort from it, so far as they can, something of the shading of their interest. Encountered in older countries, they show, on the contrary, as taking up the references, as consenting perforce to the relations, of which the air is already full, and as having thereby much rather to get themselves expressive by charm than to get themselves expressive by weight. The danger 'in Europe' is of their having too many things to say, and too many others to distinguish these from; the danger in the States is of their not having things enough—with enough tone and resonance furthermore to give them. What therefore will the multitudinous and elaborate forms of the Washington to come have to 'say' and what, above all, besides gold and silver, stone and marble and trees and flowers, will they be able to say it *with*? That is one of the questions in the mere phrasing of which the restless analyst finds a thrill. There is a thing called interest that has to be produced for him—positively as if he were a rabid usurer with a clutch of his imperilled bond. He has seen again and again how the most expensive effort often fails to lead up to interest, and he has seen how it may bloom in soil of no more worth than so many layers of dust and ashes. He has learnt in fact—he learns greatly in America—to mistrust any plea for it *directly* made by money, which operates too often as the great puffing motor-car framed for whirling him, in his dismay, quite away from it. And he has inevitably noted, at the same time, from how comparatively few other sources this rewarding dividend on his invested attention may be drawn. He thinks of these sources as few, that is, because he sees the same ones, which are the references by which interest is fed, used again and again, with a desperate economy; sees the same ones, even as the human heroes, celebrities, extemporized lions or scapegoats, required social and educational figure-heads and 'values' having to serve in *all* the connections and adorn all the tales. That is one of the liveliest of his American impressions. He has at moments his sense that, in presence of such vast populations, and instilled, emulous demands, there is not, outside the mere economic, enough native history, recorded or current, to go round.

V

It seemed to me on the spot, moreover, that such reflections were rather more than less pertinent in face of the fact that I was again to find the Capitol, whenever I approached, and above all whenever I entered it, a vast and many-voiced creation. The thing depends of course somewhat on the visitor, who will be the more responsive, I think, the further back into the 'origins' of the whole American spectacle his personal vision shall carry him; but this hugest, as I suppose it, of all the homes of debate only asks to put forth, on opportunity, an incongruous, a various, an inexhaustible charm. I may as well say at once that I had found myself from the first adoring the Capitol, though I may not pretend here to dot all the i's of all my reasons—since some of these might appear below the dignity of the subject and other alien to its simplicity. The ark of the American covenant may strike one thus, at any rate, as a compendium of all the national terms and standards, weights and measures and emblems of greatness and glory, and indeed as a builded record of half the collective vibrations of a people; their conscious spirit, their public faith, their bewildered taste, their ceaseless curiosity, their arduous and interrupted education. Such were to my vision at least some of its aspects, but the place had a hundred sides, and if I had had time to look for others still I felt I should have found them. What it comes to—whereby the 'pull' in America, is of the greatest—is that association really reigns there, and in the richest, and even again and again in the drollest, forms; it is thick and vivid and almost gross, it assaults the wondering mind. The labyrinthine pile becomes thus inordinately *amusing*—taking the term in its finer modern sense. The analogy may seem forced, but it affected me as playing in Washington life very much the part that St Peter's, of old, had seemed to me to play in Roman: it offered afternoon entertainment, at the end of a longish walk, to any spirit in the humour for the uplifted and flattered vision—and this without suggesting that the sublimities in the two cases, even as measured by the profanest mind, tend at all to be equal. The Washington dome is indeed, capable, in the Washington air, of admirable, of sublime effects; and there are cases in which, seen at a distance above its yellow Potomac, it varies but by a shade from the sense—yes, absolutely the divine campagna-sense—of St Peter's and the like-coloured Tiber.

But the question is positively of the impressiveness of the great terraced Capitol hill, with its stages and slopes, staircases and fountains, its general presentation of its charge. And if the whole mass and prospect 'amuse' as I say, from the moment they are embraced, the visitor curious of the *democratic assimilation* of the greater dignities and majesties will least miss the general logic. That is the light in which the whole thing is supremely interesting; the light of the fact, illustrated at every turn, that the populations maintaining it deal with it so directly and intimately, so sociably and humorously. We promptly take in that, if ever we are to commune in a concentrated way with the sovereign people and see their exercised power raise a side-wind of irony for forms and arrangements other than theirs, the occasion here will amply serve. Indubitably, moreover, at a hundred points, the irony operates, and all the more markedly under such possible interference; the interference of the monumental spittoons, that of the immense amount of vulgar, of barbaric, decoration, that of the terrible artistic tributes from, and scarce less to, the different States—the unassorted marble mannikins in particular, each a portrayal by one of the commonwealths of her highest worthy, which make the great Rotunda, the intended Valhalla, resemble a stonecutter's collection of priced sorts and sizes. Discretion exists, throughout, only as a flower of the very first or of these very latest years; the large middle time, corresponding, and even that unequally, with the English Victorian, of sinister memory, was unacquainted with the name, and waits there now, in its fruits, but for a huge sacrificial fire, some far-flaring act-of-faith of the future: a tribute to the aesthetic law which one already feels stirring the air, so that it may arrive, I think, with an unexampled stride. Nothing will have been more interesting, surely, than so public a wiping-over of the aesthetic slate, with all the involved collective compunctions and repudiations, the general exhibition of a colossal conscience, a conscience proportionate to the size and wealth of the country. To such grand gestures does the American scene lend itself!

The elements in question are meanwhile there, in any case, just as the sovereign people are there, 'going over' their property; but we are aware none the less of impressions—that of the ponderous proud Senate, for instance, so sensibly massive; that of the Supreme Court, so simply, one almost says so chastely, yet, while it breathes supremacy, so elegantly, so all intellectually, in session—under which the view, taking one extravagance with another, recurs rather ruefully to glimpses elsewhere caught, glimpses of authority emblazoned, bewigged, bemantled, bemarshalled, in almost direct defeat of its intention of gravity. For the reinstated absentee, in these presences, the mere recovery of native privilege was at all events a balm—after too many challenged appeals and abused patiences, too many hushed circuitous creepings, among the downtrodden, in other and more bristling halls of state. The sense of a certain large, final benignity in the Capitol comes then, I think, from this impression that the national relation to it is that of a huge flourishing Family to the place of business, the estate-office, where, in a myriad open ledgers, which offer no obscurity to the hereditary head for figures, the account of their colossal revenue is kept. They meet there in safe sociability, as all equally initiated and interested—not as in a temple or a citadel, but by the warm domestic hearth of Columbia herself; a motherly, chatty, clear-spectacled Columbia, who reads all the newspapers, knows, to the last man, every one of her sons by name, and, to the last boy, even her grandsons, and is fenced off, at the worst, but by concentric circles of rocking-chairs. It is impossible, as I say, not to be fondly conscious of her welcome—unless again, and yet again, I read into the general air, confusedly, too much of the happy accident of the basis of my introduction. But if my sensibility responds with intensity to this, so much the better; for what were such felt personal aids and influences, after all, but cases and examples, embodied expressions of character, type, distinction, products of the *working* of the whole thing?—specimens, indeed, highly concentrated and refined, and made thereby, I admit, more charming and insidious.

It must also be admitted that to exchange the inner aspects of the vast monument for the outer is to be reminded with some sharpness of a Washington in which half the sides that have held our attention drop, as if rather abashed, out of sight. Not its pleasant brightness as of a winter watering-place, not its connections, however indirect, with the older, but those with the newer, the newest, civilization, seem matter of recognition for its various marble fronts; it rakes the prospect, it rakes the continent, to a much more sweeping purpose, and is visibly concerned but in immeasurable schemes of which it can consciously remain the centre. Here, in the vast spaces—mere empty light and air, though such pleasant air and such pretty light as yet—the great Federal future seems, under vague bright forms, to hover and to stalk, making the horizon recede to take it in, making the terraces too, below the long colonnades, the admirable standpoints, the sheltering porches, of political philosophy. The comparatively new wings of the building filled me, whenever I walked here, with thanksgiving for their large and perfect elegance: so, in Paris, might the wide mated fronts that are of such a noble effect on either side of the Rue Royale shine in multiplied majesty and recovered youth over an infinite Place de la Concorde. These parts of the Capitol, on their Acropolis height, are ideally constructed for 'raking' and for this suggestion of their dominating the American scene in playhouse gallery fashion. You are somehow possessed of it *all* while you tread them—their marble embrace appears to the complement of the vast democratic lap. Though I had them in general, for contemplation, quite to myself, I met one morning a trio of Indian braves, braves dispossessed of forest and prairie, but as free of the builded labyrinth as they had ever been of these; also arrayed in neat pot-hats, shoddy suits and light overcoats, with their pockets, I am sure, full of photographs and cigarettes: circumstances all that quickened their resemblance, on the much bigger scale, to Japanese celebrities, or to specimens, on show, of what the Government can do with people with whom it is supposed able to do nothing. They seemed just then and there, for a mind fed betimes on the Leatherstocking Tales, to project as in a flash an image in itself immense, but foreshortened and simplified—reducing to a single smooth stride the bloody footsteps of time. One rubbed one's eyes, but there, at its highest polish, shining in the beautiful day, was the brazen face of history, and there, all about one, immaculate, the printless pavements of the State.

Florida

HARRIET BEECHER STOWE

*After the Civil War Harriet Beecher Stowe lived mainly
in Florida, and these extracts from some of her letters
(compiled in one volume by her son in 1889) provide a
fascinating insight into the change of scenery and climate
that she experienced there.*

AFTER VISITING FLORIDA during the winter of 1866–67, at which time her
attention was drawn to the beauties and superior advantages of Mandarin on the east side of the river, Mrs Stowe writes from Hartford,
May 29, 1867, to Rev Charles Beecher:—

MY DEAR BROTHER
We are now thinking seriously of a place in Mandarin much more beautiful than any other in the vicinity. It has on it five large date palms,
an olive grove in full bearing, besides a fine orange grove which this

year will yield about seventy-five thousand oranges. If we get that, then I want you to consider the expediency of buying the one next to it. It contains about two hundred acres of land, on which is a fine orange grove, the fruit from which last year brought in two thousand dollars as sold at the wharf. It is right on the river, and four steamboats pass it each week, on their way to Savannah and Charleston. There is on the place a very comfortable cottage, as houses go out there, where they do not need to be built as substantially as with us.

I am now in correspondence with the Bishop of Florida, with a view to establishing a line of churches along the St John's River, and if I settle at Mandarin, it will be one of my stations. Will you consent to enter the Episcopal Church and be our clergyman? You are just the man we want. If my tasks and feelings did not incline me toward the Church, I should still choose it as the best system for training immature minds such as those of our negroes. The system was composed with reference to the wants of the laboring class of England, at a time when they were as ignorant as our negroes now are.

I long to be at this work, and cannot think of it without my heart burning within me. Still I leave all with my God, and only hope He will open the way for me to do all that I want to for this poor people. Affectionately yours,

                                                            H. B. STOWE.

In April, 1869, Mrs Stowe was obliged to hurry North in order to visit Canada in time to protect her English rights in 'Oldtown Folks' which she had just finished.

About this time she secured a plot of land, and made arrangements for the erection on it of a building that should be used as a schoolhouse through the week, and as a church on Sunday. For several years Professor Stowe preached during the winter in this little schoolhouse, and Mrs Stowe conducted Sunday-school, sewing classes, singing classes, and various other gatherings for instruction and amusement, all of which were well attended and highly appreciated by both the white and colored residents of the neighborhood.

Upon one occasion, having just arrived at her Mandarin home, Mrs Stowe writes:—

'At last, after waiting a day and a half in Charleston, we arrived here about ten o'clock Saturday morning, just a week from the day we sailed. The house looked so pretty, and quiet, and restful, the day was so calm and lovely, it seemed as though I had passed away from all trouble, and was looking back upon you all from a secure resting-place. Mr Stowe is very happy here, and is constantly saying how pleasant it is, and how glad he is that he is here. He is so much improved in health that already he is able to take a considerable walk every day.

'We are all well, contented, and happy, and we have six birds, two dogs, and a pony. Do write more and oftener. Tell me all the little nothings and nowheres. You can't imagine how they are magnified by the time they have reached into this remote corner.'

The return to her Mandarin home each succeeding winter was always a source of intense pleasure to this true lover of nature in its brightest and tenderest moods. Each recurring season was filled with new delights. In December, 1879, she writes to her son, now married and settled as a minister in Saco, Me.:—

DEAR CHILDREN,

Well, we have stepped from December to June, and this morning is sunny and dewy, with a fresh sea-breeze giving life to the air. I have just been out to cut a great bunch of roses and lilies, though the garden is grown into such a jungle that I could hardly get about in it. The cannas, and dwarf bananas, and roses are all tangled together, so that I can hardly thread my way among them. I never in my life saw anything range and run rampant over the ground as cannas do. The ground is littered with fallen oranges, and the place looks shockingly untidy, but so beautiful that I am quite willing to forgive its disorder.

We got here Wednesday evening about nine o'clock, and found all the neighbors waiting to welcome us on the wharf. The Meads, and Cranes, and Webbs, and all the rest were there, while the black population was in a frenzy of joy. Your father is quite well. The sea had its usual exhilarating effect upon him. Before we left New York he was quite meek, and exhibited such signs of grace and submission that I had great hopes of him. He promised to do exactly as I told him, and stated that he had entire confidence in my guidance. What woman couldn't call such a spirit evidence of being prepared for speedy translation? I was almost afraid he could not be long for this world. But on the second day at sea his spirits rose, and his appetite reasserted itself. He declared in loud tones how well he felt, and quite resented my efforts to take care of him. I reminded him of his gracious vows and promises in the days of his low spirits, but to no effect. The fact is, his self-will has not left him yet, and I have now no fear of his immediate translation. He is going to preach for us this morning.

The last winter passed in this well-loved Southern home was that of 1883–84, for the following season Professor Stowe's health was in too precarious a state to permit him to undertake the long journey from Hartford. By this time one of Mrs Stowe's fondest hopes had been realized; and, largely through her efforts, Mandarin had been provided with a pretty little Episcopal church, to which was attached a comfortable rectory, and over which was installed a regular clergyman.

In January, 1884, Mrs Stowe writes:—

'Mandarin looks very gay and airy now with its new villas, and our new church and rectory. Our minister is perfect. I wish you could know him. He wants only physical strength. In everything else he is all one could ask.'

A Trip Through North Florida

GEORGE M. BARBOUR

*In this chapter from his traveler's guide to Florida (1883),
George M. Barbour evokes a vivid picture of the towns and
countryside of northern Florida.*

IT WAS THE middle of March when Captain Samuel Fairbanks, Assistant
Commissioner of Immigration, set out on an official pilgrimage through
the northern section of the State, in search of information for the use
of his bureau. The Captain was peculiarly well adapted for his official
position, and especially to investigate this portion of the State, which
had in all its parts become familiar to him, through a residence of over
forty years. He came originally from central New York, and there are
many other people here from that favorite section of the Empire State.

The writer accepted a cordial invitation to join Captain Fairbanks on the proposed trip, and enjoyed a delightful time, for the Captain was a pleasant, entertaining traveling companion, full of interesting information, anecdotes, and reminiscences of the State and the people. The previously described journey in the other portions of the State had given me a fine opportunity to see the wilder and more remote regions, and the present trip gave me an opportunity to learn of the older and more populous sections. Our route lay through the counties of all the northern and western portions of the State, where, in the 'piping times of peace,' the ante-war days, the true era of Southern prosperity, the planters of Florida lived and flourished and waxed wealthy. In those days Cotton was King, and the broad rolling acres of the vast plantations that covered the hills and beautiful valleys of the charming region were everywhere white with their great crops of the snowy staple. 'Every acre meant another bale, and every bale meant another nigger' was the current saying in regard to it. This was always, from the days of its transfer to American rule, a favorite region with the cotton-planters; here were obtained the largest yields per acre, of the best quality (the famous sea-island variety), and the earliest in market.

We left Jacksonville late one afternoon, by the Florida Central Railroad, changing at Live Oak (the county-seat of Suwanee County) to the Jacksonville, Pensacola and Mobile Railroad. The early morning hours found us speeding through Ohio, Wisconsin, or central New York; certainly, it was not Florida in appearance—hilly, with a rich, brown, clayey soil, solid roads, rocks, and fields of grass, just like the Northern States. Early in the forenoon we arrived at Quincy, the county-seat of Gadsden County, and took the stage from the depot to the town, one and a half mile distant by a road which winds prettily over hills and through fine forests.

Quincy is a quaint, old-fashioned town, Southern in appearance (not, however, of the dingy, miserable, 'cracker' style), a representative type of once-flourishing industry. It has a large, park-like, well-fenced square, with the court-house standing in the center, one of the old Southern regulation kind of square four-roomed-on-two-floors buildings. Huge oaks and similar trees shade the park, and around it or adjacent to it are the 'city' buildings, jail, etc., with plain and rather faded brick stores, the usual number of offices, pumps and water-trough, and the universal Southern hitching-rail on high posts, with always a number of saddle mules and horses attached. Over all is an impalpable but unmistakable mantle of mildewy decay, of neglect rapidly verging on dilapidation. Such is the general appearance of the business portion of Quincy.

The suburbs make an impression altogether more favorable. The residences here are mostly large, well-built structures, with handsome house-grounds, gardens, lawns, out-houses, shade-trees, sidewalks, etc.—in all respects, except that of a few semi-tropical products, closely resembling the usual thrifty appearance of a steady, old, agricultural center in the North. The weather at the time of our visit was lovely (it was March 10th); fruits, flowers, and gardens of thrifty vegetables were everywhere visible; the doors and windows stood wide open, verandas were occupied, croquet-parties dotted the lawns; and 'The Pirates of Penzance' and other latest music, was everywhere heard floating through the open windows, from the keys of skillfully played pianos. At the handsome residence of Postmaster Davidson, we were shown some of the finest specimens of the exquisitely beautiful, golden-hued, feathery pampas-grass that I ever saw, and it grows in many other gardens thereabout.

The views across the country in all directions are fine, ranging over broad fields, hills, valleys, hard-wood forests, orchards, good fences, and roomy residences—in all a beautiful region exhibiting unmistakable signs of agricultural prosperity. Nowhere does live-stock grow better. In the near future, when the old (but worthy) class of men and women shall have passed away with their *ante-bellum* ideas of business, crops, social 'ranks,' education, slave-labor, and their bitter memories of the war, with its defeated hopes and its 'lost cause'—when this race, with such memories in their hearts, shall be gone, and the young generation of their offspring, filled with new ideas, new aspirations, new hopes, shall be in full control, then, I believe, Quincy and all the other towns of that fair, fertile region will be among the pleasantest garden-spots in all America. At present the goodly people are 'brooding upon memories.'

Chattahoochee, the present terminus of the Jacksonville, Pensacola and Mobile Railroad, is merely a little hamlet on the Chattahoochee River, close to the Alabama line, and has stage connection with Marianna, the county-seat of Jackson County, another of those old-style, quiet inland towns, a description of one of which answers for all. The State Insane Asylum is located at Chattahoochee, a roomy old structure, clean, and having an air of comfort and adaptation to its purpose, and containing about thirty inmates. The river, in that region, is quite a large, respectable stream, the outlet of an extensive back country—once the water-way of an immense traffic—to the Gulf-port of Appalachicola. The scenery thereabout is very fine, and the atmosphere noticeably soft and clear. This is attributed to the fact that it is due north of the Gulf, and is always tempered by the famous 'Gulf-breezes.'

From Marianna, a long ride by stage-coach brought us to Pensacola. The ride was tedious and fatiguing, but not really monotonous, for the scenery was very attractive, except in occasional tracts. Vernon, Euchee Anna, and Milton, passed *en route*, are all three county-seats, and are small, drowsy-looking towns, old-fashioned, and in all respects typical specimens of the better class of representative Southern county-seats. A square, an old-fashioned tavern, a court-house, and a few shops, may be said to compose each and all of them.

On every side, in all that region, including Gadsden and adjoining counties, were seen large old plantations, and roomy, old, Southern-style planters' residences, giving evidence of a long-settled region, that had suddenly been arrested in its growth, and was in a state of suspended animation. Yet it is a good country, and has, in fact, a steady growth though it is of a kind not strikingly perceptible, being in crops and products, instead of houses, factories, and such town improvements, that are more likely to catch the attention.

The great, crying need of all that portion of the State is a railroad, and the series of causes that have prevented the completion of the Jacksonville, Pensacola and Mobile Railroad are disgraceful to all concerned. All the parties—the moneyed cliques, railroad-wreckers, lawyers, and agents—that have for years defeated the construction of that road across this fine region to its natural terminus at Pensacola, deserve the honest execrations of all who reside there; for they have greatly damaged and retarded the growth and prosperity of what ought to be one of the most flourishing sections of Florida.

Pensacola is a charming city, clean, nicely laid out, with great shade-trees, handsome homes, the houses generally of good architectural taste, with pretty lawns, arbors, gardens, etc. The navy-yard and fortifications, with their garrisons and official staffs of both branches of the service, give it an animated appearance; and the officers and their families contribute very much to the high reputation for culture and refinement enjoyed by the society there. The city has a large commerce, and is one of the most important lumber-shipping ports in the United States.

In respect to attractions for tourists and visitors, Pensacola is one of the most important places in Florida; and, instead of attempting a detailed description of my own, I will quote the following passages from a well-written and tastefully printed local hand-book:

'The splendid Bay of Pensacola, unrivaled for its beauty, depth, and security, was discovered by Pamfilo de Narvaez, in 1525. Various adventurers gave it different names, as Port de Ancluse and St Mary's Bay, but that of Pensacola, which prevailed, was the true name among the Indians, the natives of the country. The first settlement was made by the Spaniards, in 1686. The first Governor was André Arivola, who constructed a small fort, called San Carlos, and erected a church upon the present site of Fort Barrancas. The French took Pensacola in 1719; the Spaniards retook it, and the French again took it in the same year and kept it until 1722, when it was restored to Spain. In the mean time, Pensacola had been removed to the west end of Santa Rosa Island, near the present site of Fort Pickens, where the Spaniards constructed a fort, which afterward was improved by the English General Haldemand. The settlement remained on the island until 1754, when, the town being partly inundated, the site was removed to the magnificent location which it now occupies. Pensacola was ceded to the English in 1763, by whom it was laid off in regular form in 1765. The town surrendered to the Spanish arms in 1781. On the 7th of November, 1814, General Andrew Jackson, with the American army, entered the town, when the English fleet in the bay destroyed the forts, San Carlos (at Barrancas) and Santa Rosa.

'By consulting the map of Pensacola and its surroundings, the reader will observe the network of water-courses, bays, and bayous centering at that city. The water is clear, bright, and beautiful. Surf-bathing upon Santa Rosa beach, as enjoyable as language can express, the salt-water bathing in the bath-houses of the bay, and bathing in fresh water as clear as crystal, can all be had within a distance of seven miles. The Perdido Bay is one of the loveliest sheets of water in the State, rivaled by the Escambia Bay, with its bluffs and ever-moving fleets. Any attempt to particularize becomes confusing, as the special beauties and attractions of the different bays and bayous are remembered. Escambia River is the 'Ocklawaha' of West Florida. The stranger who wishes to enjoy a short trip will be pleased as the steamer plows through the broad, placid waters

of Escambia Bay, and then delighted with the luxuriance of the tropical growth as the vessel winds its way up the narrow and tortuous
channel of Escambia River to Molino. At this point the excursionist
can take the train and return by rail to Pensacola.

'The fresh-water fishing is superb. The waters literally swarm with
all kinds of fish, notably trout, black bass, and pike. All varieties
of perch abound, including a special kind, a very game fish, called
bream. It is not unusual for a good angler to pull out fifty to sixty
of these fish in an hour, weighing from a half to one pound. Both
in salt and fresh water, fishing is carried on with pleasure and profit
the entire year. In the bay and bayous every description of salt-water
fish abounds, and, in the season, fifty cents will purchase half a
dozen Spanish mackerel of the size for which the epicure pays
seventy-five cents for one half in the restaurants of New York City.
These fish, and the saltwater trout, give special excitement to those
who love a contest with a very game fish. No one can claim to
have seen what fishing is until he has visited the snapper banks
off Santa Rosa Island. There the famous red snapper can be caught,
two at a time, weighing from five pounds to sixty, as rapidly as
the line is thrown in. The limit to the quantity catchable is commensurate with the physical endurance of the catcher.

'The pleasure of boating at Pensacola is not confined to fishing
or idly rolling on the mighty wave, or smoothly plowing the placid
waters; but added to these charms are the numerous places in the
vicinity to go to. The stranger who may visit it will not wonder
at finding first on this list Santa Rosa Island. Upon its beach, mid-
day, in its overflowing brilliancy, makes the beholder feel as if,
according to Milton, 'another morn had risen on mid-noon.' The
sunset comes with a splendor and glory unknown to more northern
climes . . . Santa Rosa Island is a sand-key of the Gulf, forty miles
long, and varying in breadth from a fifth of a mile to over a mile
across; it is the breakwater of Pensacola Harbor, and receives the
shock of the rolling seas of the Gulf of Mexico, which often break
against it in fury, while the waters of the bay within are still as
a millpond, and scarce a ripple washes the beach of the city front,
seven miles away, though the water at the city is as salt as that
in the center of the Gulf. The sea-beach of the island is a gently
sloping expanse of white sand, back and forth on which the advancing and receding waves will glide for hundreds of feet. You can

stand where no water is one moment, and the next be struggling waist-deep against a surging wave that is climbing up the strand. This beach is the incubator of the great turtles of the Gulf. Its gradual incline, the easily excavated sand beyond, and the warm southern exposure, adapt it to their approach, the making of nests, and hatching of their eggs. So they resort to it for this purpose, and in due time the young turtles are hatched, unless the eggs are captured by the various creatures, biped and quadruped, who seek them in the season. From Pensacola over to the island is about seven miles, and as the land-breeze of the night sets fair across the bay, it is a pleasant trip of moonlight nights to run over on a sail-boat, land on the bay-shore, walk across the island, which is not a third of a mile wide opposite the city, and seek for 'turtle-crawls' on the Gulf-beach, or bathe luxuriously in the surf. The 'crawl' shows on the sand where the under-shell has been dragged along, and, following this up to a point above the wash of the highest waves, the nest is found, usually about two and a half feet below the surface. A single nest will contain from one hundred to three hundred eggs. At Sabine Pass, on Santa Rosa Island, alligators are found by the ten thousand, and are killed in large numbers by hunters who frequent the place.

'While on the island, very few visitors fail to find an interest in collecting shells and sea-beans. Then comes a visit to Fort Pickens. This grand and historic old edifice, though denuded of a portion of the iron dogs of war that used to bay, not 'deep-mouthed welcome home' but roars of defiance, still possesses a multitude of pleasant and interesting sights and objects that made a visit there both profitable and agreeable. Across the bay is the navy-yard, and just west of the navy-yard is Fort Barrancas. Both are beautiful, and will interest the most indifferent. Added to the novelties to be seen is the delightful society enjoyed by all who know the hospitable and intelligent officers of both the garrisons. Below Barrancas is the Pensacola Lighthouse.'

An interesting and agreeable route from Pensacola to Tallahassee is *via* one of the popular Henderson line of steamers to St Mark's, and thence by the railroad. The pleasures of a Gulf trip are detailed at length in another chapter. St Mark's is a very ancient port, one of the settlements made by the original Spanish explorers of Florida. Shortly after its settlement a large stone fort and pier were built; but they were long ago permitted to decay, and were finally destroyed by the settlers desiring the cut rock for their own uses. It is now a deserted village, only two or three small and unpretentious buildings marking this famous spot, romantic in historical events, beautiful in scenery, and once a busy mart, the second seaport in all the United States to boast of a railroad terminus. From here to Tallahassee, twenty-one miles distant, runs a railroad, built in 1835–'36. This was, in its early days, a very busy little road, the outlet of all the productive cotton region lying inland. At that time the planters lived in princely style, fairly rolling in wealth; for those were the halcyon days of the slave-owning cotton-planters, and *this* was their paradise. The road is now almost disused, trains only passing over it twice a week, on 'steamer-day' connecting with the weekly Henderson steamers.

Tallahassee, the capital of the State, 'the floral city of the flowery South' is one of the loveliest places in all America. It is built upon the broad, gently rolling surface of a high hill, surrounded on all sides by other lovely hills, valleys, and lakes. It is laid out in squares, with Main Street—which is its principal business street—lined mostly on one side with plain, old-fashioned brick stores for a distance of four blocks. This street is fairly level and wide. All the other streets are charmingly irregular and uneven—in fact, many are quite declivitous—and are lined with grand, old, mammoth-sized magnolias, oaks, maples, elms, and other magnificent shade-trees. Broad, roomy, open squares are frequent, all shady, park-like, and inviting.

At one end of the city stands the State-House, a large and very plain brick structure, painted a light color, with a front and rear portico, having each six great two-story columns. It stands in a spacious square on the crest of the hill, and can be seen from a long distance. The grounds are laid out with winding paths and lawns, shaded by many grand old magnolias, oaks, and the like, and the air is redolent with perfume from the many flowers always blooming there.

It is an unpretentious old city, with an air of village-like rustic simplicity; no factories (except one cotton-mill); all is quiet, country life. The residence avenues are mostly lined with cozy little cottages, and comfortable, roomy substantial mansions of the good old-time style of architecture, and all are surrounded by neatly fenced lawns and gardens, almost all having quite ample grounds, well kept—and flowers, flowers, flowers! Everywhere in the greatest abundance are flowers. A most creditable pride in their lovely home-grounds is exhibited by the citizens, who seem to have a friendly rivalry in this beautiful ornament of nature, that is expressive of culture and a fine taste for the beautiful. Tallahassee is truly a 'floral' city.

The suburbs are everywhere lovely, and the views from the streets or house-tops—especially the roof of the State-House—are exceedingly fine. The surrounding country is a vast range of hills, valleys, brooks, lakes, park-like clusters of large trees, broad, well-cultivated fields, large plantation dwellings and cotton-gins, and distant forests—in all, a remarkable beautiful natural panorama of nature, such as is seen nowhere else in Florida.

Here we remained several delightful days at the quaint, old, tavern-like 'City Hotel' enjoying numerous drives about the surrounding country. One beautiful day I rode out to 'Goodwood' the grand old estate of Major Arvah Hopkins, several miles out of town. This residence was well worth visiting, because it affords a striking evidence of how elegantly the old-time planters enjoyed life. Erected in 1844, it comprises numerous buildings ranged around a large square in the rear, used for laundry, cook-house, milk-house, saddle and harness house, etc., etc.; and the spacious surrounding grounds are laid out in park-like style, with paths, lawns, and innumerable strange plants, ferns, and flowers. Another day a party of us went on a trip to Lake Jackson, a large and long lake, six miles from the city. It closely resembles Cayuga Lake in New York, surrounded by high bluffs, all cleared, and everywhere the broad fields reaching down to the water's edge.

Captain C. E. Dyke, our escort on this trip, and in whose company I enjoyed many other rides and trips, besides evenings at his elegant home, is one of the most notable residents of Florida. A native of new Hampshire, where he long ago learned the printer's trade, he came to this State in 1839, and at once found a 'job' in the office of 'The Floridian' established in 1828. In 1847 he had worked his way up from the case to the editorial chair, and in that year assumed control of the paper, which he has ever since so ably conducted, without a single failure to 'go to press' regularly each week in all that long period of time. Besides being the Nestor of Florida editors, he has for many years been State's printer; and his office, close by the State-House, is a favorite consultation-room for all State officials, who, as a rule, have always placed implicit confidence in his opinions and advice. He is undoubtedly the best informed upon all matters, political and legal, pertaining to

Florida, as a Territory and as a State, of any one living. For upward of forty years he has been the intimate friend, confidant, or adviser of nearly all public officials. Knowing all the secret and unwritten history of the State, his stock of historical and personal reminiscences is very great, and, if 'written up' would make a volume at once interesting and instructive.

One of the pleasantest resorts in the capital at the time of our visit was the official apartments of Governor W. H. Bloxham, then Secretary of State. An unusually genial, off-hand, sociable gentleman, utterly free from ostentation, he is the favorite of all the State officials, and of a large circle of life-long, intimate friends. Governor Bloxham is a native of Florida, and is the first gentleman elected to that position who has been able to boast of such a distinction. He was born very nearly within sight of the capital, where he now sits as Governor; and his comfortable old home near the city, standing in the midst of an immense plantation of several hundred carefully cleared and cultivated acres, is one of the genuine, old-style cotton-plantations of the most hospitable sort. In the electoral campaign of 1880 he was chosen Governor, and it was unquestionably a good choice, for he is heart and hand in favor of any and all proper efforts to aid the cause of education, of immigration, and development of the State by railroads and similar improvements. He is, in particular, a warm friend of the public-school system, and greatly admires the Northern and Western States for their earnest efforts in this cause. He also believes in extending liberal aid to immigration, hoping to see Florida the home of at least one million people, and covered with a network of railroads and canals. A staunch Democrat, he is not a 'Bourbon' but is one who did not believe in the initial secession movement, and is heartily satisfied with the result. So far as he can control or influence the peculiarly retrogressive elements that as yet exert much influence in the political councils of this State, all may be sure that the rights and interests of new-comers will be protected.

An exceedingly pleasant circle of gentlemen to be met in Tallahassee are Chief-Justice E. M. Randall and his Associate Justices, R. B. Van Valkenburg and T. D. Wescott, of the Supreme Court; also Mr Charles H. Foster, their Clerk. Judge Randall is from Milwaukeee, has lived here many years, and has an elegant home in Jacksonville. Judge Van Valkenburg is from western New York, was a distinguished General in the Union army, and Minister to Japan. He is also a long-time resident here, is warmly attached to the State, and owns a very fine estate on the St John's River just opposite Jacksonville. Judge Wescott is a resident of Tallahassee, where he dispenses an elegant hospitality. These gentlemen are profoundly respected by all, irrespective of political creeds, and are of great benefit to the State as an encouragement to immigration. They are an unimpeachable guarantee that life and property are and shall be safe in this State, and that lawless desperadoism of the semi-political character—the 'Mississippi plan'—will not be permitted or tolerated. The fact that these Northern-born gentlemen are members of the Supreme Court of the State is a greater aid to the cause of immigration than may be supposed, even by the most observing and best-disposed native resident.

Near the city stands the famous Murat estate, once the property of Prince Achille Murat, brother-in-law of the first Napoleon, members of whose family are buried in the beautiful city cemetery. The estate is finely located, and the building-site is unsurpassed but the house now standing upon it is quite plain and unpretentious. Another local 'lion' is the noted Wakulla Spring, which I reached by a pleasant drive of sixteen miles. The spring lies in a rather flat, uninteresting, pine-wooded region, near several cultivated cotton-plantations. It is nearly circular in shape, about four hundred feet in diameter, and the shores are densely wooded to the water's edge. A rude landing has been constructed, and an old darkey is always present with his boat to row the visitor about the glassily smooth surface of the pond. The sides are very nearly perpendicular, and are composed of smooth and solid rock. Sixty-feet below the surface of the water is the first or upper level, a broad, shelving surface of clean rock; and through this is a large irregularly circular opening apparently about one hundred feet in diameter, through which can be seen the lower level or bottom of this wonderful spring, a total depth of one hundred and nine feet. The rock that forms the upper level is evidently not very thick, for in one place there is a perfectly round opening about three feet in diameter, through which can be plainly seen the second bottom, fifty-five feet farther below. It is a great, thin fringe of rock, like a crust, with a vast opening a little to one side of its center.

The water is so marvelously blue that indigo would look pale in comparison with it, and so clear that small gravel and bits of tin one inch square could all be seen plainly on the bottom. Countless fish, some quite large and some very small, could also be seen lazily floating about in the distant depths. While the water is blue, the rocks are of the most intensely brilliant green, over which occasional phosphorescent flashes of shimmering light play fitfully, producing a weird and phantasmal effect. There is neither a ripple nor a motion observable in the water, yet here is a stream that comes pouring up from the bowels of the earth and forms a river (the Wakulla River) sixty feet wide and four feet deep.

This is the spring that Ponce de Leon, the Spanish adventurer and discoverer, romantically supposed to be the long-sought 'Fountain of Youth.' He and his superstitious soldiers seem to have completely misunderstood their interpreters or the Indians, who probably meant to convey the information that it was a spring of clear, healthy water, that had a beneficial effect upon the bather therein. He and his followers, being where St Mark's now stands, sought out the Wakulla River and followed it up to this spring, into which they eagerly plunged. It need hardly be said that they came out cleaner, but no younger; and the lives of many innocent savages were at once sacrificed to appease their disappointed anger. They found, or could see on the distant bottom, the skeletons of two gigantic mastodons, their flesh all gone, but their bare bones perfect and white, their great curling tusks interlocked, evidently fallen in and drowned while engaged in a terrific combat on the brink. There the bones lay until, in 1835, Professor King, of Philadelphia, engaged several men, some of whom are now living in Tallahassee, to recover them. This was successfully accomplished, and they were shipped on board a schooner, to be placed in the museum in Philadelphia; but, unfortunately, the vessel was lost at sea, in a gale off Cape Hatteras, and these interesting skeletons were finally lost for ever.

Returning home from our visit to this romantic spring, our party visited another smaller but very interesting spring, and also examined a number of the many mysterious 'sinks' that are found in that Wakulla region. These sinks are mostly circular in form, about fifty feet in diameter and fifty to one hundred and fifty feet deep, with smooth sides, like great wells, only they are dry, or have but little water in their deep bottoms, while large lakes or rivers may be but a few hundred feet distant, with their waters nearly level with the surface of the ground. The wonder is, how there can be such a difference between the levels of the waters in the lake and in the sink; and where the waters of the sink come from and go to. These sinks are found in all portions of Florida, and are a remarkable and characteristic feature of the peninsula.

In Wakulla Country is a vast jungle of trees, vines, water, and marsh, that has never yet been fully explored. Neither the United States nor the State Government has ever attempted to survey it (in fact, there has never been a geological survey of this State). Several adventurous gentlemen in Tallahassee have, on various occasions, attempted to penetrate its depths, but found it impossible except at much expense. As far as they penetrated, they found a strange country of volcanic appearance. Everywhere were seen great masses of rocks, often an acre in extent, all cracked and ragged, as if upheaved from a great depth. Traces of gold, lead, copper, silver and iron are said to have been discovered; and abundant traces of petroleum are found there, and in numerous other localities in that region. It is in this impenetrable jungle that the famous 'Florida volcano' is supposed to exist, for a column of light, hazy smoke or vapor may be (and has been for years) seen rising from some portion of it, and provokes the conundrum, 'What is it?'

Among other strange freaks of nature in that region in Lost Creek, where a large stream suddenly ends, evidently plunging downward into the earth, in an abyss that is bottomless. Also the Natural Bridge across St Mark's River, about seventy feet in width and the same in span, over which people pass. A volume could be written about the natural curiosities of Florida that would be deeply interesting and of scientific value. A thorough scientific survey of this State should be ordered by the State authorities; but, with the present class of able tax-reducers, it is a futile hope to expect any such measure to be authorized.

The people of Tallahassee have a beautiful custom of holding a fair, early each spring, that probably differs from anything in the way of the fair exhibitions held elsewhere in the South. It is a floral fair, held at their spacious fair-grounds, open to all, but of course nearly or quite all the exhibits are made by the Tallahasseeans. The exhibits are vegetables, fruits, and flowers, especially flowers. As might be conjectured, the managers, exhibitors, and patrons generally, are the ladies, who take great interest and pride in this exhibition, so distinctively local, so pleasant, and so indicative of refined taste and culture. I attended the fair of 1880, held in March. Floral Hall was a beautiful sight, with a profuse display of flowers, of all varieties, kinds, forms, colors, and perfumes, all artistically arranged and exhibited in the best advantage.

Nowhere, it may be said in conclusion, is there more refined and cultured society than in Tallahassee. Among them are many descendants of the most prominent and aristocratic old families of America, with names that recall old colonial, Revolutionary, and 1812 days in the battlefields and in State councils; and their large, well-attended schools, numerous, handsome churches, beautiful homes and surroundings, all attest to the high standard of the best society of Tallahassee.

From Tallahassee to Jacksonsville the traveler passes over the Jacksonville, Pensacola and Mobile to Live Oak, and thence *via* the Savannah, Florida and Western Railroad. The other important towns in this section, besides those mentioned, may be briefly dealt with.

Monticello, in Jefferson County, thirty-three miles east of Tallahassee, is the terminus of a branch railroad about five miles long, and is a flourishing town of some two thousand inhabitants. It contains two hotels, good schools, a weekly newspaper and churches of the several denominations, Episcopalian, Presbyterian, Methodist, and Baptist. The climate is almost identical with that of Tallahassee, and the adjacent country is very similar in appearance to that which surrounds the capital. Near Monticello is the Lipona plantation, where Murat resided for some time while in Florida; and in the vicinity is Lake Miccosukee, whose banks figure in history as the camping-ground of De Soto, and as the scene of a bloody battle between General Jackson and the Miccosukee Indians.

Madison is a pretty town of about eight hundred inhabitants, situated on the railway, fifty-five miles east of Tallahassee. It is the capital of Madison County, is built on a plain near a small lake, and contains Presbyterian, Baptist, and Methodist churches. The Suwanee River is near by, and in the county are Lakes Rachel, Francis, Mary, and Cherry.

Live Oak, the county-seat of Suwanee County, is at the junction of the Jacksonville, Pensacola and Mobile and the Savannah, Florida and Western Railways, and is the half-way point between Tallahassee and Jacksonville. The surrounding country is pine-woods with sandy soil, which looks poor, but which, with a little manure and good cultivation, produces excellent crops. There are a number of market-gardens in the vicinity, and great quantities of vegetables are shipped from this point to Northern markets. The town spreads over a good deal of ground, and contains about eight hundred inhabitants. A live weekly newspaper, 'The Bulletin' is published here, the schools are good, and there are churches of several denominations, with some respectable store-buildings and a number of pleasant residences. Five miles south of the town (connected with it by a 'tram-road' or wooden railway) is Padlock, and four miles north is the little village of Rixford.

Houston lies six miles east of Live Oak, on the railroad, and is surrounded by a good farming country. Near the town are some fine springs, and in the vicinity are several beautiful lakes containing an abundance of excellent fish. Wellborn, twelve miles east of Live Oak, is a much larger place, and among its population are a number of settlers who have come thither from Indiana, Illinois, and Iowa. There are some fine hammock-lands near the town, and in the neighborhood are Lake Wellborn and other lakes teeming with fish. Only eight miles away are the famous Suwanee White Sulphur Springs, attractively situated on the banks of the Suwanee River.

Lake City, the most important place in this region, is on the railroad about fifty miles west of Jacksonville. It is a prosperous and substantially built town of some twenty-five hundred inhabitants, with a number of brick stores, well-kept hotels, seven or eight churches, good schools, tasteful private residences, and a large trade in vegetables and other products of the surrounding country, including lumber and turpentine. Its climate, being drier than that of Jacksonville, is thought to be more favorable to those consumptives who are in advanced stages of the disease, and the place is a favorite winter retreat for such invalids. Lakes almost surround the town, hence its name. Three miles south is Alligator Lake, which has no visible outlet. In the wet season it is three or four miles across, but in winter it retires into a deep sinkhole, and the former bottom is transformed into a grassy meadow.

The following description of Suwanee County is from a letter written by Mr N. C. Rippey to the Tallahassee 'Floridian'. We quote it because it is applicable to all this portion of the State, and contains information of value to immigrants:

'The county lies in a big bend of the Suwanee River, or at least the river forms the boundary-line on three sides. There is a high ridge extending across the county east and west, or nearly so, near the center north and south, some four miles or so in width. It is covered with the finest growth of pine-timber in the county. In it is an abundance of stone, in ledges and in bowlders. It is of a gray color, very soft; can be easily cut with a knife or saw, and, on being exposed to the air for some time, it becomes as hard and durable as granite, and makes a very fine material for building purposes.

'The country north of the ridge is pine-woods with sandy soil. Here and there are to be found tracts of hammock-lands, varying in size from a few acres to several hundred. These lands contain a rich, loamy soil, and a great variety of excellent hard-wood timber, suitable for all kinds of building and manufacturing purposes. There are a number of beautiful lakes scattered over the country, containing an abundance of excellent fish. There are numerous springs, some of them white sulphur, famed for their medical virtues. There are branches or creeks gushing out of the earth, and after flowing a few miles entirely disappear. The country south of ''The Ridge'' is more rolling and fertile, and is underlaid with limestone that frequently comes within a few inches of the surface. There are no lakes or streams of running water. There are a great number of natural wells that appear as though they were cut by the hand of man through solid rock; they are round, or nearly so, varying in size from a few inches to forty feet or more in diameter, and from a few feet to forty or more to the edge of the water; fish are frequently found in the largest; the water is clear and cool. There are a number of caves of considerable size, but they have never been explored to see how far they extend under the earth.

'The pine-lands produce about fifteen bushels of corn per acre. A little manure and good cultivation will yield more than double that; cotton, about a bale to two acres, sometimes three; upland rice, from forty to sixty bushels per acre; oats and rye are raised in considerable quantities, but I was unable to learn the yield per acre; sugar-cane does well, and is a very profitable crop; a great variety of fine vegetables are raised and shipped to Northern markets; there are a number of small vineyards in the county, and some excellent wine is made from the grapes; there are quite a number of small orange-groves, and, strange to say, they are nearly all planted by the hands of women; it is a fine country for peaches and pears. The people are just beginning to find out what a great variety of fruits and vegetables they can raise, and everybody seems determined to have an orchard of all kinds of fruit. ''Turpentining'' has become quite an industry, and there are several large turpentine farms in the county that are reported to be very profitable.

'The Suwanee River is navigable for small steamboats to the crossing of the Jacksonville, Pensacola and Mobile Railroad, and for large steamers to Rowland's Bluff, near the southeast corner of the county. The river frequently has rocky bluffs and bottoms, and many fine springs are to be seen along the banks, and some rich lands.

'The population of the county in 1880 was 7,379, of which 4,166 were white and 3,213 were black. Judging from the number of grants that have gone into the county this past fall and winter, the white population must now be about five thousand.'

Dr D. G. Brinton says; 'The climate of this part of Florida is dry and equable. Many invalids would find it a very pleasant and beneficial change from the seacoast or the river-side and immigrants would do well to visit it. Game and fish are abundant, and the sportsman need never be at a loss for occupation.'

New Orleans

MARK TWAIN

This extract from Mark Twain's autobiographical account of his life as a river pilot, Life on the Mississippi *(1883), captures the ambience of life in New Orleans and the Southern States.*

THE APPROACHES TO New Orleans were familiar; general aspects were unchanged. When one goes flying through London along a railway propped in the air on tall arches, he may inspect miles of upper bedrooms through the open windows, but the lower half of the houses is under his level and out of sight. Similarly, in high-river stage, in the New Orleans region, the water is up to the top of the enclosing levee-rim, the flat country behind it lies low—representing the bottom of a dish—and as the boat swims along, high on the flood, one looks down upon the houses and into the upper windows. There is nothing but that frail breastwork of earth between the people and destruction.

The old brick salt-warehouses clustered at the upper end of the city looked as they had always looked; warehouses which had had a kind of Aladdin's lamp experience, however, since I had seen them; for when the war broke out the proprietor went to bed one night leaving them packed with thousands of sacks of vulgar salt, worth a couple of dollars a sack, and got up in the morning and found his mountain of salt turned into a mountain of gold, so to speak, so suddenly and to so dizzy a height had the war news sent up the price of the article.

The vast reach of plank wharves remained unchanged, and there were as many ships as ever: but the long array of steamboats had vanished; not altogether, of course, but not much of it was left.

The city itself had not changed—to the eye. It had greatly increased in spread and population, but the look of the town was not altered. The dust, waste-paper-littered, was still deep in the streets; the deep, trough-like gutters alongside the kerbstones were still half full of reposeful water with a dusty surface; the sidewalks were still—in the sugar and bacon region—encumbered by casks and barrels and hogsheads; the great blocks of austerely plain commercial houses were as dusty-looking as ever.

Canal Street was finer, and more attractive and stirring than formerly, with its drifting crowds of people, its several processions of hurrying street-cars, and—toward evening—its broad second-story verandas crowded with gentlemen and ladies clothed according to the latest mode.

Not that there is any 'architecture' in Canal Street to speak in broad, general terms, there is no architecture in New Orleans, except in the cemeteries. It seems a strange thing to say of a wealthy, far-seeing, and energetic city of a quarter of a million inhabitants, but it is true. There is a huge granite US Custom-house—costly enough, genuine enough, but as a decoration it is inferior to a gasometer. It looks like a state prison. But it was built before the war. Architecture in America may be said to have been born since the war. New Orleans, I believe, has had the good luck—and in a sense the bad luck—to have had no great fire in late years. It must be so. If the opposite had been the case, I think one would be able to tell the 'burnt district' by the radical improvement in its architecture over the old forms. One can do this in Boston and Chicago. The 'burnt district' of Boston was common place before the fire; but now there is no commercial district in any city in the world that can surpass it—or perhaps even rival it—in beauty, elegance, and tastefulness.

However, New Orleans has begun—just this moment, as one may say. When completed, the new Cotton Exchange will be a stately and beautiful building; massive, substantial, full of architectural graces; no shams or false pretences or ugliness about it anywhere. To the city, it will be worth many times its cost, for it will breed its species. What has been lacking hitherto, was a model to build toward; something to educate eye and taste; a *suggester*, so to speak.

The city is well outfitted with progressive men—thinking, sagacious, long-headed men. The contrast between the spirit of the city and the city's architecture is like the contrast between waking and sleep. Apparently there is a 'boom' in everything but that one dead feature. The water in the gutters used to be stagnant and slimy, and a potent disease-breeder; but the gutters are flushed now, two or three times a day, by powerful machinery; in many of the gutters the water never stands still, but has a steady current. Other sanitary improvements have been made; and with such effect that New Orleans claims to be (during the long intervals between the occasional yellow-fever assaults) one of the healthiest cities in the Union. There's plenty of ice now for everybody, manufactured in the town. It is a driving place commercially, and has a great river, ocean, and railway business. At the date of our visit, it was the best lighted city in the Union, electrically speaking. The New Orleans electric lights were more numerous than those of New York, and very much better. One had this modified noonday not only in Canal and some neighbouring chief streets, but all along a stretch of five miles of river frontage. There are good clubs in the city now—several of them but recently organised—and inviting modern-style pleasure resorts at West End and Spanish Fort. The telephone is everywhere. One of the most notable advances is in journalism. The newspapers, as I remember them, were not a striking feature. Now they are. Money is spent upon them with a free hand. They get the news, let it cost what it may. The editorial work is not hack-grinding, but literature. As an example of New Orleans journalistic achievement, it may be mentioned that the 'Times Democrat' of August 26, 1882, contained a report of the year's business of the towns of the Mississippi Valley, from New Orleans all the way to St Paul—two thousand miles. That issue of the paper consisted of *forty* pages; seven columns to the page; two hundred and eighty columns in all; fifteen hundred words to the column; an aggregate of four hundred and twenty thousand words. That is to say, not much short of three times as many words as there are in this book. One may with sorrow contrast this with the architecture of New Orleans.

I have been speaking of public architecture only. The domestic article in New Orleans is reproachless, notwithstanding it remains as it always was. All the dwellings are of wood—in the American part of the town, I mean—and all have a comfortable look. Those in the wealthy quarter are spacious; painted snow-white double-verandas, supported by ornamental columns. These mansions stand in the centre of large grounds, and rise, garlanded with roses, out of the midst of swelling masses of shining green foliage and many-coloured blossoms. No houses could well be in better harmony with their surroundings, or more pleasing to the eye, or more home-like and comfortable-looking.

One even becomes reconciled to the cistern presently; this is a mighty cash, painted green, and sometimes a couple of stories high, which is propped against the house-corner on stilts. There is a mansion-and-brewery suggestion about the combination which seems very incongruous at first. But the people cannot have wells, and so they take rain-water. Neither can they conveniently have cellars, or graves; the town being built upon 'made' ground; so they do without both, and few of the living complain, and none of the others.

They bury their dead in vaults, above the ground. These vaults have a resemblance to houses—sometimes to temples; are built of marble, generally; are architecturally graceful and shapely; they face the walks and driveways of the cemetery; and when one moves through the midst of a thousand or so of them and sees their white roofs and gables stretching into the distance on every hand, the phase 'city of the dead' has all at once a meaning to him. Many of the cemeteries are beautiful, and are kept in perfect order. When one goes from the levee or the business streets near it, to a cemetery, he observes to himself that if those people down there would live as neatly while they are alive as they do after they are dead, they would find many advantages in it;

and besides, their quarter would be the wonder and admiration of the business world. Fresh flowers, in vases of water, are to be seen at the portals of many of the vaults: placed there by the pious hands of bereaved parents and children, husbands and wives, and renewed daily. A milder form of sorrow finds it's inexpensive and lasting remembrancer in the coarse and ugly but indestructible 'immortelle'—which is a wreath or cross or some such emblem, made of rosettes of black linen, with sometimes a yellow rosette at the conjunction of the cross's bars—kind of sorrowful breast-pin, so to say. The immortelle requires no attention: you just hang it up, and there you are; just leave it alone, it will take care of your grief for you, and keep it in mind better than you can; stands weather first-rate, and lasts like boiler-iron.

On sunny days, pretty little chameleons—gracefullest of legged reptiles—creep along the marble fronts of the vaults, and catch flies. Their changes of colour—as to variety—are not up to the creature's reputation. They change colour when a person comes along and hangs up an immortelle; but that is nothing: any right-feeling reptile would do that.

I will gradually drop this subject of graveyards. I have been trying all I could to get down to the sentimental part of it, but I cannot accomplish it. I think there is no genuinely sentimental part to it. It is all grotesque, ghastly, horrible. Graveyards may have been justifiable in the bygone ages, when nobody knew that for every dead body put into the ground, to glut the earth and the plant-roots, and the air with disease-germs, five or fifty, or maybe a hundred persons must die before their proper time; but they are hardly justifiable now, when even the children know that a dead saint enters upon a century-long career of assassination the moment the earth closes over his corpse. It is a grim sort of a thought. The relics of St Anne, up in Canada, have now, after nineteen hundred years, gone to curing the sick by the dozen. But it is merest matter-of-course that these same relics, within a generation after St Anne's death and burial, *made* several thousand people sick. Therefore these miracle-performances are simply compensation, nothing more. St Anne is somewhat slow pay, for a Saint, it is true; but better a debt paid after nineteen hundred years, and outlawed by the statute of limitations, than not paid at all; and most of the knights of the halo do not pay at all. Where you find one that pays—like St Anne—you find a hundred and fifty that take the benefit of the statute. And none of them pay any more than the principal of what they owe—they pay none of the interest either simple or compound. A Saint can never *quite* return the principal; however; for his dead body *kills* people, whereas his relics *heal* only—they never restore the dead to life. That part of the account is always left unsettled.

'Dr F. Julius Le Moyne, after fifty years of medical practice, wrote: ''The inhumation of human bodies, dead from infectious diseases, results in constantly loading the atmosphere, and polluting the waters, with not only the germs that rise from simply putrefaction, but also with the *specific* germs of the diseases from which death resulted.''

'The gases (from buried corpses) will rise to the surface through eight or ten feet of gravel, just as coal-gas will do, and there is practically no limit to their power of escape.

'During the epidemic in New Orleans in 1853. Dr E. H. Barton reported that in the Fourth District the mortality was four hundred and fifty-two per thousand—more than double that of any other. In this district were three large cemeteries, in which during the previous year more than three thousand bodies had been buried. In other districts the proximity of cemeteries seemed to aggravate the disease.

'In 1828 Professor Bianchi demonstrated how the fearful reappearance of the plague at Modena was caused by excavations in ground where, *three hundred years previously*, the victims of the pestilence had been buried. Mr Cooper, in explaining the causes of some epidemics, remarks that the opening of the plague burial-grounds at Eyam resulted in an immediate outbreak of disease.'—*North American Review, No. 3, Vol.* 135.

In an address before the Chicago Medical Society, in advocacy of cremation, Dr Charles W. Purdy made some striking comparisons to show what a burden is laid upon society by the burial of the dead:—

'One and one-fourth times more money is expended annually in funerals in the United States than the Government expends for public-school purposes. Funerals cost this country in 1880 enough money to pay the liabilities of all the commercial failures in the United States during the same year, and give each bankrupt a capital of $8,630 with which to resume business. Funerals cost annually more money than the value of the combined gold and silver yield of the United States in the year 1880! These figures do not include the sums invested in burial-grounds and expended in tombs and monuments, nor the loss from depreciation of property in the vicinity of cemeter-ies.'

For the rich, cremation would answer as well as burial; for the ceremonies connected with it could be made as costly and ostentatious as a Hindoo *suttee*; while for the poor, cremation would be better than burial, because so cheap—so cheap until the poor got to imitating the rich, which they would do by-and-bye. The adoption of cremation would relieve us of a muck of threadbare burial-witticisms; but, on the other hand, it would resurrect a lot of mildewed old cremation-jokes that have had a rest for two thousand years.

I have a coloured acquaintance who earns his living by odd jobs and heavy manual labour. He never earns above four hundred dollars in a year, and as he has a wife and several young children, the closest scrimping is necessary to get him through to the end of the twelve months debtless. To such a man a funeral is a colossal financial disaster. While I was writing one of the preceding chapters, this man lost a little child. He walked the town over with a friend, trying to find a coffin that was within his means. He bought the very cheapest one he could find, plain wood, stained. It cost him *twenty-six dollars*. It would have cost less than four, probably, if it had been built to put something useful into. He and his family will feel that outlay a good many months.

About the same time, I encountered a man in the street, whom I had not seen for six or seven years; and something like this talk followed. I said—

'But you used to look sad and oldish; you don't now. Where did you get all this youth and bubbling cheerfulness? Give me the address.'

He chuckled blithely, took off his shining tile, pointed to a notched pink circlet of paper pasted into its crown, with something lettered on it, and went on chuckling while I read, 'J. B--, UNDERTAKER.' Then he clapped his hat on, gave it an irreverent tilt to leeward, and cried out—

'That's what's the matter! It used to be rough times with me when you knew me—insurance-agency business, you know; mighty irregular. Big fire, all right—brisk trade for ten days while people scared; after that, dull policy-business till next fire. Town like this don't have fires often enough—a fellow strikes so many dull weeks in a row that he gets discouraged. But you bet you, *this* is the business! People don't wait for examples to *die*. No, sir, they drop off right along—there ain't any dull spots in the undertaker line. I just started in with two or three little old coffins and a hired hearse, and *now* look at the thing! I've worked up a business here that would satisfy any man, don't care who he is. Five years ago, lodged in an attic; live in a swell house now, with a mansard roof, and all the modern inconveniences.'

'Does a coffin pay so well? Is there much profit on a coffin?'

'*Go*-way! How you talk!' Then, with a confidential wink, a dropping of the voice, and an impressive laying of his hand on my arm; 'Look here; there's one thing in this world which isn't ever cheap. That's a coffin. There's one thing in this world which a person don't ever try to jew you down on. That's a coffin. There's one thing in this world which a person don't say—'I'll look around a little, and if I find I can't do better I'll come back and take it.'' That's a coffin. There's one thing in this world which a person won't take in pine if he can go walnut; and won't take in walnut if he can go mahogany; and won't take in mahogany if he can go an iron casket with silver door-plate and bronze handles. That's a coffin. And there's one thing in this world which you don't have to worry around after a person to get him to pay for. And *that's* a coffin. Undertaking?—why it's the dead-surest business in Christendom, and the nobbiest.

'Why, just look at it. A rich man won't have anything but your very best; and you can just pile it on, too—pile it on and sock it to him—he won't ever holler. And you take in a poor man, and if you work him right he'll bust himself on a single lay-out. Or especially a woman. F'r instance: Mrs O'Flaherty comes in—widow—wiping her eyes and kind of moaning. Un-handkerchiefs one eye, bats it around tearfully over the stock; says—

'"And fhat might ye ask for that wan?"

'"Thirty-nine dollars, madam," says I.

'''It's a foine big price, sure, but Pat shall be buried like a gintleman, as he was, if I have to work me fingers off for it. I'll have that wan, sor.''

'''Yes, madam,'' says I, ''and it is a very good one, too; not costly, to be sure, but in this life we must cut our garment to our clothes, as the saying is.'' And as she starts out, I heave in, kind of casually, ''This one with the white satin lining is a beauty, but I am afraid—well, sixty-five dollars *is* a rather—rather—but no matter, I felt obliged to say to Mrs O'Shaughnessy—''

'''D'ye mane to soy that Bridget O'Shaughnessy bought the mate to that joo-ul box to ship that dhrunken divil to Purgatory in?''

'''Yes, madam.''

'''Then Pat shall go to heaven in the twin to it, if it takes the last rap the O'Flaherties can raise; and moind you, stick on some extras, too, and I'll give ye another dollar.''

'And as I lay-in with the livery stables, of course I don't forget to mention that Mrs O'Shaughnessy hired fifty-four dollars' worth of hacks and flung as much style into Dennis's funeral as if he had been a duke or an assassin. And of course she sails in and goes the O'Shaughnessy about four hacks and an omnibus better. That *used* to be, but that's all played now; that is, in this particular town. The Irish got to piling up hacks so, on their funerals, that a funeral left them ragged and hungry for two years afterward; so the priest pitched in and broke it all up. He don't allow them to have but two hacks now, and sometimes only one.'

'Well,' said I, 'if you are so light-hearted and jolly in ordinary times, what *must* you be in an epidemic?'

He shook his head.

'No, you're off, there. We don't like to see an epidemic. An epidemic don't pay. Well, of course I don't mean that, exactly; but it don't pay in proportion to the regular thing. Don't it occur to you, why?'

'No.'

'Think.'

'I can't imagine. What is it?'

'It's just two things.'

'Well, what *are* they?'

'One's Embamming.'

'And what's the other?'

'Ice.'

'How is that?'

'Well, in ordinary times, a person dies, and we lay him up in ice; one day, two days, maybe three, to wait for friends to come. Takes a lot of it—melts fast. We charge jewellery rates for that ice, and war-prices for attendance. Well, don't you know, when there's an epidemic, they rush 'em to the cemetery the minute the breath's out. No market for ice in an epidemic. Same with Embamming. You take a family that's able to embam, and you've got a soft thing. You can mention sixteen different ways to do it—though there *ain't* only one or two ways, when you come down to the bottom facts of it—and they'll take the highest-priced way, every time. It's human nature—human nature in grief. It don't reason, you see. 'Time being, it don't care a dam. All it wants is physical immortality for deceased, and they're willing to pay for it. All you've got to do is just be ca'm and stack it up—they'll stand the racket. Why, man you can take a defunct that you couldn't *give* away; and get your embamming traps around you and go to work; and in a couple of hours he is worth a cool six hundred—that's what *he's* worth. There ain't anything equal to it but trading rats for di'monds in time of famine. Well, don't you see, when there's an epidemic, people don't wait to embam. No, indeed they don't; and it hurts the business like hellth, as we say—hurts it like hell-th, *health*, see?—Our little joke in the trade. Well I must be going. Give me a call whenever you need any—I mean, when you're going by, sometime.'

In his joyful high spirits, he did the exaggerating himself, if any has been done. I have not enlarged on him.

With the above brief references to inhumation, let us leave the subject. As for me, I hope to be cremated. I made that remark to my pastor once, who said, with what he seemed to think was an impressive manner—

'I wouldn't worry about that, if I had your chances.'

Much he knew about it—the family all so opposed to it.

The old French part of New Orleans—anciently the Spanish part—bears no resemblance to the American end of the city: the American end which lies beyond the intervening brick business-centre. The houses are massed in blocks; are austerely plain and dignified; uniform of pattern, with here and there a departure from it with pleasant effect; all are plastered on the outside, and nearly all have long, iron-railed verandas running along the several storeys. Their chief beauty is the deep, warm, vari-coloured stain with which time and the weather have enriched the plaster. It harmonises with all the surroundings, and has as natural a look of belonging there as has the flush upon sunset clouds. This charming decoration cannot be successfully imitated; neither is it to be found elsewhere in America.

The iron railings are a speciality, also. The pattern is often exceedingly light and dainty, and airy and graceful—with a large cipher or monogram in the centre, a delicate cobweb of baffling, intricate forms, wrought in steel. The ancient railings are hand-made, and are now comparatively rare and proportionately valuable. They are become *bric-à-brac*.

The party had the privilege of idling through this ancient quarter of New Orleans with the South's finest literary genius, the author of 'the Grandissimes.' In him the south has found a masterly delineator of its interior life and its history. In truth, I find by experience, that the untrained eye and vacant mind can inspect it, and learn of it, and judge of it, more clearly and profitably in his books than by personal contact with it.

With Mr Cable along to see for you, and describe and explain and illuminate, a job through that old quarter is a vivid pleasure. And you have a vivid *sense* as of unseen or dimly seen things—vivid, and yet fitful and darkling; you glimpse salient features, but lose the fine shades or catch them imperfectly through the vision of the imagination: a case, as it were, of ignorant near-sighted stranger traversing the rim of wide vague horizons of Alps with an inspired and enlightened long-sighted native.

We visited the old St Louis Hotel, now occupied by municipal offices. There is nothing strikingly remarkable about it; but one can say of it as of the Academy of Music in New York, that if a broom or a shovel has ever been used in it there is no circumstantial evidence to back up the fact. It is curious that cabbages and hay and things do not grow in the Academy of Music; but no doubt it is on account of the interruption of the light by the benches, and the impossibility of hoeing the crop except in the aisles. The fact that the ushers grow their buttonhole-bouquets on the premises shows what might be done if they had the right kind of an agricultural head to the establishment.

We visited also the venerable Cathedral, and the pretty square in front of it; the one dim with religious light, the other brilliant with the worldly sort, and lovely with orange-trees and blossomy shrubs; then we drove in the hot sun through the wilderness of houses and out on to the wide dead level beyond where the villas are, and the water wheels to drain the town, and the commons populous with cows and children; passing by an old cemetery where we were told lie the ashes of an early pirate with a tremendous and sanguinary history; and as long as he preserved unspotted, in retirement, the dignity of his name and the grandeur of his ancient calling, homage and reverence were from his high and low; but when at last he descended into politics and became a paltry alderman, the public 'shook' him, and turned aside and wept. When he died, they set up a monument over him; and little by little he has come into respect again; but it is respect for the pirate, not the alderman. To-day the loyal and generous remember only what he was, and charitably forget what he became.

Thence, we drove a few miles across a swamp, along a raised shell road, with a canal on one hand and a dense wood on the other; and here and there, in the distance, a ragged and angular-limbed and moss-bearded cypress, top standing out, clear cut against the sky, and as quaint of form as the apple-trees in Japanese pictures—such was our course and the surroundings of it. There was an occasional alligator swimming comfortably along in the canal, and an occasional picturesque coloured person on the bank, flinging his statue-rigid reflection upon the still water and watching for a bite.

And by-and-bye we reached the West End, a collection of hotels of the usual light summer-resort pattern, with broad verandas all around, and the waves of the wide and blue Lake Pontchartrain lapping the thresholds. We had dinner on a ground-veranda over the water—the chief dish the renowned fish called the pompano, delicious as the less criminal forms of sin.

Thousands of people come by rail and carriage to West End and to Spanish Fort every evening, and dine, listen to the bands, take strolls in the open air under the electric lights, go sailing on the lake, and entertain themselves in various and sundry other ways.

We had opportunities on other days and in other places to test the pompano. Notably, at an editorial dinner at one of the clubs in the city. He was in his last possible perfection there, and justified his fame. In his suite was a tall pyramid of scarlet cray-fish—large ones; as large as one's thumb—delicate, palatable, appetising. Also devilled whitebait; also shrimps of choice quality; and a platter of small soft-shell crabs of a most superior breed. The other dishes were what one might get at Delmonico's, or Buckingham Palace; those I have spoken of can be had in similar perfection in New Orleans only, I suppose.

In the West and South they have a new institution—the Broom Brigade. It is composed of young ladies who dress in a uniform costume, and go through the infantry drill, with broom in place of musket. It is a very pretty sight, on private view. When they perform on the stage of a theatre, in the blaze of coloured fires, it must be a fine and fascinating spectacle. I saw them go through their complex manual with grace, spirit, and admirable precision. I saw them do everything which a human being can possibly do with a broom, except sweep. I did not see them sweep. But I know they could learn. What they have already learned proves that. And if they ever should learn, and should go on the war-path down Tchoupitoulas or some of those other streets around there, those thoroughfares would bear a greatly improved aspect in a very few minutes. But the girls themselves wouldn't; so nothing would be really gained, after all.

The drill was in the Washington Artillery building. In this building we saw many interesting relics of the war. Also a fine oil-painting representing Stonewall Jackson's last interview with General Lee. Both men are on horseback. Jackson has just ridden up, and is accosting Lee. The picture is very valuable, on account of the portraits, which are authentic. But, like many another historical picture, it means nothing without its label. And one label will fit it as well as another—

First Interview between Lee and Jackson.

Last Interview between Lee and Jackson.

Jackson Introducing Himself to Lee.

Jackson Accepting Lee's Invitation to Dinner.

Jackson Declining Lee's Invitation to Dinner—with Thanks.

Jackson Apologising for a Heavy Defeat.

Jackson Reporting a Great Victory.

Jackson Asking Lee for a Match.

It tells *one* story, and a sufficient one; for it says quite plainly and satisfactorily, 'Here are Lee and Jackson together.' The artist would have made it tell that this is Lee and Jackson's last interview if he could have done it. But he couldn't, for there wasn't any way to do it. A good legible label is usually worth, for information, a ton of significant attitude and expression in a historical picture. In Rome, people with fine sympathetic natures stand up and weep in front of the celebrated 'Beatrice Cenci the Day before her Execution.' It shows what a label can do. If they did not know the picture, they would inspect it unmoved, and say, 'Young girl with hay fever; young girl with her head in a bag.'

I found the half-forgotten Southern intonations and elisions as pleasing to my ear as they had formerly been. A Southerner talks music. At least it is music to me, but then I was born in the South. The educated Southerner has no use for an *r*, except at the beginning of a word. He says 'honah' and 'dinnah' and 'Gove'nuh' and 'befo' the waw' and so on. The words may lack charm to the eye, in print, but they have it to the ear. When did the *r* disappear from Southern speech, and how did it come to disappear? The custom of dropping it was not borrowed from the North, nor inherited from England. Many Southerners—most Southerners—put a *y* into occasional words that begin with the *k* sound. For instance, they say Mr K'yahtah (Carter) and speak of playing k'yahds or of riding in the k'yahs. And they have the pleasant custom—long ago fallen into decay in the North—of frequently employing the respectful 'Sir.' Instead of the curt Yes, and the abrupt No, they say 'Yes, Suh', 'No, Suh.'

But there are some infelicities. Such as 'like' for 'as,' and the addition of an 'at' where it isn't needed. I heard an educated gentleman say, 'Like the flag-officer did.' His cook or his butler would have said, 'Like the flag-officer done.' You hear gentlemen say, 'Where have you been at?' And here is the aggravated form—heard a ragged street Arab say it to a comrade: 'I was a-ask'n' Tom whah you was a-sett'n' at.' The very elect carelessly say 'will' when they mean 'shall'; and many of them say, 'I didn't go to do it' meaning 'I didn't mean to do it.' The Northern word 'guess'—imported from England, where it used to be common, and now regarded by satirical Englishmen as a Yankee original—is but little used among Southerners. They say 'reckon.' They haven't any 'doesn't' in their language; they say 'don't' instead. The unpolished often use 'went' for 'gone'. It is nearly as bad as the Northern hadn't ought.' This reminds me that a remark of a very peculiar nature was made here in my neighbourhood (in the North) a few days ago: 'He hadn't ought to have went.' How is that? Isn't that a good deal of a triumph? One knows the orders combined in this half-breed's architecture without inquiring: one parent Northern, the other Southern. To-day I heard a schoolmistress ask, 'Where is John gone?' This form is so common—so nearly universal, in fact—that if she had used 'whither' instead of 'where' I think it would have sounded like an affectation.

We picked up one excellent word—a word worth travelling to New Orleans to get; a nice limber, expressive, handy word—'langniappe.' They pronounce it lanny-*yap*. It is Spanish—so they said. We discovered it at the head of a column of odds and ends in the Picayune, the first day; heard twenty people use it the second; inquired what it meant the third; adopted it and got facility in swinging it the fourth. It has a restricted meaning, but I think the people spread it out a little when they choose. It is the equivalent of the thirteenth roll in a 'baker's dozen.' It is something thrown in, gratis, for good measure. The custom originated in the Spanish quarter of the city. When a child or a servant buys something in a shop—or even the mayor or the governor, for aught I know—he finished the operation by saying—

'Give me something for lagniappe.'

The shopman always responds; gives the child a bit of liquorice-root, gives the servant a cheap cigar or a spool of thread, gives the governor—I don't know what he gives the governor; support, likely.

When you are invited to drink, and this does occur now and then in New Orleans—and you say, 'What, again?—no, I've had enough;' the other party says, 'But just this one time more—this is for lagniappe.' When the beau perceives that he is stacking his compliments a trifle too high, and sees by the young lady's countenance that the edifice would have been better with the top compliment left off, he puts his, 'I beg pardon—no harm intended' into the briefer form of 'Oh, that's for lagniappe.' If the waiter in the restaurant stumbles and spills a gill of coffee down the back of your neck, he says 'For lagniappe, sah' and gets you another cup without extra charge.

In the North one hears the war mentioned, in social conversation, once a month; sometimes as often as once a week; but as a distinct subject for talk, it has long ago been relieved of duty. There are sufficient reasons for this. Given a dinner company of six gentlemen to-day, it can easily happen that four of them—and possibly five—were not in the field at all. So the chances are four to two, or five to one, that the war will at no time during the evening become the topic of conversation; and the chances are still greater that if it become the topic it will remain so but a little while. If you add six ladies to the company, you have added six people who saw so little of the dread realities of the war that they ran out of talk concerning them years ago, and now would soon weary of the war topic if you brought it up.

The case is very different in the South. There, every man you meet was in the war; and every lady you meet saw the war. The war is the great chief topic of conversation. The interest in it is vivid and constant; the interest in other topics is fleeting. Mention of the war will wake up a dull company and set their tongues going, when nearly any other topic would fail. In the South, the war is what A.D. is elsewhere: they date from it. All day long you hear things 'placed' as having happened since the waw; or du'in' the waw; or befo' the waw; or right aftah the waw; or 'bout two yeahs or five yeahs or ten yeahs befo' the waw or aftah the waw. It shows how intimately every individual was visited, in his own person, by that tremendous episode. It gives the inexperienced stranger a better idea of what a vast and comprehensive calamity invasion is than he can ever get by reading books at the fireside.

At a club one evening, a gentleman turned to me and said, in an aside—

'You notice, of course, that we are nearly always talking about the war. It isn't because we haven't anything else to talk about, but because nothing else has so strong an interest for us. And there is another reason: In the war, each of us, in his own person, seems to have sampled all the different varieties of human experience; as a consequence, you can't mention an outside matter of any sort but it will certainly remind some listener of something that happened during the war—and out he comes with it. Of course that brings the talk back to the war. You may try all you want to, to keep other subjects before the house, and we may all join in and help, but there can be but one result: the most random topic would load every man up with war reminiscences, and *shut* him up, too; and talk would be likely to stop presently, because you can't talk pale inconsequentialities when you've got a crimson fact or fancy in your head that you are burning to fetch out.'

The poet was sitting some little distance away; and presently he began to speak—about the moon.

The gentleman who had been talking to me remarked in an 'aside:' 'There, the moon is far enough from the seat of war, but you will see that it will suggest something to somebody about the war; in ten minutes from now the moon, as a topic, will be shelved.'

The poet was saying he had noticed something which was a surprise to him; had had the impression that down here, toward the equator, the moonlight was much stronger and brighter than up north; had had the impression that when he visited New Orleans, many years ago, the moon—

Interruption from the other end of the room—

'Let me explain that. Reminds me of an anecdote. Everything is changed since the war, for better or for worse; but you'll find people down here born grumblers, who see no change except the change for the worse. There was an old negro woman of this sort. A young New-Yorker said in her presence, ''What a wonderful moon you have down here!'' She sighed and said, ''Ah, bless yo' heart, honey, you ought to seen dat moon befo' de waw!'''

The new topic was dead already. But the poet resurrected it, and gave it a new start.

A brief dispute followed, as to whether the difference between Northern and Southern moonlight really existed or was only imagined. Moonlight talk drifted easily into talk about artificial methods of dispelling darkness. Then somebody remembered that when Farragut advanced upon Port Hudson on a dark night—and did not wish to assist the aim of the Confederate gunners—he carried no battle-lanterns, but painted the decks of his ships white, and thus created a dim but valuable light, which enabled his own men to grope their way around with considerable facility. At this point the war got the floor again—the ten minutes not quite up yet.

I was not sorry, for war talk by men who have been in a war is always interesting; whereas moon talk by a poet who has not been in the moon is likely to be dull.

We went to a cockpit in New Orleans on a Saturday afternoon. I had never seen a cock-fight before. There were men and boys there of all ages and all colours, and of many languages and nationalities. But I noticed one quite conspicuous and surprising absence: the traditional brutal faces. There were no brutal faces. With no cock-fighting going on, you could have played the gathering on a stranger for a prayer-meeting; and after it began, for a revival—provided you blindfolded your stranger—for the shouting was something prodigious.

A negro and a white man were in the ring; everybody else outside. The cocks were brought in in sacks; and when time was called, they were taken out by the two bottle-holders, stroked, caressed, poked toward each other, and finally liberated. The big black cock plunged instantly at the little grey one and struck him on the head with his spur. The grey responded with spirit. Then the Babel of many-tongued shoutings broke out, and ceased not thenceforth. When the cocks had been fighting some little time, I was expecting them momently to drop dead, for both were blind, red with blood, and so exhausted that they frequently fell down. Yet they would not give up, neither would they die. The negro and the white man would pick them up every few seconds, wipe them off, blow cold water on them in a fine spray, and take their heads in their mouths and hold them there a moment—to warm back the perishing life perhaps; I do not know. Then, being set down again, the dying creatures would totter gropingly about, with dragging wings, find each other, strike a guess-work blow or two, and fall exhausted once more.

I did not see the end of the battle. I forced myself to endure it as long as I could, but it was too pitiful a sight; so I made frank confession to that effect, and we retired. We heard afterward that the black cock died in the ring, and fighting to the last.

Evidently there is abundant fascination about this 'sport' for such as have had a degree of familiarity with it. I never saw people enjoy anything more than this gathering enjoyed this fight. The case was the same with old grey-heads and with boys of ten. They lost themselves in frenzies of delight. The 'cocking-main' is an inhuman sort of entertainment, there is no question about that; still, it seems a much more respectable and far less cruel sport than fox-hunting—for the cocks like it; they experience, as well as confer enjoyment; which is not the fox's case.

We assisted—in the French sense—at a mule race, one day. I believe I enjoyed this contest more than any other mule there. I enjoyed it more than I remember having enjoyed any other animal race I ever saw. The grand stand was well filled with the beauty and the chivalry of New Orleans. That phrase is not original with me. It is the Southern reporter's. He has used it for two generations. He uses it twenty times a day, or twenty thousand times a day; or a million times a day—according to the exigencies. He is obliged to use it a million times a day, if he have occasion to speak of respectable men and women that often; for he has no other phrase for such service except that single one. He never tires of it; it always has a fine sound to him. There is a kind of swell mediæval bulliness and tinsel about it that pleases his gaudy barbaric soul. If he had been in Palestine in the early times, we should have had no references to 'much people' out of him. No, he would have said 'the beauty and the chivalry of Galilee' assembled to hear the Sermon on the Mount. It is likely that the men and women of the South are sick enough of that phrase by this time, and would like a change, but there is no immediate prospect of their getting it.

The New Orleans editor has a strong, compact, direct, unflowery style; wastes no words, and does not gush. Not so with his average correspondent. In the Appendix I have quoted a good letter, penned by a trained hand; but the average correspondent hurls a style which differs from that. For instance—

The 'Times-Democrat' sent a relief-steamer up one of the bayous, last April. This steamer landed at a village, up there somewhere, and the Captain invited some of the ladies of the village to make a short trip with him. They accepted and came aboard, and the steamboat shoved out up the creek. That was all there was 'to it.' And that is all that the editor of the 'Times-Democrat' would have got out of it. There was nothing in the thing but statistics, and he would have got nothing else out of it. He would probably have even tabulated them, partly to secure perfect clearness of statement, and partly to save space. But his special correspondent knows other methods of handling statistics. He just throws off all restraint and wallows in them—

'On Saturday, early in the morning, the beauty of the place graced our cabin, and proud of fair freight the gallant little boat glided up the bayou.'

Twenty-two words to say the ladies came aboard and the boat shoved out up the creek, is a clean waste of ten good words, and is also destructive of compactness of statement.

The trouble with the Southern reporter is—Women. They unsettle him; they throw him off his balance. He is plain, and sensible, and satisfactory, until a woman heaves in sight. Then he goes all to pieces; his mind totters, he becomes flowery and idiotic. From reading the above extract, you would imagine that this student of Sir Walter Scott is an apprentice, and knows next to nothing about handling a pen. On the contrary, he furnishes plenty of proofs, in his long letter, that he knows well enough how to handle it when the women are not around to give him the artificial-flower complaint. For instance—

'At 4 o'clock ominous clouds began to gather in the south-east, and presently from the Gulf there came a blow which increased in severity every moment. It was not safe to leave the landing then, and there was a delay. The oaks shook off long tresses of their mossy beards to the tugging of the wind, and the bayou in its ambition put on miniature waves in mocking of much larger bodies of water. A lull permitted a start, and homewards we steamed, an inky sky overhead and a heavy wind blowing. As darkness crept on, there were few on board who did not wish themselves nearer home.'

There is nothing the matter with that. It is good description, compactly put. Yet there was great temptation, there, to drop into lurid writing.

But let us return to the mule. Since I left him, I have rummaged around and found a full report of the race. In it I find confirmation of the theory which I broached just now—namely, that the trouble with the Southern reporter is Women: Women, supplemented by Walter Scott and his knights and beauty and chivalry, and so on. This is an excellent report, as long as the women stay out of it. But when they intrude, we have this frantic result—

'It will be probably a long time before the ladies' stand presents such a sea of foam-like loveliness as it did yesterday. The New Orleans women are always charming, but never so much so as at this time of the year, when in their dainty spring costumes they bring with them a breath of balmy freshness and an odour of sanctity unspeakable. The stand was so crowded with them that, walking at their feet and seeing no possibility of approach, many a man appreciated as he never did before the Peri's feeling at the Gates of Paradise, and wondered what was the priceless boon that would admit him to their sacred presence. Sparkling on their white-robed breasts or shoulders were the colours of their favourite knights, and were it not for the fact that the doughty heroes appeared on un-romantic mules, it would have been easy to imagine one of King Arthur's gala-days.'

There were thirteen mules in the first heat; all sorts of mules, they were; all sorts of complexions, gaits, dispositions, aspects. Some were handsome creatures, some were not; some were sleek, some hadn't had their fur brushed lately; some were innocently gay and frisky; some were full of malice and all unrighteousness; guessing from looks, some of them thought the matter on hand was war, some thought it was a lark, the rest took it for a religious occasion. And each mule acted according to his convictions. The result was an absence of harmony well compensated by a conspicuous presence of variety—variety of a picturesque and entertaining sort.

All the riders were young gentlemen in fashionable society. If the reader has been wondering why it is that the ladies of New Orleans attend so humble an orgy as a mule-race, the thing is explained now. It is a fashion-freak; all connected with it are people of fashion.

It is great fun, and cordially liked. The mule-race is one of the marked occasions of the year. It has brought some pretty fast mules to the front. One of these had to be ruled out, because he was so fast that he turned the thing into a one-mule contest, and robbed it of one of its best features—variety. But every now and then somebody disguises him with a new name and a new complexion, and rings him in again.

The riders dress in full jockey costumes of bright-coloured silks, satins, and velvets.

The thirteen mules got away in a body, after a couple of false starts, and scampered off with prodigious spirit. As each mule and each rider had a distinct opinion of his own as to how the race ought to be run, and which side of the track ought to be crossed, and when a collision ought to be accomplished, and when it ought to be avoided, these twenty-six conflicting opinions created a most fantastic and picturesque confusion, and the resulting spectacle was killingly comical.

Mile heat; time 2.22. Eight of the thirteen mules distanced. I had a bet on a mule which would have won if the procession had been reversed. The second heat was good fun; and so was the 'consolation race for beaten mules' which followed later; but the first heat was the best in that respect.

I think that much the most enjoyable of all races is a steamboat race; but next to that, I prefer the gay and joyous mule-rush. Two red-hot steamboats raging along, neck-and-neck, straining every nerve—that is to say, ever rivet in the boilers—quaking and shaking and groaning from stem to stern, spouting white steam from the pipes, pouring black smoke from the chimneys, raining down sparks, parting the river into long breaks of hissing foam—this is sport that makes a body's very liver curl with enjoyment. A horse-race is pretty tame and colourless in comparison. Still, a horse-race might be well enough, in its way, perhaps, if it were not for the tiresome false starts. But then, nobody is ever killed. At least, nobody was ever killed when I was at a horse-race. They have been crippled, it is true; but this is little to the purpose.

The largest annual event in New Orleans is a something which we arrived too late to sample—the Mardi-Gras festivities. I saw the procession of the Mystic Crew of Comus there, twenty-four years ago—with knights and nobles and so on, clothed in silken and golden Paris-made gorgeousnesses, planned and bought for that single night's use; and in their train all manner of giants, dwarfs, monstrosities, and other diverting grotesquerie—a startling and wonderful sort of show, as it filed solemnly and silently down the street in the light of its smoking and flickering torches; but it is said that in these latter days the spectacle is mightily augmented, as to cost, splendour, and variety. There is a chief personage—'Rex;' and if I remember rightly, neither this king nor any of his great following of subordinates is known to any outsider. All these people are gentlemen of position and consequence; and it is a proud thing to belong to the organisation; so the mystery in which they hide their personality is merely for romance's sake, and not on account of the police.

Mardi-Gras is of course a relic of the French and Spanish occupation; but I judge that the religious feature has been pretty well knocked out of it now. Sir Walter has got the advantage of the gentlemen of the cowl and rosary, and he will stay. His mediæval business, supplemented by the monsters and the oddities, and the pleasant creatures from fairyland, is finer to look at than the poor fantastic inventions and performances of the revelling rabble of the priest's day, and serves quite as well, perhaps, to emphasize the day and admonish men that the graceline between the worldly season and the holy one is reached.

This Mardi-Gras pageant was the exclusive possession of New Orleans until recently. But now it has spread to Memphis and St Louis and Baltimore. It has probably reached its limit. It is a thing which could hardly exist in the practical North; would certainly last but a very brief time; as brief a time as it would last in London. For the soul of it is the romantic, not the funny and the grotesque. Take away the romantic mysteries, the kings and knights and big-sounding titles, and Mardi-Gras would die, down there in the South. The very feature that keeps it alive in the South—girly-girly romance—would kill it in the North or in London. Puck and Punch, and the press universal, would fall upon it and make merciless fun of it, and its first exhibition would be also its last.

Against the crimes of the French Revolution and of Bonaparte may be set two compensating benefactions: the Revolution broke the chains of the *ancien régime* and of the Church, and made of a nation of abject slaves a nation of freemen; and Bonaparte instituted the setting of merit above birth, and also so completely stripped the divinity from royalty, that whereas crowned heads in Europe were gods before, they are only men, since, and can never be gods again, but only figure-heads, and answerable for their acts like common clay. Such benefactions as these compensate the temporary harm which Bonaparte and the Revolution did, and leave the world in debt to them for these great and permanent services to liberty, humanity, and progress.

Then comes Sir Walter Scott with his enchantments, and by his single might checks this wave of progress, and even turns it back; sets the world in love with dreams and phantoms; with decayed and swinish forms of religion; with decayed and degraded systems of government; with the sillinesses and emptinesses, sham grandeurs, sham gauds, and sham chivalries of a brainless and worthless long-vanished society. He did measureless harm; more real and lasting harm, perhaps, than any other individual that ever wrote. Most of the world has now outlived good part of these harms, though by no means all of them; but in our South they flourish pretty forcefully still. Not so forcefully as half a generation ago, perhaps, but still forcefully. There, the genuine and wholesome civilisation of the nineteenth century is curiously confused and commingled with the Walter Scott Middle-Age sham civilisation; and so you have practical, common-sense, progressive ideas, and progressive works, mixed up with the duel, the inflated speech, and the jejune romanticism of an absurd past that is dead, and out of charity ought to be buried. But for the Sir Walter disease, the character of the Southerner—or Southron, according to Sir Walter's starchier way of phrasing it—would be wholly modern, in place of modern and mediæval mixed, and the South would be fully a generation further advanced than it is. It was Sir Walter that made every gentleman in the South a Major or a Colonel, or a General or a Judge, before the war; and it was he, also, that made these gentlemen value these bogus decorations. For it was he that created rank and caste down there, and also reverence for rank and caste, and pride and pleasure in them. Enough is laid on slavery, without fathering upon it these creations and contributions of Sir Walter.

Sir Walter had so large a hand in making Southern character, as it existed before the war, that he is in great measure responsible for the war. It seems a little harsh toward a dead man to say that we never should have had any war but for Sir Walter; and yet something of a plausible argument might, perhaps, be made in support of that wild proposition. The Southerner of the American Revolution owned slaves; so did the Southerner of the Civil War: but the former resembles the latter as an Englishman resembles a Frenchman. The change of character can be traced rather more easily to Sir Walter's influence than to that of any other thing or person.

One may observe, by one or two signs, how deeply that influence penetrated, and how strongly it holds. If one take up a Northern or Southern literary periodical of forty or fifty years ago, he will find it filled with wordy, windy, flowery 'eloquence' romanticism, sentimentality—all imitated from Sir Walter, and sufficiently badly done, too— innocent travesties of his style and methods, in fact. This sort of literature being the fashion in both sections of the country, there was opportunity for the fairest competition; and as a consequence, the South was able to show as many well-known literary names, proportioned to population, as the North could.

But a change has come, and there is no opportunity now for a fair competition between North and South. For the North has thrown out that old inflated style, whereas the Southern writer still clings to it— clings to it and has a restricted market for his wares, as a consequence. There is as much literary talent in the South, now, as ever there was, of course; but its work can gain but slight currency under present conditions; the authors write for the past, not the present; they use obsolete forms, and a dead language. But when a Southerner of genius writes modern English, his book goes upon crutches no longer, but upon wings; and they carry it swiftly all about America and England, and through the great English reprint publishing houses of Germany—as witness the experience of Mr Cable and Uncle Remus, two of the very few Southern authors who do not write in the Southern style. Instead of three or four widely-known literary names, the South ought to have a dozen or two—and will have them when Sir Walter's time is out.

A curious exemplification of the power of a single book for good or harm is shown in the effects wrought by 'Don Quixote' and those wrought by 'Ivanhoe.' The first swept the world's admiration for the mediæval chivalry-silliness out of existence; and the other restored it. As far as our South is concerned, the good work done by Cervantes is pretty nearly a dead letter, so effectually has Scott's pernicious work undermined it.

Arkansas

WASHINGTON IRVING

*Following an adventurous trip to the Western frontier,
Washington Irving wrote a collection of essays entitled* A
Tour on the Prairies *(1835). The following extract
describes his hazardous crossing of the Arkansas River.*

WE HAD NOW arrived at the river, about a quarter of a mile above the
junction of the Red Fork; but the banks were steep and crumbling, and
the current was deep and rapid. It was impossible, therefore, to cross
at this place, and we resumed our painful course through the forest,
despatching Beatte ahead, in search of a fording place. We had proceeded
about a mile further, when he rejoined us, bringing intelligence of a
place hard by, where the river, for a great part of its breadth, was rendered fordable by sandbars, and the remainder might easily be swum
by the horses.

Here, then, we made a halt. Some of the rangers set to work vigorously with their axes, felling trees on the edge of the river, wherewith to form rafts for the transportation of the baggage and camp equipage: others patrolled the banks of the river farther up, in hopes of finding a better fording-place, being unwilling to risk their horses in the deep channel.

It was now that our worthies, Beatte and Tonish, had an opportunity of displaying their Indian adroitness and resource. At the Osage village which we had passed a day or two before, they had procured a dried buffalo skin. This was now produced; cords were passed through a number of small eyelet holes with which it was bordered, and it was drawn up until it formed a kind of deep trough. Sticks were then placed athwart it on the inside, to keep it in shape; our camp equipage and a part of our baggage were placed within, and the singular bark was carried down the bank and set afloat. A cord was attached to the prow, which Beatte took between his teeth, and, throwing himself into the water, went ahead, towing the bark after him, while Tonish followed behind, to keep it steady and to propel it. Part of the way they had foot-hold, and were enabled to wade, but in the main current they were obliged to swim. The whole way they whooped and yelled in the Indian style, until they landed safely on the opposite shore.

The Commissioner and myself were so well pleased with this Indian mode of ferriage, that we determined to trust ourselves in the buffalo hide. Our companions, the Count and Mr L----, had proceeded with the horses along the river bank, in search of a ford, which some of the rangers had discovered about a mile and a half distant. While we were waiting for the return of our ferryman, I happened to cast my eyes upon a heap of luggage under a bush, and descried the sleek carcass of the polecat, snugly trussed up, and ready for roasting before the evening fire. I could not resist the temptation to plump it into the river, where it sank to the bottom like a lump of lead; and thus our lodge was relieved from the bad odour which this savoury viand had threatened to bring upon it.

Our men having recrossed with their cockle-shell bark, it was drawn on shore, half filled with saddles, saddle-bags, and other luggage, amounting to at least a hundred weight, and being again placed in the water, I was invited to take my seat. It appeared to me pretty much like the embarkation of the wise men of Jotham, who went to sea in a bowl: I stepped in, however, without hesitation, though as cautiously as possible, and sat down on top of the luggage, the margin of the hide sinking to within a hand's breadth of the water's edge. Rifles, fowling-pieces, and other articles of small bulk were then handed in, until I protested against receiving any more freight. We then launched forth upon the stream, the bark being towed and propelled as before.

It was with a sensation, half serious, half comic, that I found myself thus afloat, on the skin of a buffalo, in the midst of a wild river, surrounded by wilderness, and towed along by a half savage, whooping and yelling like a devil incarnate. To please the vanity of little Tonish, I discharged the double-barrelled gun to the right and left, when in the centre of the stream. The report echoed along the woody shores, and was answered by shouts from some of the rangers, to the great exultation of the little Frenchman, who took to himself the whole glory of this Indian mode of navigation.

Our voyage was accomplished happily: the Commissioner was ferried across with equal success, and all our effects were brought over in the same manner. Nothing could equal the vainglorious vapouring of little Tonish, as he strutted about the shore, and exulted in his superior skill and knowledge to the rangers. Beatte, however, kept his proud saturnine look, without a smile. He had a vast contempt for the ignorance of the rangers, and felt that he had been undervalued by them. His only observation was 'Dey now see de Indian good for someting, any how!'

The broad sandy shore where we had landed, was intersected by innumerable tracks of elk, deer, bears, raccoons, turkeys, and water-fowl. The river scenery at this place was beautifully diversified: presenting long shining reaches, bordered by willows and cotton-wood trees; rich bottoms, with lofty forests, among which towered enormous plane trees; and the distance was closed in by high embowered promontories. The foliage had a yellow autumnal tint, which gave to the sunny landscape the golden tone of one of the landscapes of Claude Lorraine. There was animation given to the scene by a raft of logs and branches, on which the Captain, and his prime companion the Doctor, were ferrying their effects across the stream, and by a long line of rangers on horseback, fording the river obliquely along a series of sand-bars, about a mile and a half distant.

Kansas

HORACE GREELEY

Horace Greeley, famous newspaper man and noted for his exhortation 'Go West, Young Man' followed his own advice in 1859 when he embarked on a journey from New York to California. The following year a record of his experiences was published entitled Overland Journey *and in this extract from it, he describes his impressions of Kansas.*

IT RESUMED RAINING in Kansas, after a few dry days, on Thursday, the 12th inst., and rained off and on till Saturday night. Sunday, the 15th, was cloudy and chilly, but without rain, until evening, when thunder-showers came up from every side, and kept flashing, rumbling, and pouring nearly throughout the night. Kansas brags on its thunder and lightning; and the boast is well founded. I never before observed a display of celestial pyrotechny so protracted, incessant and vivid as that of last Sunday night. The country, already saturated with water, was fairly drenched by this deluge, which rendered many streams ordinarily insignificant either dangerous or for a season impassable.

At 6 a.m. on Monday morning, four of us left Atchison in a two-horse wagon, intent on reaching Osawatomie (some eighty miles rather east of south—one hundred by any practicable route) next evening. The sky was still threatening; we knew that the streams were swelled beyond reason; but our pilot was a most experienced pioneer, who had forded, been ferried over or swam every stream in eastern Kansas, and was confident of his ability to go through by some route or other. So we went ahead in a southerly direction, across swells of prairie rather steep-sided for Kansas, and through ravines in which what were usually rills were swelled into torrents. From the high level of the prairies, little but a broad sweep of grass on every side was visible; but soon we were descending into a new ravine, and now belts and spurs of timber were seen, generally widening as they tend toward the Missouri. I noted that these woody spurs, composed mainly of black oak and cottonwood (the latter a very poor but quick-growing timber, ranging somewhere between poplar and basswood), began to spread on every side wherever the annual fires were repelled from the adjacent prairie, whether by the interposition of a road or otherwise, and that the young trees that thus spring up along the sides of the ravines and run out into the level prairie, are quite often hickory, white ash, etc., even where none such are visible among the adjacent timber. I was fully convinced that wood becomes more abundant with the progress of settlement and cultivation. Of course, there is timber enough today in the territory, but the better portion of it is too generally confined to the intervales of the larger streams, too far for their comfort from most settlers on the prairies. Could prairie fires be wholly arrested, the increase of timber would over-balance tenfold the annual use and waste; and the quality improves even faster than the quantity. This is real progress. For, though there is quite enough in Kansas, and a pretty good variety of all species except the evergreens, which are lamentably deficient, there are points at which there is none within several miles—the little that formerly ran up the small ravines which here cut in upon the great high prairies being soon exhausted by use for building, fuel, and fencing, and requiring years for its reproduction.

Twelve or fifteen miles south of Atchison, we struck the great California trail from Leavenworth, and thence followed it east by south into that city, some fifteen to eighteen miles. I should have liked Gerrit Smith as one of our party, that I might show him the practical working of his theory that government has no other legitimate business than to keep one man's fingers off another man's throat and out of any pocket but his own. The great California trail, like the Santa Fé and all other primitive roads through this prairie country, keeps along the highest 'divides' or prairie swells, avoiding the miry 'bottoms' of the streams and (so far as possible) the ravines which the water falling on the high prairie has cut down to them, of course winding considerably, but making the best and most serviceable natural road that can be, and one that in dry weather is excellent, and in wet as good as possible. But each settler along this trail, in the absence of any legal establishment of the trail as a highway, is at liberty to run his fences right across it as the line of his land runs, and so crowd it off the high 'divides' into all manner of angles and zigzags, across the ravine and into that slough, until the trail is fast becoming the very worst road in all Kansas. I have had a pretty full experience of bad roads during the week; but the very worst and miriest was that portion of the California trail (and United States military road from Fort Leavenworth west to other forts) which works its sinuous way through the region generally settled by thrifty farmers, lying directly west of Leavenworth. And the worst hill for teams I have seen in Kansas is traversed by this road within five miles of Leavenworth, between the fort and the rich but miry valley of Salt Creek on the west. This road, unless it can be restored, will soon have to be abandoned, and thence Leavenworth must suffer.

As we neared the California trail, the white coverings of the many emigrant and transport wagons dotted the landscape, giving the trail the appearance of a river running through great meadows, with many ships sailing on its bosom. Most of the independent wagoners were still encamped by the wayside, unable or unwilling to brave the deep mud; their cattle feeding on the broad prairie; the emigrants cooking or sitting beside the wagons; women sometimes washing, and all trying to dry their clothing, drenched and soaked by the pouring rain of the past night. One great night was still in corral with its cattle feeding and men lounging about; the others might better have been, as it was clearly impossible to make their lean, wild-looking oxen (mainly of the long-horned stripe, which indicates Texas as their native land, and which had probably first felt the yoke within the past week) draw them up the slightest ascent through that deep, slippery mire. A great deal of yelling, beating, swearing, was being expended to little purpose, as I presume each train corraled for the ensuing night within a mile of the point it left in the morning. These contractors' wagons are very large and strong, each carrying a couple of good extra axles lashed under its body, to be used in case an old one gives way under a heavy jerk; the drivers are as rough and wild-looking as their teams, though not quite so awkward at their business; but to keep six yoke of such oxen in line in the road, and all pulling on the load, is beyond human skill. It is a sore trial to patience, that first start of these trains on their long journey—to Utah, Fort Hall, Green River, and some of these to New Mexico, though this is not the Santa Fé trail. The loads are generally fifty hundred weight; the wagons must weigh at least fifteen hundred each; and, though this would seem moderate for twelve oxen, it must be remembered that they are at this season poor and at first unbroken, and that the road is in spots a very bad one. A train consists of ten to thirty wagons; each train has its reliable and experienced master or director; and when a team is stalled, another is unhitched from its own wagon and sent to the aid of the one in trouble. The rate of progress is necessarily snail-like; these trains will do very well if they make twenty miles the first week, considering the weather. But then the feeding of the teams (like the lodging of the men) costs nothing, as they live on the broad prairie, and though they will often be fearfully hungry or dry in traversing grassless tracts on their route, they are said generally to gain in flesh (for which there is ample room) during a journey of three or four months. Of course, they improve in docility and effective-ness, being at first so wild that, in order to be yoked, they have to be driven into the corral (formed, as I may have explained, by the wagons closely ranged in a hollow square, the tongue of each being run under its next neighbor, for defense against Indians or other prowlers). Very few wagons or cattle ever come back; the freighting is all one way; and both wagons and cattle are usually sold at or near their point of destination for whatever they will fetch—to be taken to California or disposed of as they best may.

We drove into Leavenworth City about 11 a.m., and found that the delegates from this county had generally given up the idea of reaching Osawatomie, judging that the Convention would have to be adjourned or postponed on account of the swollen and impassable streams. Stranger Creek barred all egress by way of Lawrence, which we had intended to make our resting place for the night; a creek nine miles south of Leavenworth had turned back the stage running in that direction; in fact, no stage made its way out of Leavenworth that day in any direction which was not forced to return, baffled by the high water. So at 3 p.m. we shipped our horses and wagons on board the steamboat *D. A. January*, and dropped down the Missouri some fifty miles, past the bleaching bones of several dead cities (not including Quindaro, which insists that it is still alive) to Wyandotte, in the lower corner of Kansas, with Kansas City, Missouri, three miles off, in plain sight across the mouth of the Kansas or Kaw River. Wyandotte, though hemmed in and impeded, like Quindaro, by an Indian reserve back of it, is alive, and is becoming, what it ought fully to be, the outlet and inlet between Southern Kansas and the Missouri River. It has a beautiful location, and decided natural advantages over Kansas City, which, with other border-ruffian strongholds south of it, has hitherto engrossed too much of the travel and trade of Kansas. We halted at Wyandotte over night, had an impromptu Republican gathering and some offhand talk in the evening, and set forth at six next morning for Osawatomie (forty-six miles a little west of south by a beeline, but over fifty by any practicable route), which we were desirous of reaching before night, as the Convention was to be held next day.

Our route led southwest over rolling woodland through the Wyandotte Reserve, descending into the bottom of the Kansas or Kaw River—said bottom being from one to two miles wide, and very heavily timbered with elm, yellow oak, black walnut, hickory, cottonwood, sycamore, basswood, etc. Nearly all the rivers and larger creeks of Kansas run through similar bottoms or intervales, from half a mile to three miles wide, and timbered much like this. These intervales are composed of a dark, rich mold, oftener over than under three feet in depth, but they are so level that they could hardly be cultivated without drainage, even were it advisable to strip them by wholesale of timber, as it decidedly is not. The houses and barns that shall yet thickly dot the adjacent prairies are now mainly growing in these bottoms, and should stand there as trees till they are wanted. When cleared and drained—and in some places the rotting out of the stumps, and thorough plowing thereafter will go far toward effecting the drainage required—they will yield bounteous crops of almost anything that does not dread frost. Though it seems hardly possible that their soil should be richer than that of the prairies, it is deeper, and probably contains a more varied and choice admixture of the elements of vegetation. But the Kansas or Kaw bottom was not only soaked but covered with water—for it had rained here smartly only the preceding morning after it ceased at Atchison, and the road across the bottom was for the time an all but impassable morass. I trust the citizens of Wyandotte will not long leave it thus.

We crossed the Kaw on a fair wooden toll bridge, one thousand two hundred feet long, just erected—or, rather, not quite completed. In default of a tollhouse or gatekeeper, a man at work on the bridge in his shirtsleeves, took the toll. I believe no other bridge across the Kaw is now standing, though there has been one at Topeka, fifty miles up, and perhaps at other points. Bridges are sorely needed throughout Kansas, not only because the streams are addicted to rapid and vast augmentations from thaws or rains, but because their banks are almost perpendicular, and often miry toward the bottom, while the streams are nearly as deep at either shore as in the middle, making the attempt to ford difficult, even when it is not dangerous.

The Kaw was, of course, nearly full (all the rivers of Kansas have low banks), and was running very swiftly; still, it seems of moderate size, for a river which leads about six hundred miles westward of its mouth; but all rivers of this region, the Missouri included, seem small, considering the area drained by them. The facts that they run rapidly, are apt to be deep, and that their depth is nearly uniform from side to side, account in part for this appearance.

Half an hour after crossing the Kaw, we emerged from the road and the reserve upon the high prairie, the clouds of the morning broke away, and the day was henceforth perfect. The young grass of the prairie, refreshed by the heavy rains, appeared in its freshest, tenderest green; the delicate early flowers were abundant, yet not so numerous as to pall by satiety the pleasure of looking at them, and the panorama presented was magnificent. Passing Shawnee, a prairie village of twenty or thirty houses, with a large hotel, our road bore more directly south, and soon brought us in sight of the great Santa Fé trail, with its white-topped emigrant wagons, and three great contract trains, one of them still in corral, the others with six pair of mules to each wagon, attempting to make progress toward New Mexico—attempting it, for the most part, in vain. The mules were small, and new to work—to *this* work, at all events—and drew badly; while the wheels cut so deeply into the yielding paste beneath them that little or no advance was made. I presume they all corraled for the night within two miles of the places where we saw them.

Crossing the trail almost at right angles, we left the smart village of Olathe (county seat of Johnson county) a mile or so to the west, and struck off nearly due south, over high prairies sloped as gently and grassed as richly as could be desired, with timber visible along the water-courses on either hand. Yet there was little or no settlement below Olathe—for the next twenty miles that we traveled there was hardly an improvement to each four square miles of the country in sight. And yet, if the Garden of Eden exceeded this land in beauty or fertility, I pity Adam for having to leave it. The earth was thoroughly sodden with rain, so that temporary springs were bursting out on almost every acre, while the watercourses, including those usually dry, ran heavy streams, each of them requiring skill in the charioteer and good conduct on the part of the horses to pass them without balk or break. We must have crossed over a hundred of these 'runs' in the course of this day's travel, each of them with a trying jerk on the carriage, and generally with a spring on the part of the horses. These waterways have generally a limestone bottom not far below the surface of their bed; but their banks are apt to be steep, and are continually growing more so by reason of the water washing away the earth which has been denuded of grass and worked loose by hoofs and wheels. Traveling by jerks like this is not so pleasant as over a macadamized road, yet our day was a bright and pleasant one.

Thirty miles of progress, twenty of them over prairie, brought us to Spring Hill, a hamlet of five or six dwellings, including a store, but no tavern. Our horses needed food and rest—for the wagon, with its four inmates, was a heavy drag over such going—so we stopped and tried to find refreshment, but with limited success. There was no grain to be had, save a homeopathic dose sold us for a quarter by a passing wagoner, and thankfully received; we gave this to our steeds, regaled ourselves on crackers and herring, and pushed on.

Our direct route led due south to Paoli, county seat of Lykins; but persons we met here assured us that there was no crossing Bull Creek on this road, and that we must bear away to the west through Marysville (a village of perhaps a dozen houses, including a store and a tavern), so as to cross at Rock Ford, three miles beyond, which opened the only chance of getting over. We did so, and crossed in safety, with the usual jokes when we were fairly over; but I confess that the wide, impetuous stream, so impenetrable to the eye, and so far above its average level, wore a vicious look to me when we approached and plunged into it. Its bottom is here hardly half a mile wide, but is capitally wooded with hickory, oak, black walnut, etc. Emerging from it, we rode over twelve miles more of high, gently rolling prairie, with wood in the ravines on either side, which brought us to the village of Stanton (of twenty or thirty houses, including two stores and a tavern) which we reached before sunset, having traveled at least fifty miles since we started in the morning. Night and the Marais des Cygnes here brought us to a halt—the creek being at this time impassable—and we had to forego our determination to reach Osawatomie before sleeping. So we halted at the little tavern, where we found five or six others bound to Osawatomie, like ourselves, at least one of whom had swam three creeks since the morning. Fifteen or twenty others drove up during the evening; we had supper, a neighborhood meeting and a Republican talk at the schoolhouse, and adjourned to fill all the beds and floors of the tavern as full as they could hold. The kind, active, efficient landlady did her best, which was good enough; and all were snugly bestowed except another editor and myself, who accepted the kindly proferred hospitality of a Republican farmer, and were capitally entertained at his house, half a mile distant.

As night fell, the lightning had begun to gleam and flash nearly around the horizon; by ten o'clock, the thunder rolled; at twelve, a high gale could be heard sweeping over the prairies some moments before it struck us. The lightning blazed almost incessantly for hours; yet the rainfall at Stanton was very slight. But there were heavy showers at Marysville, at Paoli, and almost everywhere else around us, still further raising the streams, so that many who had come part way were unable to reach Osawatomie next day.

We were early on the bank (a mile from Stanton) of the Marais des Cygnes, which was running heavy driftwood, and otherwise misbehaving itself. It had buried up the ferry rope, without whose aid the boat could not be propelled across its sweeping current; one of the trees to which that rope was attached was now nearly in the middle of the stream; and there had been no crossing for a day or two. But a new rope had been procured and somehow stretched across the stream, whereby we were taken across in our turn, after waiting somewhat over an hour. A mile or so of well-timbered and too-well-watered bottom brought us again to prairie, over which we drove rapidly into Osawatomie, which we reached before 10 a.m.

Osawatomie is a village of at most one hundred and fifty houses, situated in the forks of the Marais des Cygnes and Potawatomie, a somewhat smaller creek, which comes in from the southwest. The location is a pleasant and favorable but not a commanding one; the surrounding country is more considerably cultivated than any I had passed south of the Kaw. The two creeks supply abundant and good timber; an excellent steam sawmill has taken the place of that which the border ruffians burned; a flouring mill, tannery, brewery and a large hotel are being erected or completed. I presume there is a larger town somewhere in what is known as Southern Kansas, though I do not know which it is.

But Osawatomie has a higher interest than any other spot in Kansas, except possibly Lawrence, because of her honorable eminence in the struggle which has secured Kansas to free labor. She was long the only settlement near the Missouri border which was avowedly, decidedly free-state; the only free-state village that could be reached by a night's march from Missouri. To be known as a free-state man at Topeka, Waubonsee, Emporia, or any other post well inland, involved struggles and sacrifices; to be one at Osawatomie, was to live in nightly and well-grounded apprehension of robbery, arson and murder. The pro-slavery settlements in the neighborhood were strong and malignant; and they had only to draw upon Missouri at sight for any amount of force, and the draft would be honored. Yet to surrender this outpost was virtually to give up all Kansas south of the Marais des Cygnes; and, though its maintenance was sure to cost property and blood it was not surrendered, for OLD JOHN BROWN was among its early settlers. Twice was it sacked and laid in ashes, once after a desperate fight of two hours, in which Old Brown with forty of his neighbors held at bay four hundred well-armed Missourians, who had the advantage of a cannon. So fearfully outnumbered, Old Brown, after seeing his son and several of his neighbors shot dead by his side, and after killing at least as many Missourians as there were of his own party altogether, was gradually driven back through the open timber north of the village, and across the Marais des Cygnes, the ruffians not venturing to pursue their victory, though they had attacked from the west, and so were driving the free-state men toward Missouri.

The women and children had meantime fled to the woods on the south; the village was burned after being robbed, the only iron safe therein having been blown open by firing a cannon into its side; and so plundered of some silverware and a considerable sum in money, Osawatomie was thus a second time 'wiped out.' But it has risen again from its ashes, and is once more the home of an undaunted, freedom-loving people, who are striving to forget their bereavements and sacrifices in view of the rich fruits they have borne to liberty and human good. They have gathered the dust of their martyred dead into a common grave on a prairie knoll just west of their village, and propose to erect there a monument which shall teach their children and grandchildren to love and cherish the cause for which those heroes joyfully laid down their lives. I beg leave to suggest an enlargement of the scope of this enterprise—that this monument be reared to *all* martyrs of freedom in Kansas, and that the name of each be inscribed upon it, and his mortal remains, if his relatives make no objection, be placed beneath the column which shall here be reared as a memorial of the struggle which secured Kansas to free labor, and is destined finally to hasten the expulsion of slavery from Missouri. Should a monument be proposed on this basis, I feel confident that subscriptions in aid of its erection might reasonably be asked of all who prefer freedom to slavery, and would not be asked in vain.

North Dakota

THEODORE ROOSEVELT

In this chapter from Ranch Life and the Hunting Trail
(1888), Theodore Roosevelt gives a vivid account of life in
North Dakota.

MY HOME RANCH lies on both sides of the Little Missouri, the nearest ranchman above me being about twelve, and the nearest below me about ten, miles distant. The general course of the stream here is northerly, but, while flowing through my ranch, it takes a great westerly reach of some three miles, walled in, as always, between chains of steep, high bluffs half a mile or more apart. The stream twists down through the valley in long sweeps, leaving oval wooded bottoms, first on one side and then on the other; and in an open glade among the thick-growing timber stands the long, low house of hewn logs.

Just in front of the ranch veranda is a line of old cottonwoods that shade it during the fierce heats of summer, rendering it always cool and pleasant. But a few feet beyond these trees comes the cut-off bank of the river, through whose broad, sandy bed the shallow stream winds as if lost, except when a freshet fills it from brim to brim with foaming yellow water. The bluffs that wall in the river-valley curve back in semicircles, rising from its alluvial bottom generally as abrupt cliffs, but often as steep, grassy slopes that lead up to great level plateaus; and the line is broken every mile or two by the entrance of a coulee, or dry creek, whose head branches may be twenty miles back. Above us, where the river comes round the bend, the valley is very narrow, and the high buttes bounding it rise, sheer and barren, into scalped hill-peaks and naked knife-blade ridges.

The other buildings stand in the same open glade with the ranch house, the dense growth of cottonwoods and matted, thorny underbrush making a wall all about, through which we have chopped our wagon roads and trodden out our own bridle-paths. The cattle have now trampled down this brush a little, but deer still lie in it, only a couple of hundred yards from the house; and from the door sometimes in the evening one can see them peer out into the open, or make their way down, timidly and cautiously, to drink at the river. The stable, sheds, and other out-buildings, with the hayricks and the pens for such cattle as we bring in during winter, are near the house; the patch of fenced garden land is on the edge of the woods; and near the middle of the glade stands the high, circular horse-corral, with a snubbing-post in the center, and a wing built out from one side of the gate entrance, so that the saddle-band can be driven in without trouble. As it is very hard to work cattle where there is much brush, the larger cow-corral is some four miles off on an open bottom.

A ranchman's life is certainly a very pleasant one, albeit generally varied with plenty of hardship and anxiety. Although occasionally he passes days of severe toil,—for example, if he goes on the round-up he works as hard as any of his men,—yet he no longer has to undergo the monotonous drudgery attendant upon the tasks of the cowboy or of the apprentice in the business. His fare is simple; but, if he chooses, it is good enough. Many ranches are provided with nothing at all but salt pork, canned goods, and bread; indeed, it is a curious fact that in traveling through the cow country it is often impossible to get any milk or butter; but this is only because the owners or managers are too lazy to take enough trouble to insure their own comfort. We ourselves always keep up two or three cows, choosing such as are naturally tame, and so we invariably have plenty of milk and, when there is time for churning, a good deal of butter. We also keep hens, which, in spite of the damaging inroads of hawks, bob-cats, and foxes, supply us with eggs, and in time of need, when our rifles have failed to keep us in game, with stewed, roast, or fried chicken also. From our garden we get potatoes, and unless drought, frost, or grasshoppers interfere (which they do about every second year), other vegetables as well. For fresh meat we depend chiefly upon our prowess as hunters.

During much of the time we are away on the different round-ups, that 'wheeled house' the great four-horse wagon, being then our home; but when at the ranch our routine of life is always much the same, save during the excessively bitter weather of midwinter, when there is little to do except to hunt, if the days are fine enough. We breakfast early—before dawn when the nights have grown long, and rarely later than sunrise, even in midsummer. Perhaps before this meal, certainly the instant it is over, the man whose duty it is rides off to hunt up and drive in the saddle-band. Each of us has his own string of horses, eight or ten in number, and the whole band usually split up into two or three companies. In addition to the scattered groups of the saddle-band, our six or eight mares, with their colts, keep by themselves, and are rarely bothered by us, as no cowboy ever rides anything but horses, because mares give great trouble where all the animals have to be herded together. Once every two or three days somebody rides round and finds out where each of these smaller bands is, but the man who goes out in the morning merely gathers one bunch. He drives these into the corral, the other men (who have been lolling idly about the house or stable, fixing their saddles or doing any odd job) coming out with their ropes as soon as they hear the patter of the unshod hoofs and the shouts of the cowboy driver. Going into the corral, and standing near the center, each of us picks out some one of his own string from among the animals that are trotting and running in a compact mass round the circle; and after one or more trials, according to his skill, ropes it and leads it out. When all have caught their horses the rest are again turned loose, together with those that have been kept up overnight. Some horses soon get tame and do not need to be roped: my pet cutting pony, little Muley, and good old Manitou, my companion in so many hunting trips, will neither of them stay with the rest of their fellows that are jamming and jostling each other as they rush round in the dust of the corral, but they very sensibly walk up and stand quietly with the men in the middle, by the snubbing-post. Both are great pets, Manitou in particular; the wise old fellow being very fond of bread and sometimes coming up of his own accord to the ranch house and even putting his head into the door to beg for it.

Once saddled, the men ride off on their different tasks; for almost everything is done in the saddle, except that in winter we cut our fire-wood and quarry our coal,—both on the ranch,—and in summer attend to the garden and put up what wild hay we need.

If any horses have strayed, one or two of the men will be sent off to look for them; for hunting lost horses is one of the commonest and most irksome of our duties. Every outfit always has certain of its horses at large; and if they remain out long enough they become as wild and wary as deer and have to be regularly surrounded and run down. On one occasion, when three of mine had been running loose for a couple of months, we had to follow at full speed for at least fifteen miles before exhausting them enough to enable us to get some control over them and heard them towards a corral. Twice I have had horses absent nearly a year before they were recovered. One of them, after being on the ranch nine months, went off one night and traveled about two hundred miles in a straight line back to its old haunts, swimming the Yellowstone on the way. Two others were at one time away nearly eighteen months, during which time we saw them twice, and on one occasion a couple of the men fairly ran their horses down in following them. We began to think they were lost for good, as they were all the time going farther down towards the Sioux country, but we finally recovered them.

If the men do not go horse-hunting they may ride off over the range; for there is generally some work to be done among the cattle, such as driving in and branding calves that have been overlooked by the round-up, or getting some animal out of a bog-hole. During the early spring months, before the round-up begins, the chief work is in hauling out mired cows and steers; and if we did not keep a sharp lookout, the losses at this season would be very serious. As long as everything is frozen solid there is, of course, no danger from miring; but when the thaw comes, along towards the beginning of March, a period of new danger to the cattle sets in. When the ice breaks up, the streams are left with an edging of deep bog, while the quicksand is at its worst. As the frost goes out of the soil, the ground round every little alkali-spring changes into a trembling quagmire, and deep holes of slimy, tenacious mud form in the bottom of all the gullies. The cattle, which have had to live on snow for three or four months, are very eager for water, and are weak and in poor condition. They rush heedlessly into any pool and stand there, drinking gallons of the icy water and sinking steadily into the mud. When they try to get out they are already too deep down, and are too weak to make a prolonged struggle. After one or two fits of desperate floundering, they resign themselves to their fate with dumb apathy and are lost, unless some one of us riding about discovers and hauls them out. They may be thus lost in wonderfully small mud-holes; often they will be found dead in a gulch but two or three feet across, or in the quicksand of a creek so narrow that it could almost be jumped. An alkali-hole, where the water oozes out through the thick clay, is the worst of all, owing to the ropy tenacity with which the horrible substance sticks and clings to any unfortunate beast that gets into it.

In the spring these mud-holes cause very serious losses among the cattle, and are at all times fruitful sources of danger; indeed, during an ordinary year more cattle die from getting mired than from any other cause. In addition to this they also often prove very annoying to the rider himself, as getting his steed mired or caught in a quicksand is one of the commonest of the accidents that beset a horseman in the far West. This usually happens in fording a river, if the latter is at all high, or else in crossing one of the numerous creeks; although I once saw a horse and rider suddenly engulfed while leisurely walking over what appeared to be dry land. They had come to an alkali mud-hole, an old buffalo-wallow, which had filled up and was covered with a sun-baked crust, that let them through as if they had stepped on a trap-door. There being several of us along, we got down our ropes and dragged both unfortunates out in short order.

When the river is up it is a very common thing for a horseman to have great difficulty in crossing, for the swift, brown water runs over a bed of deep quicksand that is ever shifting. An inexperienced horse, or a mule,—for a mule is useless in mud or quicksand,— becomes mad with fright in such a crossing, and, after speedily exhausting its strength in wild struggles, will throw itself on its side and drown unless the rider gets it out. An old horse used to such work will, on the contrary, take matters quietly and often push along through really dangerous quicksand. Old Manitou never loses his head for an instant; but, now resting a few seconds, now feeling his way cautiously forward, and now making two or three desperate plunges, will go on wherever a horse possibly can. It is really dangerous crossing some of the creeks, as the bottom may give way where it seems hardest; and if one is alone he may work hours in vain before getting his horse out, even after taking off both saddle and bridle, the only hope being to head it so that every plunge takes it an inch or two in the right direction.

Nor are mud-holes the only danger the horseman has to fear; for in much of the Bad Lands the buttes are so steep and broken that it needs genuine mountaineering skill to get through them, and no horse but a Western one, bred to the business, could accomplish the feat. In many parts of our country it is impossible for a horseman who does not know the land to cross it, and it is difficult enough even for an experienced hand. For a stretch of nearly ten miles along the Little Missouri above my range, and where it passes through it, there are but three or four places where it is possible for a horseman to get out to the eastern prairie through the exceedingly broken country lying back from the river. In places this very rough ground comes down to the water; elsewhere it lies back near the heads of the creeks. In such very bad ground the whole country seems to be one tangled chaos of canyon-like valleys, winding gullies and washouts with abrupt, unbroken sides, isolated peaks of sandstone, marl, or 'gumbo' clay, which rain turns into slippery glue, and hill chains the ridges of which always end in sheer cliffs. After a man has made his way with infinite toil for half a mile, a point will be reached around which it is an absolute impossibility to go, and the adventurer has nothing to do but painfully retrace his steps and try again in a new direction, as likely as not with the same result. In such a place the rider dismounts and leads his horse, the latter climbing with cat-like agility up seemingly inaccessible heights, scrambling across the steep, sloping shoulders of the bluffs, sliding down the faces of the clay cliffs with all four legs rigid, or dropping from ledge to ledge like a goat, and accepting with unruffled composure an occasional roll from top to bottom. But, in spite of the climbing abilities of the ponies, it is difficult, and at times—for our steeds, at any rate— dangerous work to go through such places, and we only do it when it cannot be avoided. Once I was overtaken by darkness while trying to get through a great tract of very rough land, and, after once or twice nearly breaking my neck, in despair had to give up all attempts to get out, and until daybreak simply staid where I was, in a kind of ledge or pocket on the side of the cliff, luckily sheltered from the wind. It was midsummer and the nights were short, but this particular one seemed quite long enough; and though I was on the move by dawn, it was three hours later before I led the horse, as hungry, numb, and stiff as myself, out on the prairie again.

Occasionally it is imperatively necessary to cross some of the worst parts of the Bad Lands with a wagon, and such a trip is exhausting and laborious beyond belief. Often the wagon will have to be taken to pieces every few hundred yards in order to get it over a ravine, lower it into a valley, or drag it up a cliff. One outfit, that a year ago tried to take a short cut through some of the Bad Lands of the Powder River, made just four miles in three days, and then had to come back to their starting-point after all. But with only saddle-horses we feel that it must be a very extraordinary country indeed, if, in case of necessity, we cannot go through it.

The long forenoon's work, with its attendant mishaps to man and beast, being over, the men who have been out among the horses and cattle come riding in, to be joined by their fellows—if any there be—who have been hunting, or haying, or chopping wood. The midday dinner is variable as to time, for it comes when the men have returned from their work; but, whatever be the hour, it is the most substantial meal of the day, and we feel that we have little fault to find with a table on the clean cloth of which are spread platters of smoked elk meat, loaves of good bread, jugs and bowls of milk, saddles of venison or broiled antelope steaks, perhaps roast and fried prairie chickens, with eggs, butter, wild plums, and tea or coffee.

The afternoon's tasks are usually much the same as the morning's, but this time is often spent in doing the odds and ends; as, for instance, it may be devoted to breaking-in a new horse. Large outfits generally hire a bronco-buster to do this; but we ourselves almost always break our own horses, two or three of my men being pretty good riders, although none of them can claim to be anything out of the common. A first-class flash rider or bronco-buster receives high wages, and deserves them, for he follows a most dangerous trade, at which no man can hope to grow old; his work being infinitely harder than that of an Eastern horse-breaker or rough-rider, because he has to do it in such a limited time. A good rider is a good rider all the world over; but an Eastern or English horse-breaker and Western bronco-buster have so little in common with each other as regards style or surroundings, and are so totally out of place in doing each other's work, that it is almost impossible to get either to admit that the other has any merits at all as a horseman, for neither could sit in the saddle of the other or could without great difficulty perform his task. The ordinary Eastern seat, which approaches more or less the seat of a cross-country rider or fox-hunter, is nearly as different from the cowboy's seat as from that of a man who rides bareback. The stirrups on a stock saddle are much farther back than they are on an ordinary English one (a difference far more important than the high horn and cantle of the former), and the man stands nearly erect in them, instead of having his legs bent; and he grips with the thighs and not with the knees, throwing his feet well out. Some of the things he teaches his horse would be wholly useless to an Eastern equestrian: for example, one of the first lessons the newly-caught animal has to learn is not to 'run on a rope'; and he is taught this by being violently snubbed up, probably turning a somersault, the first two or three times that he feels the noose settle round his neck, and makes a mad rush for liberty. The snubbing-post is the usual adjunct in teaching such a lesson; but a skillful man can do without any help and throw a horse clean over by holding the rope tight against the left haunch, at the same time leaning so far back, with the legs straight in front, that the heels dig deep into the ground when the strain comes, and the horse, running out with the slack of the rope, is brought up standing, or even turned head over heels by the shock. Cowboys are probably the only working-men in the world who invariably wear gloves, buckskin gauntlets being preferred, as otherwise the ropes would soon take every particle of skin off their hands.

A bronco-buster has to work by such violent methods in consequence of the short amount of time at his command. Horses are cheap, each outfit has a great many, and the wages for breaking an animal are but five or ten dollars. Three rides, of an hour or two each, on as many consecutive days, are the outside number a bronco-buster deems necessary before turning an animal over as 'broken.' The average bronco-buster, however, handles horses so very rudely that we prefer, aside from motives of economy, to break our own; and this is always possible, if we take enough time. The best and quietest horses on the ranch are far from being those broken by the best riders; on the contrary, they are those that have been handled most gently, although firmly, and that have had the greatest number of days devoted to their education.

Some horses, of course, are almost incurably vicious, and must be conquered by main force. One pleasing brute on my ranch will at times rush at a man open-mouthed like a wolf, and this is a regular trick of the range-stallions. In a great many—indeed, in most—localities there are wild horses to be found, which, although invariably of domestic descent, being either themselves runaways from some ranch or Indian outfit, or else claiming such for their sires and dams, yet are quite as wild as the antelope on whose domain they have intruded. Ranchmen run in these wild horses whenever possible, and they are but little more difficult to break than the so-called 'tame' animals. But the wild stallions are, whenever possible, shot; both because of their propensity for driving off the ranch mares, and because their incurable viciousness makes them always unsafe companions for other horses still more than for men. A wild stallion fears no beast except the grizzly, and will not always flinch from an encounter with it; yet it is a curious fact that a jack will almost always kill one in a fair fight. The particulars of a fight of this sort were related to me by a cattle man who was engaged in bringing out blooded stock from the East. Among the animals under his charge were two great stallions, one gray and one black, and a fine jackass, not much over half the size of either of the former. The animals were kept in separate pens, but one day both horses got into the same inclosure, next to the jack-pen, and began to fight as only enraged stallions can, striking like boxers with their fore feet, and biting with their teeth. The gray was getting the best of it; but while clinched with his antagonist in one tussle they rolled against the jack-pen, breaking it in. No sooner was the jack at liberty than, with ears laid back and mouth wide open, he made straight for the two horses, who had for the moment separated. The gray turned to meet him, rearing on his hind legs and striking at him with his fore feet; but the jack slipped in, and in a minute grasped his antagonist by the throat with his wide-open jaws, and then held on like a bull-dog, all four feet planted stiffly in the soil. The stallion made tremendous efforts to shake him off: he would try to whirl round and kick him, but for that the jack was too short; then he would rise up, lifting the jack off the ground, and strike at him with his fore feet; but all that he gained by this was to skin his foe's front legs without making him loose his hold. Twice they fell, and twice the stallion rose, by main strength dragging the jack with him; but all in vain. Meanwhile the black horse attacked both the combatants, with perfect impartiality, striking and kicking them with his hoofs, while his teeth, as they slipped off the tough hides, met with a snap like that of a bear-trap. Undoubtedly the jack would have killed at least one of the horses had not the men come up, and with no small difficulty separated the maddened brutes.

If not breaking horses, mending saddles, or doing something else of the sort, the cowboys will often while away their leisure moments by practicing with the rope. A man cannot practice too much with this if he wishes to attain even moderate proficiency; and as a matter of fact he soon gets to wish to practice the whole time. A cowboy is always roping something, and it especially delights him to try his skill at game. A friend of mine, a young ranchman in the Judith basin, about four years ago roped a buffalo, and by the exercise of the greatest skill, both on his own part and on his steed's, actually succeeded, by alternate bullying and coaxing, in getting the huge brute almost into camp. I have occasionally known men on fast horses to rope deer, and even antelope, when circumstances all joined to favor them; and last summer one of the cowboys on a ranch about thirty miles off ran into and roped a wounded elk. A forty-foot lariat is the one commonly used, for the ordinary range at which a man can throw it is only about twenty-five feet. Few men can throw forty feet; and to do this, taking into account the coil, needs a sixty-foot rope.

When the day's work is over we take supper, and bed-time comes soon afterward, for the men who live on ranches sleep well and soundly. As a rule, the nights are cool and bracing, even in midsummer; except when we occasionally have a spell of burning weather, with a steady, hot wind that blows in our faces like a furnace blast, sending the ther-mometer far up above a hundred and making us gasp for breath, even at night, in the dry-baked heat of the air. But it is only rarely that we get a few days of this sort; generally, no matter how unbearable the heat of the day has been, we can at least sleep pleasantly at night.

A ranchman's work is, of course, free from much of the sameness attendant upon that of a mere cowboy. One day he will ride out with his men among the cattle, or after strayed horses; the next he may hunt, so as to keep the ranch in meat; then he can make the tour of his outlying camps; or, again, may join one of the round-ups for a week or two, perhaps keeping with it the entire time it is working. On occasions he will have a good deal of spare time on his hands, which, if he chooses, he can spend in reading or writing. If he cares for books, there will be many a worn volume in the primitive little sitting-room, with its log walls and huge fire-place; but after a hard day's work a man will not read much but will rock to and fro in the flickering firelight, talking sleepily over his success in the day's chase and the difficulty he has had with the cattle; or else may simply lie stretched at full length on the elk-hides and wolf-skins in front of the hearthstone, listening in drowsy silence to the roar and crackle of the blazing logs and to the moaning of the wind outside.

In the sharp fall weather the riding is delicious all day long; but even in the late spring, and all through the summer, we try, if we can, to do our work before the heat of the day, and if going on a long ride, whether to hunt or for other purposes, leave the ranch house by dawn.

The early rides in the spring mornings have a charm all their own, for they are taken when, for the one and only time during the year, the same brown landscape of these high plains turns to a vivid green, as the new grass sprouts and the trees and bushes thrust forth the young leaves; and at dawn, with the dew glittering everywhere, all things show at their best and freshest. The flowers are out and a man may gallop for miles at a stretch with his horse's hoofs sinking at every stride into the carpet of prairie roses, whose short stalks lift the beautiful blossoms but a few inches from the ground. Even in the waste places the cactuses are blooming; and one kind in particular, a dwarfish, globular plant, with its mass of splendid crimson flowers glows against the sides of the gray buttes like a splash of flame.

The ravines, winding about and splitting into a labyrinth of coulees, with chains of rounded hills to separate them, have groves of trees in their bottoms, along the sides of the water courses. In these are found the blacktail deer, and his cousin, the whitetail, too, with his flaunting flag; but in the spring-time, when we are after antelope only, we must go out farther to the flat prairie land on the divide. Here, in places, the level, grassy plains are strewn with mounds and hillocks of red or gray scoria, that stand singly or clustered into little groups, their tops crested, or their sides covered, by queer detached masses of volcanic rock, wrought into strange shapes by the dead forces whose blind, hidden strength long ago called them into being. The road our wagons take, when the water is too high for us to come down the river bottom, stretches far ahead—two dark, straight, parallel furrows which merge into one in the distance. Quaint little horned frogs crawl sluggishly along in the wheel tracks, and the sickle-billed curlews run over the ground or soar above and around the horsemen, uttering their mournful, never-ceasing clamor. The grassland stretches out in the sunlight like a sea, every wind bending the blades into a ripple, and flecking the prairie with shifting patches of a different green from that around, exactly as the touch of a light squall or wind-gust will fleck the smooth surface of the ocean. Our Western plains differ widely in detail from those of Asia; yet they always call to mind

> . . . . The Scythian
> On the wide steppe, unharnessing
> His wheel'd house at noon.
> He tethers his beast down, and makes his meal—
> Mares' milk, and bread
> Baked on the embers;—all around
> The boundless, waving grass-plains stretch . . .
> . . .; before him, for long miles,
> Alive with bright green lizards
> And the springing bustard fowl,
> The track, a straight black line,
> Furrows the rich soil; here and there
> Clusters of lonely mounds
> Topp'd with rough hewn,
> Gray, rain-blear'd statues, overpeer
> The sunny waste.

In the spring mornings the rider on the plains will hear bird songs unknown in the East. The Missouri skylark sings while soaring above the great plateaus so high in the air that it is impossible to see the bird; and this habit of singing while soaring it shares with some sparrow-like birds that are often found in company with it. The white-shouldered lark-bunting, in its livery of black, has rich, full notes, and as it sings on the wing it reminds one of the bobolink; and the sweet-voiced lark-finch also utters its song in the air. These birds, and most of the sparrows of the plains, are characteristic of this region.

But many of our birds, especially those found in the wooded river bottoms, answer to those of the East; only almost each one has some marked point of difference from its Eastern representative. The bluebird out West is very much of a blue bird indeed, for it has no 'earth tinge' on its breast at all; while the indigo-bird, on the contrary, has gained the ruddy markings that the other has lost. The flicker has the shafts of its wing and tail quills colored orange instead of yellow. The towhee has lost all title to its name, for its only cry is a mew like that of a cat-bird; while, most wonderful of all, the meadow-lark has found a rich, strong voice, and is one of the sweetest and most incessant singers we have.

Throughout June the thickets and groves about the ranch house are loud with bird music from before dawn till long after sunrise. The thrashers have sung all the night through from among the thorn-bushes if there has been a moon, or even if there has been bright starlight; and before the first glimmer of gray the bell-like, silvery songs of the shy woodland thrushes chime in; while meadow-lark, robin, bluebird, and song sparrow, together with many rarer singers, like the grosbeak, join in swelling the chorus. There are some would-be singers whose intention is better than their execution. Blackbirds of several kinds are plenty round the house and stables, walking about with a knowing air, like so many dwarf crows; and now and then a flock of yellow-heads will mix for a few days with their purple or rusty-colored brethren. The males of these yellow-headed grakles are really handsome, their orange and yellow heads contrasting finely with the black of the rest of their plumage; but their voices are discordant to a degree. When a flock has done feeding it will often light in straggling order among the trees in front of the veranda, and then the males will begin to sing, or rather to utter the most extraordinary collection of broken sounds—creakings, gurglings, hisses, twitters, and every now and then a liquid note or two. It is like an accentuated representation of the noise made by a flock of common blackbirds. At nightfall the poor-wills begin to utter their boding call from the wooded ravines back in the hills; not 'whip-poor-will,' as in the East, but with two syllables only. They often come round the ranch house. Late one evening I had been sitting motionless on the veranda, looking out across the water and watching the green and brown of the hill-tops change to purple and umber and then fade off into shadowy gray as the somber darkness deepened. Suddenly a poor-will lit on the floor beside me and stayed some little time; now and then uttering its mournful cries, then ceasing for a few moments as it flitted round after insects, and again returning to the same place to begin anew. The little owls, too, call to each other with tremulous, quavering voices throughout the livelong night, as they sit in the creaking trees that overhang the roof. Now and then we hear the wilder voices of the wilderness, from animals that in the hours of darkness do not fear the neighborhood of man; the coyotes wail like dismal ventriloquists, or the silence may be broken by the strident challenge of a lynx, or by the snorting and stamping of a deer that has come to the edge of the open.

In the hot noontide hours of midsummer the broad ranch veranda, always in the shade, is almost the only spot where a man can be comfortable; but here he can sit for hours at a time, leaning back in his rocking-chair, as he reads or smokes, or with half-closed, dreamy eyes gazes across the shallow, nearly dry river-bed to the wooded bottoms opposite, and to the plateaus lying back of them. Against the sheer white faces of the cliffs, that come down without a break, the dark green tree-tops stand out in bold relief. In the hot, lifeless air all objects that are not near by seem to sway and waver. There are few sounds to break the stillness. From the upper branches of the cottonwood trees overhead, whose shimmering, tremulous leaves are hardly every quiet, but if the wind stirs at all, rustle and quiver and sigh all day long, comes every now and then the soft, melancholy cooing of the mourning dove, whose voice always seems far away and expresses more than any other sound in nature the sadness of gentle, hopeless, never-ending grief. The other birds are still; and very few animals move about. Now and then the black shadow of a wheeling vulture falls on the sun-scorched ground. The cattle, that have strung down in long files from the hills, lie quietly on the sand-bars, except that some of the bulls keep traveling up and down, bellowing and routing or giving vent to long, surly grumblings as they paw the sand and toss it up with their horns. At times the horses, too, will come down to drink, and to splash and roll in the water.

The prairie-dogs alone are not daunted by the heat, but sit at the mouths of their burrows with their usual pert curiosity. They are bothersome little fellows, and most prolific, increasing in spite of the perpetual war made on them by every carnivorous bird and beast. One of their worst foes is the black-footed ferret, a handsome, rather rare animal, somewhat like a mink, with a yellow-brown body and dark feet and mask. It is a most bloodthirsty little brute, feeding on all small animals and ground birds. It will readily master a jack-rabbit, will kill very young fawns if it finds them in the mother's absence, and works extraordinary havoc in a dog town, as it can follow the wretched little beasts down into the burrows. In one instance, I knew of a black-footed ferret making a succession of inroads on a ranchman's poultry, killing and carrying off most of them before it was trapped. Coyotes, foxes, swifts, badgers, and skunks also like to lurk about the dog towns. Of the skunks, by the way, we had last year altogether too much; there was a perfect plague of them all along the river, and they took to trying to get into the huts, with the stupid pertinacity of the species. At every ranch house dozens were killed, we ourselves bagging thirty-three, all slain near the house, and one, to our unspeakable sorrow, in it.

In making a journey over ground we know, during the hot weather we often prefer to ride by moonlight. The moon shines very brightly through the dry, clear night air, turning the gray buttes into glimmering silver; and the horses travel far more readily and easily than under the glaring noonday sun. The road between my upper and lower ranch houses is about forty miles long, sometimes following the river-bed, and then again branching off inland, crossing the great plateaus and winding through the ravines of the broken country. It is a five-hours' fair ride; and so, in a hot spell, we like to take it during the cool of the night, starting at sunset. After nightfall the face of the country seems to alter marvelously, and the clear moonlight only intensifies the change. The river gleams like running quicksilver, and the moonbeams play over the grassy stretches of the plateaus and glance off the wind-rippled blades as they would from water. The Bad Lands seem to be stranger and wilder than ever, the silvery rays turning the country into a kind of grim fairyland. The grotesque, fantastic outlines of the higher cliffs stand out with startling clearness, while the lower buttes have become formless, misshapen masses, and the deep gorges are in black shadow; in the darkness there will be no sound but the rhythmic echo of the hoof-beats of the horses, and the steady, metallic clank of the steel bridle-chains.

But the fall is the time for riding; for in the keen, frosty air neither man nor beast will tire, though out from the dawn until the shadows have again waxed long and the daylight has begun to wane, warning all to push straight for home without drawing rein. Then deer-saddles and elk-haunches hang from the trees near the house; and one can have good sport right on the sand of the river-bed, for we always keep shot-gun or rifle at hand, to be ready for any prairie chickens, or for such of the passing water-fowl as light in the river near us. Occasionally we take a shot at a flock of waders, among which the pretty avocets are the most striking in looks and manners. Prairie fowl are quite plenty all round us, and occasionally small flocks come fairly down into the yard, or perch among the trees near by. At evening they fly down to the river to drink, and as they sit on the sand-bars offer fine marks for the rifles. So do the geese and ducks when they occasionally light on the same places or paddle leisurely down stream in the middle of the river; but to make much of a bag of these we have to use the heavy No. 10, choke-bore shot-gun, while the little 16-bore fowling-piece is much the handiest for prairie fowl. A good many different kinds of water-fowl pass, ranging in size from a teal duck to a Canada goose, and all of them at times help to eke out our bill of fare. Last fall a white-fronted goose lighted on the river in front of the ranch house, and three of us, armed with miscellaneous weapons, went out after him; we disabled him, and then after much bad shooting, and more violent running through thick sand and thick underbrush, finally took and most foully butchered him. The snow geese and common wild geese are what we usually kill, however.

Sometimes strings of sandbill cranes fly along the river, their guttural clangor being heard very far off. They usually light on a plateau, where sometimes they form rings and go through a series of queer antics, dancing and posturing to each other. They are exceedingly wide-awake birds, and more shy and wary than antelope, so that they are rarely shot; yet once I succeeded in stalking up to a group in the early morning, and firing into them rather at random, my bullet killed a full-grown female. Its breast, when roasted, proved to be very good eating.

Sometimes we vary our diet with fish—wall-eyed pike, ugly, slimy catfish, and other uncouth finny things, looking very fit denizens of the mud-choked water; but they are good eating withal, in spite of their uncanny appearance. We usually catch them with set lines, left out over-night in the deeper pools.

The cattle are fattest and in best condition during the fall, and it is then that the bulk of the beef steers are gathered and shipped—four-year-olds as a rule, though some threes and fives go along with them. Cattle are a nuisance while hunting on foot, as they either take fright and run off when they see the hunter, scaring all game within sight, or else, what is worse, follow him, blustering and bullying and pretending that they are on the point of charging, but rarely actually doing so. Still, they are occasionally really dangerous, and it is never entirely safe for a man to be on foot when there is a chance of meeting the droves of long-horned steers. But they will always bluster rather than fight, whether with men or beasts, or with one another. The bulls and some of the steers are forever traveling and challenging each other, never ceasing their hoarse rumbling and moaning and their long-drawn, savage bellowing, tearing up the banks with their horns and sending little spurts of dust above their shoulders with their fore hoofs; yet they do not seem especially fond of real fighting, although, of course, they do occasionally have most desperate and obstinate set-tos with one another. A large bear will make short work of a bull: a few months ago one of the former killed a very big bull near a ranch house a score of miles or so distant, and during one night tore up and devoured a large part of his victim. The ranchman poisoned the carcass and killed the bear.

Colorado

ERNEST INGERSOLL

In this chapter from Crest of the Continent (1885), *Ernest Ingersoll captures the grandeur of the Rocky Mountains and provides an incisive account of his visit to the city of Denver.*

'THERE ARE THE Rocky Mountains!' I strained my eyes in the direction of his finger, but for a minute could see nothing. Presently sight became adjusted to a new focus, and out against a bright sky dawned slowly the undefined shimmering trace of something a little bluer. Still it seemed nothing tangible. It might have passed for a vapor effect of the horizon, had not the driver called it otherwise. Another minute and it took slightly more certain shape. It cannot be described by any Eastern analogy; no other far mountain view that I ever saw is at all like it. If you have seen those sea-side albums which ladies fill with algae during their summer holiday, and in those albums have been startled, on turning over a page suddenly, to see an exquisite marine ghost appear, almost evanescent in its faint azure, but still a literal existence, which had been called up from the deeps, and laid to rest with infinite delicacy and difficulty,—then you will form some conception of the first view of the Rocky Mountains. It is impossible to imagine them built of earth, rock, anything terrestrial; to fancy them cloven by horrible chasms, or shaggy with giant woods. They are made out of the air and the sunshine which show them. Nature has dipped her pencil in the faintest solution of ultramarine, and drawn in once across the Western sky with a hand tender as Love's. Then when sight becomes still better adjusted, you find the most delicate division taking place in this pale blot of beauty, near its upper edge. It is rimmed with a mere thread of opaline and crystalline light. For a moment it sways before you and is confused. But your eagerness grows steadier, you see plainer and know that you are looking on the everlasting snow, the ice that never melts. As the entire fact in all its meaning possesses you completely, you feel a sensation which is as new to your life as it is impossible of repetition. I confess (I should be ashamed not to) that my first view of the Rocky Mountains had no way of expressing itself save in tears. To see what they looked, and to know what they were, was like a sudden revelation of the truth that the spiritual is the only real and substantial; that the eternal things of the universe are they which, afar off, seem dim and faint.'

There are the Rocky Mountains! Ludlow saw them after days of rough riding in a dusty stage-coach. Our plains journey had been a matter of a few hours only, and in the luxurious ease of a Pullman sleeping car; but *our* hearts, too, were stirred, and we eagerly watched them rise higher and higher, and perfect their ranks, as we threaded the bluffs into Pueblo. Then there they were again, all the way up to Denver; and when we arose in the morning and glanced out of the hotel window, the first objects our glad eyes rested on were the snow-tipped peaks filling the horizon.

Thither *Madame ma femme* and I proposed to ourselves to go for an early autumn ramble, gathering such friends and accomplices as presented themselves. But how? That required some study. There were no end of ways. We were given advice enough to make a substantial appendix to the present volume, though I suspect that it would be as useless to print it for you as it was to talk it to us. We could walk.

We could tramp, with burros to carry our luggage, and with or without other burros to carry ourselves. We could form an alliance, offensive and defensive, with a number of pack mules. We could hire an ambulance sort of wagon, with bedroom and kitchen and all the other attachments. We could go by railway to certain points, and there diverge. Or, as one sober youth suggested, we needn't go at all. But it remained for us to solve the problem after all. As generally happens in this life of ours, the fellow who gets on owes it to his own momentum, for the most part. It came upon us quite by inspiration. We jumped to the conclusion; which, as the Madame truly observed, is not altogether wrong if only you look before you leap. That is a good specimen of feminine logic in general, and the Madame's in particular.

But what was the inspiration—the conclusion—the decision? You are all impatience to know it, of course. It was this:

Charter a train!

Recovering our senses after this startling generalization, particulars came in order. Spreading out the crisp and squarely-folded map of Colorado, we began to study it with novel interest, and very quickly discovered that if our brilliant inspiration was really to be executed, we must confine ourselves to the narrow-gauge lines. Tracing these with one prong of a hair-pin, it was apparent that they ran almost everywhere in the mountainous parts of the State, and where they did not go now they were projected for speedy completion. Closer inspection, as to the names of the lines, discovered that nearly all of this wide-branching system bore the mystical letters D. & R. G., which evidently enough (after you had learned it) stood for—

'Why, Denver and Ryo Grand, of course' exclaims the Madame, contemptuous of any one who didn't know *that*.

'Not by a long shot!' I reply triumphantly, 'Denver and Reeo Grandy is the name of the railway—Mexican words.'

'Oh, indeed!' is what I *hear*; a very lofty nose, naturally a trifle uppish, is what I *see*.

Deciding that our best plan is to take counsel with the officers of the Denver and Rio Grande railway, we go immediately to interview Mr Hopper, the General Passenger Agent, among whose many duties is that of receiving, counseling, and arranging itineraries for all sorts of pilgrims. An hour's discussion perfected our arrangements, and set the workmen at the shops busy in preparing the cars for our migratory residence.

The realization that our scheme, which up to this point had seemed akin to a wild dream, was now rapidly growing into a promising reality, did not diminish our enthusiasm. Indeed we experienced an exhilaration which was quite phenomenal. Was it the very light wine we partook at luncheon? Perish the suspicion! Possibly it was the popularly asserted effect of the rarefied atmosphere. But kinder to our self-esteem than either of these was the thought that our approaching journey had something to do with our elevation, and we accepted it as an explanation.

But we had yet a few days to spare, and we could employ them profitably in looking over this Denver, the marvelous city of the plains. We studied it first from Capitol Hill, as our artist has done, though his picture, so excellently reproduced, can convey but the shadow of the substance. Then we nearly encompassed the town, going southward on Broadway until we had passed Cherry Creek, and *détouring* across Platte River to the westward and northward, on the high plateau which stretches away to the foothills. The city lies at an altitude of 5,197 feet, near the western border of the plains, and within twelve miles of the mountains,—the Colorado or front range of which may be seen for an extent of over two hundred miles. In the north, Long's Peak rears its majestic proportions against the azure sky. Westward, Mounts Rosalie and Evans rise grandly above the other summits of the snowy range, and Gray's and James' Peaks peer from among their gigantic brethren; while historic Pike's Peak, the mighty landmark that guided the gold-hunters of '59, plainly shows its white crest eighty miles to the south. The great plains stretch out for hundreds of miles to the north, east and south. Near the smelting works at Argo, we retrace our way and re-enter the city.

It is the metropolis of the Rocky Mountains, and a stroll through these scores of solid blocks of salesrooms and factories exhibits at once the fact that it is as the commercial center of the mountainous interior that Denver thrives, and congratulates herself upon the promise of a continually prosperous future. She long ago safely passed that crisis which has proved fatal to so many incipient Western cities. Every year proves anew the wisdom and foresight of her founders; and I think her assertion that she is to the largest city between Chicago and San Francisco is likely to be realized. Most of her leading business men came here at the beginning, but their energies were hampered when every article had to be hauled six hundred miles across the plains by teams. It frequently used to happen that merchants would sell their goods completely out, put up their shutters and go a-fishing for weeks, before the new semi-yearly supplies arrived. Everybody therefore looked forward, with good reason, to railway communication as the beginning of a new era of prosperity, and watched with keen interest the approach of the Union Pacific lines from Omaha and Kansas City. These were completed, by the northern routes, in 1869 and 1870; and a few months later the enterprising Atchison, Topeka and Santa Fe sent its tracks and trains through to the mountains, and then came the Burlington route, a most welcome acquisition, adding another link to the transcontinental chain, which now binds the East to the West, the Atlantic to the Pacific coast. At Pueblo, the Denver and Rio Grande, meeting the Atchison, Topeka and Santa Fe, was already prepared to make this new route available to Denver and much of Colorado, and adopting a liberal policy, at once exerted an immense influence upon the speedy development and prosperity of the State.

Thus, in a year or two, the young city found itself removed from total isolation to a central position on various railways, east and west, and to its mill came the varied grist of a circle hundreds of miles in radius. Now blossomed the booming season of business which sagacious eyes had foreseen. The town had less than four thousand inhabitants in 1870. A year from that time her population was nearly fifteen thousand, and her tax-valuation had increased from three to ten millions of dollars. it was a time of happy investment, of incessant building and improvement, and of grand speculation. Mines flourished, crops were abundant, cattle and sheep grazed in a hundred valleys hitherto tenanted by antelope alone, and everybody had plenty of money. Then came a shadow of storm in the East, and the sound of the thunder-clap of 1873 was heard in Denver, if the bolt of the panic was not felt. The banks suddenly became cautious in loans; speculators declined to buy, and sold at a sacrifice. Merchants found that trade was dull, and ranchmen got less for their products. It was a 'set-back' to Denver, and two years of stagnation followed. But she only dug the more money out of the ground to fill her depleted pockets, and survived the 'hard times' with far less sacrifice of fortune and price than did most of the Eastern cities. None of her banks went under, nor ever certified a check, and most of her business houses weathered the storm. The unhealthy reign of speculation was effectually checked, and business was placed upon a compact and solid foundation. Then came 1875 and 1876, which were 'grasshopper years' when no crops of consequence were raised throughout the State, and a large amount of money was sent East to pay for flour and grain. This was a particularly hard blow, but the bountiful harvest of 1877 compensated, and the export of beeves and sheep, with their wool, hides and tallow, was the largest ever made up to that time.

The issue of this successful year with miner, farmer and stock-ranger, yielding them more than $15,000,000, a large proportion of which was an addition to the intrinsic wealth of the world, had an almost magical effect upon the city. Commerce revived, a buoyant feeling prevailed among all classes, and merchants enjoyed a remunerative trade. Money was 'easy' rents advanced, and the real estate business assumed a healthier tone. Generous patronage of the productive industries throughout the whole State was made visible in the quickened trade of the city, which rendered the year an important one in the history of Denver's progress. So, out of the barrenness of the cactus-plain, and through this turbulent history, has arisen a cultivated and beautiful city of 75,000 people, which is truly a metropolis. Her streets are broad, straight, and everywhere well shaded with lines of cotton-woods and maples, abundant in foliage and of graceful shape. On each side of every street flows a constant stream of water, often as clear and cool as a mountain brook. The source is a dozen miles southward, whence the water is conducted in an open channel. There are said to be over 260 miles of these irrigating ditches or gutters, and 250,000 shade-trees.

For many blocks in the southern and western quarter of the town,—from Fourteenth to Thirtieth streets, and from Arapahoe to Broadway and the new suburbs beyond—you will see only elegant and comfortable houses. Homes succeed one another in endlessly varying styles of architecture, and vie in attractiveness, each surrounded by lawns and gardens abounding in flowers. All look new and ornate, while some of the dwellings of wealthy citizens are palatial in size and furnishing, and with porches well occupied during the long, cool twilight characteristic of the summer evening in this climate, giving a very attractive air of opulence and ease. Even the stranger may share in the general enjoyment, for never was there a city with so many and such pleasant hotels, the largest of which, the Windsor and the St. James, are worthy of Broadway or Chestnut street.

The power which has wrought all this change in a short score of years, truly making the desert to bloom, is water; or, more correctly, that is the great instrument used, for the *power* is the will and pride of the intelligent men and women who form the leading portion of the citizens.

Water is pumped from the Platte, by the Holly system, and forced over the city with such power that in case of fire no steam-engine is necessary to send a strong stream through the hose. The keeping of a turf and garden, after it is once begun, is merely a matter of watering. The garden is kept moist mainly by flooding from the irrigating ditch in the street or alley, but the turf of the lawn and the shrubbery owe their greenness to almost incessant sprinkling by the hand-hose. Fountains are placed in nearly every yard. After dinner (for Denver dines at five o'clock as a rule), the father of the house lights his cigar and turns hoseman for an hour, while he chats with friends; or the small boys bribe each other to let them lay the dust in the street, to the imminent peril of passers-by; and young ladies escape the too engrossing attention of complimentary admirers by busily sprinkling heliotrope and mignonette, hinting at a possible different use of the weapon if admiration becomes too ardent. The swish and gurgle and sparkle of water are always present, and always must be; for so Denver defies the desert and dissipates the dreaded dust.

Their climate is one of the things Denverites boast of. That the air is pure and invigorating is to be expected at a point right out on a plateau a mile above sea-level, with a range of snow-burdened mountains within sight. From the beginning to the end of warm weather it rarely rains, except occasional thunder and hail storms in July and August. September witnesses a few storms, succeeded by cool, charming weather, when the haze and smoke is filtered from the bracing air, and the landscape robes itself in its most enchanting hues. The coldest weather occurs after New Year's Day, and lasts sometimes until April. Then come the May storms and floods, followed by a charming summer. The barometer holds itself pretty steady throughout the year. There is a vast quantity of electricity in the air, and the displays of lightning are magnificent and occasionally destructive. Sunshine is very abundant. One can by no means judge from the brightest day in New York of the wonderful glow sunlight has here. During 1884 there were 205 clear days, 126 fair, and 34 cloudy, the sun being totally obscured on only 18 days; and yet this record is more unfavorable than the average for a number of years. Summer heat often reaches a hundred in the shade at midday; but with sunset comes coolness, and the nights allow refreshing sleep. In winter the mercury sometimes sinks twenty degrees below zero; but one does not feel this severity as much as he would a far less degree of cold in the damp, raw climate of the coast. Snow is frequent, but rarely plentiful enough for sleighing.

Denver is built not only with the capital of her own citizens, but constructed of materials close at hand. Very substantial bricks, kilned in the suburbs, are the favorite material. Then there is a pinkish trachyte, almost as light as pumice, and ringing under a blow with a metallic clink, that is largely employed in trimmings. Sandstone, marble and limestone are abundant enough for all needs. Coarse lumber is supplied by the high pine forests, but all the hard wood and fine lumber is brought from the East. The fuel of the city was formerly wholly lignite coal, which comes from the foothills; but the extension of the railway to Canon City, El Moro and the Gunnison, have made the harder and less sulphurous coals accessible and cheap.

And while she has been looking well after the material attractions, Denver has kept pace with the progress of the times in modern advantages. She is very proud of her school-buildings, constructed and managed upon the most improved plans; of her fine churches, of her State and county offices, her seminaries of higher learning, and of her natural history and historical association. Her Grand Opera House is the most elegant on the continent, her business blocks are extensive and costly, and the Union Depot ranks with the best of similar structures. Gas was introduced several years ago, and the system, which now includes nearly all sections of the city, is being constantly improved and extended. The Brush electric light has been in very general use for nearly three years, and the Edison incandescent lamps are now being employed. The telephone is found in hundreds of business places and residences, the exchange at the close of last year numbering 709 subscribers. The water supply is distributed through forty miles of mains, the consumption averaging three million gallons per day, exclusive of the contributions of the irrigating ditches and the numerous artesian wells. The steam heating works evaporate one hundred thousand gallons of water daily, delivering the product through three miles of mains and nearly two miles of service pipes; this being the only company out of twenty seven of its nature in the country which has proved a financial success. Street car lines traverse the thoroughfares in all directions, and transport over two million passengers annually. Two district messenger companies are generously patronized. The regular police force consists of some forty-five patrolmen and detectives, aside from the Chief and his assistants; and a distinct organization is the Merchant's Police, numbering twenty men. A paid Fire Department is maintained, at an annual expense of $56,000, and the alarm system embraces twenty-six miles of wire and fifty signal boxes. There are published six daily newspapers, one being in German, and a score of weeklies. All are well conducted and prosperous.

A branch of the United States Mint is located here, but is used for assays only, and not for coinage. An appropriation has been made by Congress for a handsome building, the site has been selected, and work is now being pushed forward. The post-office is a source of considerable revenue to the Government. There are six National and two State banks, with a paid in capital of $870,000, and showing a surplus of $754,000 at the close of 1883. The deposits for the year amounted to $8,396,200, and the loans and discounts approximated $4,500,000. The shops of the Denver and Rio Grande railway are doubtless the most extensive in the West, employing over 800 men, and turning out during the year 2 express, 8 mail, 4 combination, 522 box, 303 stock, 25 refrigerator, 197 flat, and 300 coal cars, together with 8 cabooses. In addition they have produced 350 frogs, 200 switch stands, and all the iron work for the bridges on 350 miles of new road. The year's shipments of the Boston and Colorado Smelting Company aggregate, in silver, gold, and copper, $3,907,000; and in the same time the Grant smelter has treated, in silver, lead and gold, $6,348,868. Finally, from the statistics at hand it appears that the volume of Denver's trade for the year referred to, apart from the industries above mentioned, and real estate transactions, has exceeded the snug sum of $58,856,998. In the meantime the taxable valuation of property in Arapahoe county has increased $6,600,000.

These facts establish, beyond the slightest doubt, the truth that Denver stands upon a firm financial basis. This the casual stranger can hardly fail to surmise when he glances at her magnificent buildings, and statistics will confirm the surmise.

Denver society is cosmopolitan. Famous and brilliant persons are constantly appearing from all quarters of the globe. Five hundred people a day, it is said, enter Colorado, and nine-tenths of this multitude pass through Denver. Nowadays, 'the tour' of the United States is incomplete if this mountain city is omitted. Thus the registers of her hotels bear many foreign autographs of world-wide reputation. Surprise is often expressed by the critical among these visitors (why, I do not understand) at the totally unexpected degree of intelligence, appreciation of the more refined methods of thought and handiwork, and the knowledge of science, that greet them here. Matters of art and music, particularly, find friends and cultivation among the educated and generous families who have built up society; and there are schools and associations devoted to sustaining the interest in them, just as there are reading circles and literary clubs. And, withal, there is the most charming freedom of acquaintance and intercourse—the polish and good breeding of rank delivered from all chill and exclusiveness or regard for 'who was your grandfather.' Yet this winsome good-fellowship by no means descends to vulgarity, or permits itself to be abused. After all, it is only New York and New England and Ohio, transplanted and considerably enlivened.

Returning to our consideration of Denver's resources, it will readily be seen that she stands as the supply-depot and money-receiver of three great branches of industry and wealth, namely, mining, stock-raising and agriculture.

The first of these is the most important. Many of the richest proprietors live and spend their profits here. Then, too, the machinery which the mining and reduction of the ores require, and the tools, clothing and provisions of the men, mainly come from here. Long ago ex-Governor Gilpin, worthily one of the most famous of Colorado's representative men, and an enthusiast upon the subject of her virtues and loveliness, prophesied the immense wealth which would continue to be delved from the crevices of her rocky frame, and was called a visionary for his pains; but his prophesies have aggregated more in the fulfilment than they promised in the foretelling, and his 'visions' have netted him a most satisfactory fortune. About 75,000 lodes have been discovered in Colorado, and numberless placers. Only a small proportion of these, of course, were worked remuneratively, but the cash yield of the twenty years since the discovery of the precious metals, has averaged over $7,000,000 a year, and has increased from $200,000 in 1869 to over $26,376,562 in 1883. Not half of this is gold, yet it is only since 1870 that silver has been mined at all in Colorado. These statistics show the total yield of the State in gold and silver thus far to exceed $154,000,000, not to mention tellurium, copper, iron, lead and coal. Surely this alone is sufficient employment of capital and production of original wealth— genuine making of money—to ensure the permanent support of the city.

The second great source of revenue to Denver, is the cattle and sheep of the State. The wonderful worthless-looking buffalo grass, growing in little tufts so scattered that the dust shows itself everywhere between, and turning sere and shriveled before the spring rains are fairly over, has proved one of Colorado's most prolific avenues of wealth. The herds now reported in the State count up 1,461,945 head, and the annual shipments amount to 100,000, at an average of $20 apiece, giving $2,000,000 as the yearly yield. Add the receipts for the sales of hides and tallow, and the home consumption, amounting to about $60,000, and you have a figure not far from $3,500,000 to represent the total annual income from this branch of productive industry. The whole value of the cattle investments in the State is estimated by good judges at $14,000,000, nearly one-fourth of which is the property of citizens of Denver. Yet this sum, great as it is for a pioneer region, represents only two-thirds of Colorado's live stock. Last year about 1,500,000 sheep were sheared, and more capital is being invested in them. Perhaps the total value of sheep ranches is not less than $5,000,000, the annual income from which approaches $1,300,000.

The third large item of prosperity is agriculture, although it advances in the face of much opposition. In 1883 the production of the chief crops was as follows: hay, 266,500 tons; wheat 1,750,840 bushels; oats, 1,186,534 bushels; corn, 598,975 bushels; barley, 265,180 bushels; rye 78,030 bushels, and potatoes, 851,000 bushels. Add to this vegetables and small fruits, and the yield of the soil in Colorado is brought to over $9,000,000 in value. Farmers are learning better and better how to produce the very best results by means of scientific irrigation, and the tillage is annually wider.

Nor is this the whole story. Denver is rapidly growing into a manufacturing center. Here are rolling mills, iron foundries, smelters, machine shops, woolen mills, shoe factories, glass works, carriage and harness factories, breweries, and so on through a long list. The flouring mills are very valuable, representing an investment of $350,000, and handling half the wheat crop of Colorado. I have dwelt upon these somewhat prosy statements in order to point out fully what rich resources Denver has behind her, and how it happens that she finds herself, at twenty-three years of age, amazingly strong commercially. Not only a large proportion of the money which gives existence to these enterprises (nearly every householder in the city has a financial interest in one or several mines, stock-ranges or farms), but as I have intimated, the current supplies that sustain them, are procured in Denver, and a very large percentage of their profits finds its way directly to this focus.

Denver thus becomes to all Colorado what Paris is to France. Through

all the enormous area, from Wyoming far into New Mexico, and westward to Utah, she has had no formidable rival until South Pueblo rose
to contest the trade of all the southern half of this commercial territory.
That she advances with the rapidly thickening population of the State
and its increasing needs, is apparent to everyone who has noted the
gigantic strides with which Denver has grown, and the ease with which
she wears her imperial honors. Every extension of the railways, every
good crop, every new mineral district developed, every increase of stock
ranges, directly and instantly affects the great centralmart. This sound
business basis being present, the opportunity to pleasantly dispose of
the money made is, of course, not long in preventing itself. It thus
happens that Denver shows, in a wonderful measure, the amenities
of intellectual culture that make life so attractive in the old-established
centers of civilization, where selected society, thoughtful study, and the
riches of art, have ripened to maturity, through long time and under
gracious traditions. There is an abundance here, therefore, to please
the eye and touch the heart as well as fill the pockets, and year by
year the city is becoming more and more a desirable place in which
to dwell as well as to do business.

New Mexico

ROBERT P. PORTER

This fascinating description of the nineteenth century
frontier state of New Mexico is taken from Robert P.
Porter's The West *(1882).*

THE TRAVELER IN New Mexico feels that he is in a foreign land. Nearly
all of the people are of Spanish descent, speak the Spanish language
(though by no means pure Castilian), and have the manners and customs
of the Spanish of two or three centuries ago, mingled with those of
the semi-civilized Pueblo Indians, with whom they jointly possess the
soil. The people, both Mexican and Indian, are ineffably lazy and shiftless; and the country, under their control, has remained stationary for
centuries. The progress of railroad building is now, however, bringing
into the Territory a large American element, which is already making
itself felt very decidedly in opening up the resources of the Territory,

and especially its mineral wealth.

New Mexico lies between the parallels of 31°20' and 37° north latitude, and the meridians of 26° and 32° west of Washington. On the north it is bounded by Colorado, on the east by Indian Territory, on the south by Texas and Mexico, and on the west by Arizona.

It was a part of the territory ceded to the United States by Mexico, under the treaty of Guadalupe Hidalgo, and by the Gadsden purchase. Its discovery and exploration antedated that of any other part of the country excepting the Gulf States. In 1537 to 1540, the region was penetrated and the natives conquered by Vasquez de Coronado, a Spanish adventurer, who entered the country from Mexico at the head of a small army. At that time the principal inhabitants consisted of a semi-civilized people, living in communal towns of stone or adobe brick. These are the Pueblo Indians of the present day.

Towards the close of that century the country was colonized with Spaniards, who enslaved the inhabitants of the Pueblos, and treated them with the utmost harshness. Many attempts at revolt followed, but without success, until 1680, when they succeeded in driving the Spaniards out of the country, and maintained their independence for eighteen years. In 1698, they were reconquered, and remained under the Dominion of Spain until 1822, when, joining with the other States of Mexico, they succeeded in throwing off the Spanish yoke.

The Territory, as originally organized under the United States, comprised, besides what is now New Mexico, all of Arizona and part of Colorado. Arizona was set off in 1863, and the part of Colorado in 1865.

During the late civil war, New Mexico was invaded by the rebels, under command of Gen. Sibley, who defeated some raw levies of Mexican militia, and occupied Santa Fé. Marching northward, with the intention of invading Colorado, he was met by a body of Colorado volunteers, when a drawn battle ensued; after which the rebel commander, finding it impossible to sustain himself, and being threatened constantly by large bodies of the Federals, was forced to retreat into Texas, with a loss of one-half of his command.

The growth of the Territory, until recently, has been very slow. Until within a year or two, there has been almost no immigration, and the increase has been confined almost entirely to natural growth. The Territory has now taken a vigorous start; and we may look for a very rapid increase in population and wealth.

The area of New Mexico is 122,580 square miles. Its mean elevation above the sea is placed at 5,600 feet. Its lowest point probably is near El Paso, on the Rio Grande, which is 3,800 feet above the sea; while its mountain peaks reach nearly to 14,000 ft.

Nearly one-half of the area of the Territory is between 4,000 and 5,000 ft above sea level.

New Mexico has a very varied, uneven surface, with great extents of plains, broken by small ranges and groups of mountains. The north-eastern portion consists of a part of the great plains. South of the Canadian river, these rise into the great plateau known as the Liano Estacado, which ranges in elevation from 3,500 to 5,000 ft. The surface is grassy, but is almost absolutely without water. West of this plateau is the narrow, fertile valley of the Pecos, between which and the Rio Grande the country is mainly dry and sterile, while water is extremely scarce. The surface is nearly level, but is broken here and there by a few groups as sterile as the desert at their bases. The Sangre de Cristo range, which in Colorado has an elevation of about 14,000 ft in many of its peaks, extends southward half way through New Mexico, with a gradual diminution of altitude, separating the plains on the east from the valley of the Rio Grande on the west. The northern part of the Rio Grande valley consists of the southern portion of the San Luis park, or valley, the greater portion of which is embraced in Colorado. In this Territory, the soil of this valley becomes yet more sandy, and the vegetation sparser and more desert-like than in Colorado. At its foot the valley is terminated abruptly by an outflow of volcanic rock, through which the river has a narrow valley, which extends down to Fort Craig. Thence it is in canon, or a very narrow valley, beyond the limits of the Territory.

West of the Rio Grande, in the northern part, the great Southern spur from the San Juan Mountains of Colorado enters the Territory, and extends southward in a broad mass as far as latitude 35°30′. The rest of this western half of the Territory consists of plains and plateaux, broken by numberless ranges and groups of mountains, some of considerable height. Among them the range known as the Zuni Mountains is perhaps the most important, rising to a mean height of about 12,000 ft. These plains and plateaux are for the most part covered with grass, but become more arid and desert-like toward the northwest. The higher mountains are everywhere covered with forests of coniferæ.

The rivers of the Territory are few and unimportant for other purposes than irrigation. The Canadian heads in the eastern slopes of the Sangre de Cristo Range, and flows off to the eastward. The Rio Grande, which is by far the largest stream, heads in the San Juan Mountains, in Colorado, and pursues a course nearly due south down the Territory. It receives nearly all its supply of water from the mountains about its head, and is joined by no tributary of any magnitude in its long course through New Mexico. Indeed, the net result of its journey across this Territory is a considerable loss of water owing to evaporation and sinking in this arid region. It has been known to sink entirely into the sands of its bed, in the southern part of the Territory. In the southwestern part are the sources of the Gila, and, farther north, those of the Colorado Chiquito, both of which are branches of the Colorado of the West.

The leading feature of the climate is its aridity, which, owing to its more southerly position and less altitude, is much greater than that of Colorado. The mean annual temperature ranges from 45° to 64° in the plain and valley portions, decreasing, of course, on the mountains. The rainfall in the valleys and on the plains is very slight, ranging from eight to twenty-two inches annually, an amount nowhere sufficient to produce any useful crops, except the grasses, without irrigation. Snow very rarely falls, except on the mountains; indeed, a fall of four inches, in the level country, in the winter of 1880–81, was a phenomenon almost unprecedented.

With so arid a climate, it is a singular fact that New Mexico has very little desert land; nearly all the plains and plateaux are covered with gamma grass, that most nutritious food for cattle and sheep. While there is an abundance of sage brush for all practical purposes, it does not, as in other parts of the West, even in those which are much less arid, crowd out the useful grasses.

The higher mountains are covered with forests; but they are by no means so extensive as in Colorado; nor do they furnish as large or as valuable timber. Some of the plateaux are partially covered with pinon pine and a stunted species of cedar, both of which trees are peculiar to an arid climate and are of little economic value.

Throughout the Territory, large game is scarce. The species found are not characteristically different from those of Colorado, excepting that those peculiar to an arid climate become relatively more abundant. The short, sharp bark and prolonged wail of the coyote are heard more frequently; and the traveler must take greater heed to his steps to avoid treading upon rattlesnakes.

The climate of New Mexico is adapted to the growth of all cereals and fruits of the temperate zone. Corn, which can be cultivated in only a few localities in Colorado, can here be ripened almost anywhere.

The extent of arable land being here, as almost everywhere in the West, a question of water, it is thereby limited. The utmost amount possible to place under irrigation, by utilizing all the contributions of the streams with the utmost economy, is estimated to be not more than five per cent, of the area of the Territory, or 6,060 square miles. This is distributed along the bases of the higher ranges of mountains and the valleys of the few streams of the Territory. Agriculture will probably never be a leading industry of New Mexico. It will be, as now, far eclipsed by the grazing interest, which, even under the lazy Mexican régime, is a large and important industry. In 1880, there were in the Territory no less than 400,000 head of cattle and 5,000,000 sheep. The climate is so mild that neither cattle now sheep require shelter or feed during the winter.

The surface geology of the Territory is quite complicated; and to give a sketch of it in any way approaching detail would far transcend the space allowed in this work. More than half of the Territory, including the Llano Estacado, the plains, and large proportion of the plateau region, is covered by the Cretaceous formation. In many of the canons of the latter, the Trias, and even the Jura, is exposed. The plateaux of the southwestern portion are Eozoic, as are also most of the mountain ranges of the Territory, with the earlier stratified formations exposed at their bases and on their flanks. There are outbursts and fields of volcanic rock covering considerable areas at the foot of San Luis valley, between the Rio Grande and the Guadalupe Mountains, and in the western part, about Mount Taylor.

Under the old Mexican and Indian régime, little was done toward a development of the mineral resources of the Territory. The comparatively small white population, which has been but slowly increasing since the acquisition of the Territory by the United States, has been hampered very much in this direction by the countless land grants which have been continually cropping up to disturb and invalidate titles. The grants appear to be of two kinds; those which, in terms, convey the minerals to be found on the grant, and those which do not. The latter form by far the larger proportion of the whole; and recent rulings of the courts are to the effect that they do not cover mineral land, even if it be included within the limits of the grant. It is necessary to say that these decisions are supported heartily by the Anglo-Saxon element of the population. There is no longer any danger threatening the titles to mineral lands, from an unconfirmed grant of this class.

From this and other causes, among them the great interest in mining which has recently arisen, and the extension of railroads into the Territory, the development of the mineral wealth of New Mexico has been commenced in earnest, and with the most flattering results. The Territory contains a number of very rich placers, among them the 'Old' and 'New Placers' which have been worked in only a small way, owing to a scarcity of water and want of capital. The later is now forthcoming; and great works are in progress to bring water from a distance to these deposits.

Thousands of mineral lodes have been discovered and located; and many are already being worked with profit. The most productive district at present is probably that of Silver City, toward the southwestern part of the Territory.

The total production for the year 1879 is estimated by Wells, Fargo & Co. as—gold, $19,800; silver, $603,000. In 1880, they report a total of $711,300, nearly all of which is silver.

Besides the precious metals, New Mexico is destined to be a large producer of copper. Several rich mines of this metal have been discovered and are now being worked. Among them is one on the San Pedro Grant, which consists of a bed thirty feet in thickness of ore which runs about fifteen per cent of copper.

Until within a year or two, the Territory was without railroads. Now, at the beginning of 1881, the Atchison, Topeka & Santa Fe road, entering at the north, over the Raton Hills, has traversed two-thirds of the width of the Territory, following generally the course of the Rio Grande. The Southern Pacific Railroad, coming from the west, has reached a junction with the former. Other roads are projected, which, if completed, will afford easy communication with all parts of the Territory.

In 1880, the Territory contained four National banks, with a total capital of $400,000 and an outstanding circulation of $355,670, and five private bankers.

The population of the Territory is 119,563, of which 64,499 are males, and 55,064 females. Of the total number, more than one-half are Mexicans, and about 9,000 are Pueblo Indians, who, by the terms of the treaty of Guadalupe Hidalgo, are American citizens, although still under tribal organization.

The principal city is Santa Fe, the capital of the Territory, which was settled in the sixteenth century, and is, therefore, one of the oldest cities in the country. It is situated twenty miles east of the Rio Grande, on

Santa Fe creek, at the base of the Sangre de Cristo range, and at an elevation above the sea of about 7,000 feet. The population in 1880 was 6,635.

Other settlements of some importance are Las Vegas, Silver City, and Albuquerque.

Several of the pueblos are important places, containing a thousand population or more.

Besides the Pueblo Indians, who possess a degree of civilization but little inferior to that of their Mexican neighbors, there are in the Territory a large number of Indians proper. In the northwest is the large tribe of Navajos, numbering 11,850; farther east are the Jicarillo Apaches, 627 in number; and on or about the Pecos river, in the eastern part, are the Mescalero and Hot Spring Apaches, numbering 1,350. Besides these, there are small bands of wandering Indians, more or less hostile, whose numbers can not be estimated, but are known to be small.

New Mexico is now just awakening from its sleep of centuries, and with the influx of American blood and enterprise, its great resources, which, under Spanish domination, have laid untouched, are being rapidly brought to light, and the Territory will, ere long, occupy the place in the sisterhood of States, to which it is entitled.

Southern California

THEODORE S. VAN DYKE

In these passages from his traveler's guide, Southern
California (1886), *Theodore S. Van Dyke gives a vivid
depiction of the region's scenery and climate.*

THE HIGHEST PEAK of the San Bernardino mountains is quite sharp and
bare upon the summit, and commands a circular view of a tract fully
three hundred miles in diameter, within which lies almost every variety
and combination of Southern California scenery. From the top of this
peak, eleven thousand feet above the general level of the habitable part
of the land, one may on a clear day look down upon a landscape that
embraces all possible extremes of barrenness and fertility, of wildness
and civilization, with nearly all the varieties of mountain, plain, and
valley that time and the elements can form. The prospect is best in
midsummer, for it is only then that the distinctive features of California

are brought out. Even then one needs a powerful glass, for the mountain is so lofty that it is no easy task to unravel the tangled web of shapes and colors that present themselves even at its very feet; this mountain having the peculiarity of being the highest in the United States above the general level of the country at its base.

The first thing that rivets the stranger's eye is the stupendous desert on the east, cut in two near the center by a long low range of wavy hills, bare, dry, and inexpressibly barren. The part on the north, called the Mojave Desert, is larger than Massachusetts; that on the south, called the Colorado Desert, is nearly as large. The visitor may have traveled over strips of barren land, and seen large tracts of good land called 'desert' because there is no surface-water, but nowhere else in North America can one see such barrens as these; and to comprehend them in their immensity one must see them from this mountain as they lie below, gleaming beneath an eternal sun. Nowhere does the power of man in his triumphs over nature appear more insignificant than on the line of the Southern Pacific Railroad, stretching far out upon this yellow immensity, looking with its nearest stations like a spider's web with three or four gnats sitting upon it. One scarcely realizes what desolation is until looking down upon these mighty sweeps of shimmering sand, and thinking of the fiery winds that whirl the dust in those huge drifts, and of the fate of the hundreds who have tried to cross them without water.

Yawning beneath us on the south, nine thousand feet deep, is the pass of San Gorgonio, on the other side of which Mount San Jacinto rises almost to a level with our feet, making on the desert side the swiftest mountain rise in North America—ten thousand feet in less than five miles. Far away into the south leads from it the high and rugged mountain chain that shuts off the inhabitable part of the County of San Diego from the fiery breath of the desert. Tumbling toward the coast in long lines of lower mountains, foot-hills, and table-lands, with valleys and plains lying between, until lost in the highlands of Mexico, the range presents but a rolling confusion of blue, gray, yellow, brown, and green.

Around toward the north-west sweeps the great desert of the Mojave, with the blue hills of Arizona on the east, the lofty spurs of the Sierra Nevada on the north, growing hazy with distance and bounded on the south-western rim by a continuation of the range upon which we stand. Miles away these mountains run, in a long ridge nearly five thousand feet below us, clad in green forests of heavy pine until the line dips

suddenly three thousand feet lower to form the Cajon Pass. Then in
a moment it rolls skyward again in a wild medley of rugged hills, mounting swiftly one over another until they terminate in the peak of Cuca-
munga. This peak upon the south falls away ten thousand feet in less
than six miles into the plains of San Bernardino, almost equaling San
Jacinto in suddenness, but on the north-west breaks and rises again
into another mighty mountain called 'Old Baldy' and then into lower
ridges, that wind away till lost to sight in the bristling heights of the
San Fernando range in the northern part of Los Angeles County; and
these again disappear as if merged in the last peaks of the Sierra Nevada.
The western horizon is bounded by the long bright band of the Pacific,—
in the morning, of silvery sheen; in the afternoon, when the sun hangs
over it, all aglow with golden shimmer. And this is broken by a few
dark spots with ragged edges, that one would scarcely suspect to be
islands, some of them over twenty miles long and seven or eight hundred
feet high.

Within this inclosure of desert, mountain, and ocean lies a tract that
has not its like upon the globe. One sees valleys of the brightest verdure
where the grass is fed by the drainage of the surrounding hills, and
others always green with the dense foliage of live-oaks that have stood
shoulder to shoulder for ages. There are smooth slopes brown with
the ripened alfileria; low rolling hills, silver gray with matted wild-oats,
which when green a horseman could have tied over his horse's neck;
others whitish green with the tall white sage, and others grayish brown
with the dense ranks of the wild-mustard stalks. Here a canon enters
the plain with a great wash from some ancient cloud-burst or season
of unusual rain, cutting the level with a long deep gully, and then covering it with acres of boulder and gravel; and here another enters by a
little soft valley, clad with a rich brown carpet of dried clover and flowers,
with perhaps a huge rock-pile of ancient granite in its center overshadowed by the sweeping arms of some venerable live-oak. There lies
the great plain itself, with its distant laguna glittering on its breast, with
tall slender columns of dust marching slowly over its face where the
little whirlwinds move along; the Indian girls, bright with gray calico,
jogging on their little ponies, or the eight-horse team of the farmer creep-
ing slowly, with two great wagons trailing behind. Upon a rising knoll
shine the white walls of the old Spanish ranch-house, with saddled
horses tied to the porch, beneath which the owner and his friends are
perhaps rolling cigarettes and chattering melodious Spanish, while the

herdsmen are driving the herds without.

You see the line of the water-course, now perhaps only a long dry bed of white sand, winding seaward through long green lines of syca-more, cottonwood, and willow, spreading out at times into broad groves. Perhaps the water breaks out here and there in a long shining strip, or it may flow on for miles and then sink to rise no more. Often it meanders through meadows green with perennial grass, then amid jun-gles of wild-rose, sweet-brier, and guatemote, along low bottom-lands where the grape-vine overwhelms the snowy bloom of the elder with a shower of green drapery, and feeding from its hidden waters little ponds fringed with green rushes, where black-birds of red and golden wings are darkening the air above the open water, and where the cinna-mon-teal is floating with its downy brood.

Along the edges the plains and valleys break into low hills covered with thin grayish-green brush, and the little hollows between them are often filled with prickly-pear; or the still more forbidding cholla cactus, as high as one's head. And often these low hills are themselves hard and stony, and covered with cactus, and often are only concretions of cobble-stones, with which the intervening hollows are also filled. And perhaps the whole is only a succession of little mounds a few yards apart, reaching often far out upon the plain itself, looking as though a lake of soft mud had suddenly hardened while shaken into waves, but probably made by the wind heaping dust around bushes which have since died out.

These hills break into higher ones that roll in all sorts of shapes and bristle with dense, dark brush higher than one's head, or perhaps are covered with dead grass and scattered green bushes of live-oak, sumac, and fusica. Among these bushes smooth boulders of granite often shine afar like springs on the hillside, or they stand along the crests looking against the sky like houses or chimneys. Again some of these hills are only huge undulations of bare dirt, reaching for miles like chopping waves upon a stormy sea, some gray, some dingy white, others a sickly brown or red.

Beyond these secondary hills rise others, thousands of feet high, covered with dark-green chaparral, through which perhaps a clump of bright-green sycamores marks afar the presence of water. Or they may be from base to summit studded with boulders, amid which the lilac, manzanita, and live-oak struggle for foothold. Others again have long, smooth slopes, golden with dead foxtail grass, over which venerable white-oaks stand scattered. And among the jostling shoulders of these lower mountains are often little gardens of living green, sometimes sunk like lakes into their very tops. Between the ranges of such hills may lie broad valleys or wide table-lands, with surfaces like rolling prairie, all lifted into the region of abundant rains. And far above all else rise fir-plumed mountains, whose sides are robed in dark forests, below whose heads the clouds float in long streams, whose highest gulches are white with snow far into the summer, while in winter it often lies twenty feet deep, though the orange-tree is blooming scarce twenty miles away.

Such was the view of the land but a few years ago; but now valley, slope and *mesa*, and even the mountain-sides, are dotted with bright and beautiful homes, while villages and even cities are rearing tall spires from the lately bare plains. At the western foot of the mountain rise the steeples and housetops of San Bernardino from a deep mass of green, among which may be seen the glitter of the streams and the sparkle of the artesian wells that have produced the luxuriance in which most of the city is lost to view. Nearer still lies old San Bernardino, a long line of green gardens and orchards, vineyards and rich pastures, with Mill Creek winding through it beneath an arcade of lofty alders. Farther west stands Colton, a spot fast brightening upon a lately bare waste of sand; and a few miles beyond lies Riverside, where the power of water has struck from beauty the fetters of ages and made it a veritable oasis. Hundreds upon hundreds of handsome houses, embowered in every variety of shrubbery, now rise amid orange and lemon groves, fields of alfalfa, orchards where the foliage of the apricot, prune, plum, walnut, almond, peach, or pear hide the ground beneath, vineyards where over sixty kinds of grapes are growing, and the plots of raisin-grapes alone larger than many wheat-fields of the Middle States. And that long silvery thread running far along the bare plain outside, taken from the Santa Anna River and fed by the snow-banks at our side, has done it all.

Along the foot of the dark-blue mountains that, rolling skyward farther west, shut out from view the shore-line of the distant coast, lie the fair and fertile meadows of Temescal. Over these mountains toward the coast lie the towns of Santa Anna, Orange, Tustin, and Anaheim. All these, like Riverside, were created almost entirely by the same Santa Anna River that starts here beside us, and through a gorge in the Temescal Range winds to the sea. Farther to the north we get a peep into the valley of San Gabriel—only a dim haze of green in a girdle of mountains, although its vineyards and orchards and green fields cover tens of thousands of acres; and beyond lies the city of Los Angeles, almost hidden, like San Barnardino, beneath its trees. Radiating for miles away from it are long avenues of cypress, eucalyptus, and other tall green trees; and between these avenues are great orchards of orange and lemon and every imaginable fruit, amid which stand thousands of houses surrounded by gardens of guavas, pomegranates, and other exotics, with walks lined with maguey and palm and other tropical vegetation. Dozens of villages, hamlets, and townsites dot the intervening spaces, and everywhere the spirit of development is at work. Farther north the view into Ventura and Santa Barbara counties is intercepted by the towering peaks of the Gucamunga Range. The highest peak of that range is easily ascended, however, and there another wonderful view opens below.

But to see at its best the loveliest part of Southern California as improved, one must descend into its great valley of San Gabriel. The Sierra Madre Mountains that form its northern wall rise with a sudden sweep much higher above the valley than most of the great mountains of our country rise above the land at their feet, lifting one at once into a different climate and to a country where primeval wildness still reigns supreme. Few parts of the United States are less known and less traversed than these great hills; yet they look down upon the very garden of all California. Away up there the mountain trout flashes undisturbed in the hissing brook, and the call of the mountain quail rings from the shady glen where the grizzly bear yet dozes away the day, secure as in the olden time. From the bristling points where the lilac and manzanita light up the dark hue of the surrounding chaparral the deer yet looks down upon the plain from which the antelope has long been driven; while on the lofty ridges that lie in such clear outline against the distant sky the mountain sheep still lingers, safe in its inaccessible home.

But a few years ago this valley of San Gabriel was a long open stretch of wavy slopes and low rolling hills; in winter robed in velvety green and spangled with myriads of flowers, all strange to Eastern eyes; in summer brown with sun-dried grass, or silvery gray where the light rippled over the wild oats. Here and there stood groves of huge live-oaks, beneath whose broad, time-bowed heads thousands of cattle stamped away the noons of summer. Around the old mission, whose bells have rung over the valley for a century, a few houses were grouped; but beyond this there was scarcely a sign of man's work except the far-off speck of a herdsman looming in the mirage, or the white walls of the old Spanish ranch-house glimmering afar through the hazy sunshine in which the silent land lay always sleeping.

The old bells of the mission still clang in brazen discord as before, and the midnight yelp of the coyote may yet be heard as he comes in from the outlying hills to inspect the new breeds of chickens that civilization has brought in; a few scattered live-oaks still nod to each other in memory of the past, and along the low hills far off in the south the light still plays upon the waving wild-oats; but nearly all else has changed as no other part of the world has ever changed. Nearly all is now covered with a luxuriant growth of vegetation the most diverse, yet all of it foreign to the soil. Side by side are the products of two zones, reaching the highest stages of perfection, yet none of them natives of this coast. Immense vineyards of the tenderest grapes of Southern Spain or Italy, yielding five or six tons to the acre, lie by the side of fields of wheat whose heads and berry far excel in size and fullness the finest ever seen in the famed fields of Minnesota or Dakota. Here the barley gives often a return that no Northern land can equal, and by its side the orange-tree outdoes its race in the farthest South, and keeps its fruit in perfection when those of other lands have failed.

Gay cottages now line the roads where so recently the hare cantered along the dusty cattle-trail; and villages lie brightly green with a wealth of foliage where the roaring wings of myriads of quail shook the air above impenetrable jungles of cactus. Houses furnished in all the styles of modern decorative art rise in all directions, embowered in roses, geraniums, heliotropes, and lilies that bloom the long year round and reach a size that makes them hard to recognize as old friends. Among them rise the banana, the palm, the aloe, the rubber-tree, and the pampas-grass with its tall feathery plumes. Perhaps the camphor-tree and a dozen other foreign woods are scattered around them, while the lawns shine with grasses unknown in other parts of the United States. The broad head and drooping arms of the Mexican pepper-tree fill along the road the sunny openings that the stately shaft of the Australian eucalyptus has failed to shade; and on every hand, instead of homely fences, are hedges of Monterey cypress, lime, pomegranate, arborvitae, or acacia. Here and there one sees the guava, the Japanese persimmon, Japanese plum, or some similar exotic, cultivated, like the olive and quince and lemon, for pleasure more than profit; but grapes and oranges are the principal product. Yet there are groves of English walnuts almost rivaling in size the great orange-orchards, and orchards of prunes, nectarines, apricots, plums, pears, peaches, and apples that are little behind in size or productiveness. The deep green of the alfalfa may here and there contrast with the lighter green of the grape, but vineyards of enormous size, some a mile square, make all beside them look small.

There are here but two seasons, neither of which can be exactly defined, but which are most nearly described as spring and summer. Spring is generally called winter; but, with the exception of a few frosty nights, which can only be when the sky is clear and the air quite dry, in which case the succeeding day is sure to be warm and bright, there is nothing on the greater part of the lowlands, and especially along the coast, that can be correctly called winter. It is also called by many the 'rainy season.' But this is only by way of distinction from the long, dry summer—the season when it may rain enough to make things grow, as distinguished from the season when it is quite certain not to rain enough to be worthy of mention. It is not a 'rainy season' as that term would be understood in Illinois or New England. From the first to the last rain, a period lasting in seasons unusually wet for nearly six months, the number of rainy days if never equal to that of a wet spring and summer in any of the Eastern States, and too often does not equal the number of the rainy days in the driest six months ever seen there. The floods which happen occasionally come from heavy precipitation before there is grass enough on the hills to hold back the water, and not from a long continuance of rainy days.

Sometimes this season commences with a fair rain in November, after a light shower or two in October, but some of the very best seasons begin about the time that all begin to lose hope. November adds its full tribute to the stream of sunshine that for months has poured along the land; and, perhaps, December closes the long file of cloudless days with banners of blue and gold. The plains and slopes lie bare and brown; the low hills that break away from them are yellow with dead foxtail or wild-oats, gray with mustard-stalks, or ashy green with chemical or sage. Even the chapparal, that robes the higher hills in living green, has a tired air, and the long timber-line that marks the cañon winding up the mountain-slopes is decidedly paler. The sea-breeze has fallen off to a faint breath or air; the land lies silent and dreamy with golden haze; the air grows drier, the sun hotter, and the shade cooler; the smoke of brush-fires hangs at times along the sky; the water has risen in the springs and sloughs as if to meet the coming rain, but it never looked less like rain than it now does.

Suddenly a new wind arises from the vast watery plains upon the southwest; long, fleecy streams of cloud reach out along the sky; the distant mountain-tops seem swimming in a film of haze, and the great California weather-prophet—a creature upon whom the storms of adverse experience have beaten for years without making even a weather-crack in the smooth cheek of his conceit—lavishes his wisdom as confidently as if he had never made a false prediction. After a large amount of fuss, and enough preliminary skirmishing over the sky for a dozen storms in any Easter State, the clouds at last get ready, and a soft pattering is heard upon the roof—the sweetest music that ever cheers a Californian ear, and one which the author of 'The Rain upon the Roof' should have heard before writing his poem.

When the sun again appears, it is with a softer, milder beam than before. The land looks bright and refreshed, like a tired and dirty boy who has had a good bath and a nap, and already the lately bare plains and hillsides show a greenish tinge. Fine little leaves of various kinds are springing from the ground, but nearly all are lost in a general profusion of dark green ones, of such shape and delicacy of texture that a careless eye might readily take them for ferns. This is the alfileria, the prevailing flower of the land. The rain may continue at intervals. Daily the land grows greener, while the shades of green, varied by the play of sunlight on the slopes and rolling hills, increase in number and intensity. Here the color is soft, and there bright; yonder it rolls in wavy alternations, and yonder it reaches in an unbroken shade where the plain sweeps broad and free. For many weeks green is the only color, though cold nights may, perhaps, tinge it with a rusty red. About the first of February a little star-like flower of bluish pink begins to shine along the ground. This is the bloom of the alfileria, and swiftly it spreads from the southern slopes, where it begins, and runs from meadow to hill-top. Soon after a cream-colored bell-flower begins to nod from a tall, slender stalk; another of sky-blue soon opens beside it; beneath these a little five-petaled flower of deep pink tries to outshine the blossoms of the alfileria; and above them soon stands the radiant shooting-star, with reflexed petals of white, yellow, and pink shining behind its purplish ovaries. On every side violets, here of the purest golden hue, and of overpowering fragrance, appear in numbers beyond all conception. And soon six or seven varieties of clover, all with fine delicate leaves, unfold flowers of yellow, red, and pink. Delicate little crucifers of white and yellow shine modestly below all these; little cream-colored flowers on slender scapes look skyward on every side; while others of purer white with every variety of petal crowd up among them. Standing now upon some hillside that commands miles of landscape, one is dazzled with a blaze of color, from acres and acres of pink, great fields of violets, vast reaches of blue, endless sweeps of white.

Upon this—merely the warp of the carpet about to cover the land—the sun fast weaves a woof of splendor. Along the southern slopes of the lower hills soon beams the orange light of the poppy, which swiftly kindles the adjacent slopes, then flames along the meadow, and blazes upon the northern hillsides. Spires of green, mounting on every side, soon open upon the top into lilies of deep lavender, and the scarlet bracts of the painted-cup glow side by side with the crimson of the cardinal-flower. And soon comes the iris, with its broad golden eye, fringed with rays of lavender blue, and five varieties of phacelia overwhelm some places with waves of purple, blue, indigo, and whitish pink. The evening primrose covers the lower slopes with long sheets of brightest yellow, and from the hills above, the rock-rose adds its golden bloom to that of the sorrel and the wild alfalfa, until the hills almost outshine the bright light from the slopes and plains. And through all this nods a tulip of most delicate lavender; vetches, lupins, and all the members of the wild-pea family are pushing and winding their way everywhere in every shade of crimson, purple, and white; along the ground the crow-foot weaves a mantle of white, through which, amid a thousand comrades, the orthocarpus rears its tufted head of pink. Among all these are mixed a thousand other flowers, plenty enough as plenty would be accounted in other countries, but here mere pinpoints on a great map of colors.

As the stranger gazes upon this carpet that now covers hill and dale, undulates over the table-lands, and robes even the mountain with a brilliancy and breadth of color that strikes the eye from miles away, he exhausts his vocabulary of superlatives, and goes away imagining he has seen it all. Yet he has seen only the background of an embroidery more varied, more curious and splendid, than the carpet upon which it is wrought. Asters bright with centre of gold and lavender rays soon shine high above the iris, and a new and larger tulip of deepest yellow nods where its lavender cousin is drooping its lately proud head. New bell-flowers of white and blue and indigo rise above the first, which served merely as ushers to the display, and whole acres ablaze with the orange of the poppy are fast turning with the indigo of the larkspur. Where the ground was lately aglow with the marigold and the four-o'clock the tall penstemon now reaches out a hundred arms full-hung with trumpets of purple and pink. Here the silence rears high its head with fringed corolla of scarlet; and there the wild gooseberry dazzles the eye with a perfect shower of tubular flowers of the same bright color. The mimulus alone is almost enough to color the hills. Half a dozen varieties, some with long, narrow, trumpet-shaped flowers, others with broad flaring mouths; some of them tall herbs, and others large shrubs, with varying shades of dark red, light red, orange, cream-color, and yellow, spangle hillside, rock-pile, and ravine. Among them the morning-glory twines with flowers of purest white, new lupins climb over the old ones, and the trailing vetch festoons rock and shrub and tree with long garlands of crimson, purple, and pink. Over the scarlet of the gooseberry or the gold of the highbush mimulus along the hills, the honeysuckle hangs its tubes of richest cream-color, and the wild cucumber pours a shower of white over the green leaves of the sumac or sage. Snap-dragons of blue and white, dandelions that you must look at three or four times to be certain what they are, thistles that are soft and tender with flowers too pretty for the thistle family, orchids that you may try in vain to classify, and sages and mints of which you can barely recognize the genera, with cruciferæ, compositæ, and what-not, add to the glare and confusion.

Meanwhile, the chaparral, which during the long dry season has robed the hills in somber green, begins to brighten with new life; new leaves adorn the ragged red arms of the manzanita, and among them blow thousands of little urn-shaped flowers of rose-color and white. The bright green of one lilac is almost lost in a luxuriance of sky-blue blossoms, and the white lilac looks at a distance as if drifted over with snow. The cercocarpus almost rivals the lilac in its display of white and blue, and the dark, forbidding adenostoma now showers forth dense panicles of little white flowers. Here, too, a new mimulus pours floods of yellow light, and high above them all the yucca rears its great plume of purple and white.

Thus marches on for weeks the floral procession, new turns bringing new banners into view, or casting on old ones a brighter light, but ever showing a riotous profusion of splendor until member after member drops gradually out of the ranks, and only a band of stragglers is left marching away into the summer. But myriads of ferns, twenty-one varieties of which are quite common, and of a fineness and delicacy rarely seen elsewhere, still stand green in the shade of the rocks and trees along the hills, and many a flower lingers in the timber or cañons long after its friends on the open hills or plains have faded away. In the cañons and timber are also many flowers that are not found in the open ground, and as late as the middle of September, only twenty miles from the sea, and at an elevation of but fifteen hundred feet, I have gathered bouquets that would attract immediate attention anywhere. The whole land abounds with flowers both curious and lovely; but those only have been mentioned which force themselves upon one's attention. Where the sheep have not ruined all beauty, and the rains have been sufficient, they take as full possession of the land as the daisy and wild carrot do of some Eastern meadows. There are thousands of others, which it would be a hopeless task to enumerate, which are even more numerous than most of the favorite wild flowers are in the East, yet they are not abundant enough to give character to the country. For instance, there is a great larkspur, six feet high, with a score of branching arms, all studded with spurred flowers of such brilliant red that it looks like a fountain of strontium-fire: but you will not see it every time you turn around. A tall lily grows in the same way, with a hundred golden flowers shining on its many arms, but it must be sought in certain places. So the tiger-lily and the columbine must be sought in the mountains, the rose and sweetbrier on low ground, the nightshades and the helianthus in the timbered cañons and gulches.

Delicacy and brilliancy characterize nearly all the California flowers, and nearly all are so strange, so different from the other members of their families, that they would be an ornament to any greenhouse.

The alfileria, for instance, is the richest and strongest fodder in the world. It is the mainstay of the stock-grower, and when raked up after drying makes excellent hay; yet it is a geranium, delicate and pretty, when not too rank.

But suddenly the full blaze of color is gone, and the summer is at hand. Brown tints begin to creep over the plains; the wild oats no longer ripple in silvery waves beneath the sun and wind; and the foxtail, that shone so brightly green along the hill-side, takes on a golden hue. The light-lavender tint of the chorizanthe now spreads along the hills where the poppy so lately flamed, and over the dead morning-glory the dodder weaves its orange floss. A vast army of cruciferæ and compositæ soon overruns the land with bright yellow, and numerous varieties of mint tinge it with blue or purple; but the greater portion of the annual vegetation is dead or dying. The distant peaks of granite now begin to glow at evening with a soft purple hue, the light poured into the deep ravines towards sundown floods them with a crimson mist; on the shady hill-sides the chaparral looks bluer, and on the sunny hill-sides is a brighter green than before.

The alfileria and the clovers that lately robed the plains now lie along the ground in a mat of brown hay mingled with nutritious seeds, the combination forming an unequaled fodder; and even the tallest annuals, like the mustard and the nettle, succumb to the influence of the season. Yet long after the rains have ceased and the sun rides high in the zenith the land is by no means as dreary and brown as one might suppose. The heteromeles stands brightly green along the hills the long long year, now drifted over with white blossoms, and in winter gay with clusters of red berries like the mountain-ash. The sumac, too, is green through the longest drought, and in June is all aglow with new leaves of reddish tinge, overwhelmed with white panicles also a little tinged with red. The wild buckwheat lights up whole hill-sides with a bloom similar in color to that of the sumac, and the white sage lifts its tall spires of grayish green, tasseled with a thousand flowers of city-milk blue. The great thorny arms of the cholla cactus are now adorned with flowers, the broad lobes of the prickly-pear are studded with large golden ones, while the smaller and smoother varieties rival the others with a profusion of large rose-like flowers of the deepest pink. Among the piles of granite the mimulus still stands with its trumpet-flowers of red or creamy pink; the ivy twines itself among them, and the live-oak spreads its broad green arms above them. The salt-grass, the mallow and the wire-grass keep the low meadows as green as ever, while near them the elder stands with its green leaves almost lost in snowy bloom. The wild rose and sweet-brier form dense thickets of solid green, and above them the grape-vine festoons the trees or overpowers them with its long shady arms. The sycamore, willow, cotton-wood, and other trees along the dry bed of the river are now full of lusty life. Even the dry sandy wastes are relieved by the bright pink of the abronia, the glistering leaves and whitish blossoms of the ice-plant, or the tall form of the *yerba mansa*; while from the cracks of the driest ledges of rock the cotyledon sends up its tall curving spike of chalky hue, full-hung on the under side with a fringe of long carmine trumpets.

There is nothing about autumn here that is at all saddening or sentimental. It is only the long-lingering afternoon of a long-lingering summer day. There are dreamy hazes and filmy atmospheres enough, but they are not at all peculiar to autumn. The spider occasionally weaves his thin shroud and the gossamer rides the air, dead leaves rustle to the rabbit's tread, the crow caws from the tree-top, the jay jangles and the quail pipes; but they have been doing it all summer, and, in truth, much of it in spring. It is a bad country for 'the singer' although one occasionally ventures 'a poem' in which no one without looking at the title could tell which season it described.

September brings no change along the rolling hills, except a little ashen tint upon the ramiria, and the chorizanthe, a paler brown upon the dodder that clambers over the chemical or buckwheat, a grayer shade upon the white sage and the dead phacelias, a grayer brown upon the plains and table-lands. Smiling from unclouded skies, the sun passes the central line, the nights grow a trifle cooler, the ocean breeze a trifle fresher; but instead of rain there is merely a drier air. The linnet and the mocking-bird are heard no more; the cooing of the dove sounds more seldom from the grove; the brooding call of the quail has ceased along the hills and sales, and the young coveys gather into large bands. The mimulus that has lingered long among the shady chinks of the granite piles begins to close its crimson bugles; the ivy that twines the oak above it shows a strong tinge of scarlet; the sand-verbena and other summer flowers begin to fade; the wild gourd ripens on the low grounds, and the meadows along the edge turn a trifle sere. But in nearly all else it is summer.

October comes, but the summer sun still rules the land. The low hills that are free from chaparral grow paler where the dead mustard, wild oats, clover, alfileria, and foxtail have so long lain bleaching. The *adenostoma* and *cercocarpus*, and other chaparral bushes, look perhaps a trifle weary; the green of the sumac and fusica is a little less bright than in July; the elder and the wild buckwheat look unmistakably worse for wear, and even the ever-vigorous cactus seems to think it has done full duty. But all these changes are very slight, and would scarcely be noticed by the casual observer. For the whole host of bushes and trees that cover the hills, the living grass that covers the moist lands, and the dead grass that carpets the plains, all wear the same general appearance as in July; while some plants, such as the golden-rod in the meadows, are just coming into bloom, and on the dry lands the *baccharis* is rearing its snowy plumes. Many days will now be cooler than most of the days of summer, hoar-frost will be found along the mountain valleys, some skies will be a little overcast, perhaps rain enough may fall to start the weather-prophets; but the whole will be soft and bright like the sunset hour of a lovely summer day.

November; yet no leaden skies; no sodden leaves on soaking ground; no snow-flakes riding on howling blasts; no sloughs of mud in the roads to-day and frozen hummocks to-morrow; no robin chirping out a dismal farewell high above one's head; no fish-ducks whistling down the icy margin of the pond where of late the mallard quacked; no sparrows sitting around with ruffled feathers. Only a little colder nights and shorter days; only a little frost along the bottoms of the valleys; only a stiller, drier air, often clearer than in summer, except where brush-fires make it thick or hazy. The evaporation being checked by the longer and cooler nights, the water rises in the springs and runs in places where two months ago was nothing but dry sand. The wild duck appears along the sloughs, the *honk* of the goose is heard again in its winter haunts, the bluebird and robin come down from the high mountains, and the turtle-dove almost disappears. The sycamore and cottonwood begin to look sere, the grape-vine leaves are yellowing, and the willows are fast fading. But in nearly all else it is still summer.

December comes at last, but few would suspect it. The nights are still colder, and the hoar-frost creeps higher up along the slopes of the valleys, and thin ice may form at daylight on some of the lowest grounds. Yet the days are nearly like those of summer, though the sea-breeze is almost gone, and the wind comes often from the north and east. The berries of the manzanita are now black and shining; the heteromeles is aglow with scarlet clusters; the golden-rod that lately blazed along the meadows is grown gray and fuzzy; the accords patter on the roof beneath the spreading live-oak; the plains look a little grayer, the table-lands a little browner. But the grand old oaks, the sumacs, the lilac, the fusica, manzanita, *madroña*,—all the chaparral bushes, in fact,—are very nearly as green as ever. We might as well call the whole of it summer, for it is only summer a little worn out.

'How fearfully monotonous all that must be!' remarks one who has never passed through it. 'I like something positive, some distinctive features about the seasons. It is so pleasant to sit by the fire and hear the snow-storm howl without; sleigh-riding is so delightful, skating is such a luxury! And then the winter air is so bracing and sends the pulse bounding, and makes the cheek glow with health!'

To which it might be replied: There are some things that are not always objectionable even when monotonous; such things as health and wealth, for instance. It is possible that such things appear monotonous to those who do not possess them; and also possible that after a thorough trial of them they might change their opinion of them. One who has never spent an autumn outside of an umbrella or an overcoat, and all whose winters have been largely spent sitting by the fire and listening to the raging of the storm without, is hardly a competent judge compared with one who has given both sides of the case a fair trial, as have most of the residents of California. At all events, there is always one resource for any one whom such monotony troubles,—to return to the East and try once more those good old days by the fire. Few ever stay East long enough to test them again thoroughly, and from those that do 'monotony' is the last complaint ever heard after their return to California.

Glimpses of California

REVEREND WALTER COLTON

In the following extracts from his journal Three Years in California *(1850), Reverend Walter Colton gives an intimate and detailed account of his impressions of the people, towns and countryside of California.*

SATURDAY, MARCH 6.

I have never been in a community that rivals Monterey in its spirit of hospitality and generous regard. Such is the welcome to the privileges of the private hearth, that a public hotel has never been able to maintain itself. You are not expected to wait for a particular invitation, but to come without the slightest ceremony, make yourself entirely at home, and tarry as long as it suits your inclination, be it for a day or for a month. You create no flutter in the family, awaken no apologies, and are greeted every morning with the same bright smile. It is not a smile which flits over the countenance, and passes away like a flake of moonlight over a marble tablet. It is the steady sunshine of the soul within.

If a stranger, you are not expected to bring a formal letter of introduction. No one here thinks any the better of a man who carries the credentials of his character and standing in his pocket. A word or an allusion to recognized persons or places is sufficient. If you turn out to be different from what your first impressions and fair speech promised, still you meet with no frowning looks, no impatience for your departure. You still enjoy in full that charity which suffereth long, and is kind. The children are never told that you are a burden; you enjoy their glad greetings and unsuspecting confidence to the last. And when you finally depart, it will not be without a benison; not perhaps that you are worthy of it; but you belong to the great human family, where faults often spring from misfortune, and the force of untoward circumstances. Generous, forbearing people of Monterey! there is more true hospitality in one throb of your heart, than circulates for years through the courts and capital of kings.

THURSDAY, OCT. 28.

The king of all field-sports in California is the bear-hunt: I determined to witness one, and for this purpose joined a company of native gentlemen bound out on this wild amusement. All were well mounted, armed with rifles and pistols, and provided with lassoes. A ride of fifteen miles among the mountain crags, which frown in stern wildness over the tranquil beauty of Monterey, brought us to a deserted shanty, in the midst of a gloomy forest of cypress and oak. In a break of this swinging gloom lay a natural pasture, isled in the centre by a copse of willows and birch, and on which the sunlight fell. This, it was decided, should be the arena of the sport: a wild bullock was now shot, and the quarters, after being trailed around the copse, to scent the bear, were deposited in its shade. The party now retired to the shanty, where our henchman tumbled from his panniers several rolls of bread, a boiled ham, and a few bottles of London porter. These discussed, and our horses tethered, each wrapped himself in his blanket, and with his saddle for his pillow, rolled down for repose.

At about twelve o'clock of the night our watch came into camp and informed us that a bear had just entered the copse. In an instant each sprung to his feet and into the saddle. It was a still, cloudless night, and the moonlight lay in sheets on rivulet, rock, and plain. We proceeded with a cautious, noiseless step, through the moist grass of the pasture to the copse in its centre, where each one took his station, forming a cordon around the little grove. The horse was the first to discover, through the glimmering shade, the stealthful movements of his antagonist. His ears were thrown forward, his nostrils distended, his breathing became heavy and oppressed, and his large eye was fixed immovable on the dim form of the savage animal. Each rider now uncoiled his lasso from its loggerhead, and held it ready to spring from his hand, like a hooped serpent from the brake. The bear soon discovered the trap that had been laid for him; plunged from the thicket, broke through the cordon, and was leaping, with giant bounds, over the cleared plot for the dark covert of the forest beyond. A shout arose—a hot pursuit followed, and lasso after lasso fell in curving lines around the bear, till at last one looped him around the neck and brought him to a momentary stand.

As soon as bruin felt the lasso, he growled his defiant thunder, and sprung in rage at the horse. Here came in the sagacity of that noble animal. He knew, as well as his rider, that the safety of both depended on his keeping the lasso taught, and without the admonitions or rein or spur, bounded this way and that, to the front or rear, to accomplish his object, never once taking his eye from the ferocious foe, and ever in an attitude to foil his assaults. The bear, in desperation, seized the lasso in his griping paws, and hand over hand drew it into his teeth: a moment more and he would have been within leaping distance of his victim; but the horse sprung at the instant, and, with a sudden whirl, tripped the bear and extricated the lasso. At this crowning feat the horse fairly danced with delight. A shout went up which seemed to shake the wild-wood with its echoes. The bear plunged again, when the lasso slipped from its loggerhead, and bruin was instantly leaping over the field to reach his jungle. The horse, without spur or rein, dashed after him. While his rider, throwing himself over his side, and hanging there like a lampereel to a flying sturgeon, recovered his lasso, bruin was brought up again all standing, more frantic and furious than before; while the horse pranced and curveted around him like a savage in his death-dance over his doomed captive. In all this no overpowering torture was inflicted on old bruin, unless it were through his own rage,—which sometimes towers so high he drops dead at your feet. He was now lassoed to a sturdy oak, and wound so closely to its body by riata over riata, as to leave him no scope for breaking or grinding off his clankless chain; though his struggles were often terrific as those of Laocoon, in the resistless folds of the serpent.

This accomplished, the company retired again to the shanty, but in spirits too high and noisy for sleep. Day glimmered, and four of the baccaros started off for a wild bull, which they lassoed out of a roving herd, and a few hours brought into camp, as full of fury as the bear. Bruin was now cautiously unwound, and stood front to front with his horned antagonist. We retreated on our horses to the rim of a large circle, leaving the arena to the two monarchs of the forest and field. Conjectures went wildly round on the issue, and the excitement became momently more intense. They stood motionless, as if lost in wonder and indignant astonishment at this strange encounter. Neither turned from the other his blazing eyes; while menace and defiance began to lower in the looks of each. Gathering their full strength, the terrific rush was made: the bull missed, when the bear, with one enormous bound, dashed his teeth into his back to break the spine; the bull fell, but whirled his huge horn deep into the side of his antagonist. There they lay, grappled and gored; in their convulsive struggles and death-throes. We spurred up, and with our rifles and pistols closed the tragedy; and it was time; this last scene was too full of blind rage and madness even for the wild sports of a California bear-hunt.

MONDAY, FEB. 7.

The rains in California are mostly confined to the three winter months—a few showers may come before, or a few occur after, but the body of the rain falls within that period. The rain is relieved of nearly all the chilling discomforts of a winter's storm in other climes; it falls only when the wind is from a southern quarter, and is consequently warm and refreshing. It is by no means continuous; it pays its visits like a judicious lover—with intervals sufficient to keep up the affection; and like the suitor, brings with it flowers, and leads the fair one by the side of streamlets never wrinkled with frost, and into groves where the leaf never withers, and where the songs of birds ever fill the warbling air.

MONDAY, SEPT. 25

San José is sixty-five miles from Monterey, and stands in the centre of a spacious valley which opens on the great bay of San Francisco.

It is cultivated only in spots, but the immense yield in these is sufficient evidence of what the valley is capable. A plough and harrow, at which a New England crow would laugh, are followed by fields of waving grain. Within this valley lie the rich lands of Com. Stockton, and they will yet feel the force of his vivifying enterprise. The mission buildings of Santa Clara lift their huge proportions on the eye. The bells that swing in their towers are silent, but they will yet find a tongue and fill the cliffs with their glad echoes. The Anglo-Saxon blood will yet roll here as if in its first leap.

Such are the representations of the roads between this and the mines, that we have concluded to part with our wagon and pack our mules. Mr Botts, one of our companions, has received intelligence which requires his return to Monterey. We must proceed without his agreeable society. Wm. Stewart, Esq., secretary of Com. Jones, and Lieut. Simmons of the Ohio, have just arrived on their way to the mines. Two of our mules were now packed, the third mounted by our wagoner, and the fourth driven, to guard against contingencies. Thus equipped, we started again for the mines; but we had hardly cleared the town when one of our mules took fright, plunged over the plain, burst his girth, and scattered on the winds the contents of his pack. Capt. Marcy and Mr Willkinson, with the mules and their driver, returned into town to repack, and I proceeded on in the company of Mr Stewart and Lieut. Simmons.

We passed the mission of San José, which stands three leagues from the town. The massive proportions of the church lay in shadow, but the crowning cross was lit with the rays of the descending sun. No hum of busy streets or jocund voice of childhood saluted the ear. No eye regarded us but that of the owl gazing in wise wonder from his ivy tower. He seemed to marvel at the vanity that had brought us here; and as we hurried past on our gold destination, sent after us an ominous hoot! The purple twilight was settling fast when we reached a stream singing along between the slopes of two hills. Here we camped for the night. The grass was scanty and the ground uneven, but it was now too late to look for other spots. The dry willows, which skirted the stream, furnished us with fuel. The lid of our coffee kettle was soon trembling over the steam, while the fresh steaks, curling on the coals, scented the evening air. Our supper over, we talked of friends far away, and spread our blankets for the night. The ground was so descending I put a stone at my feet to keep from slipping down, but must have rolled from my pedestal, for on awaking at daybreak, I found myself at the foot of the slope, and close on the verge of the bubbling stream. My ground-blanket remained where it had been spread, though it seemed higher up the hill, as I clambered back to it from my somnambulic roll.

WEDNESDAY, NOV. 15.

Another day had dawned fresh and brilliant; we breakfasted with our friends, who ordered up their horses, and started with us for Stockton, twelve miles distant. Our lady hostess and myself led off; she had crossed the Rocky Mountains on horseback into California, and was, of course, at home in the saddle. She was mounted on a spirited animal, and my little Indian almost blew the wind out of him to keep up. My companion, though accomplished in all the refinements of metropolitan life, was yet in love with the wild scenes in which her lot had been cast. The rose of health blushed in her cheek, and the light of a salient soul revelled in her eye. 'I would not exchange' she said, 'my cabin for any palace in Christendom. I have all that I want here, and what more could I have elsewhere? I have tried luxury without health, and a wild mountain life with it. Give me the latter, with the free air, the dashing streams, the swinging woods, the laughing flowers, and the exulting birds; and

> ''Let him who crawls enamored of decay,
> Cling to his couch, and sicken years away.'' '

Nevada

HENRY BRAINARD KENT

In this extract from Graphic Sketches of the West
*(1890), Henry Brainard Kent describes the magnificence
of the Yosemite Valley and its surroundings.*

THERE IS ONLY one Yosemite Valley, and only one trip to this enchanted
reserve ever made exactly after the fashion of the one in which the
writer was implicated.

My associates in this excursion among the Sierras were an Ohio real
estate operator (who has lately removed to California), the private secretary of an eminent New York official, and a Chicago merchant. These,
whom I have already alluded to, have constituted the *dramatis personae*
in a number of successful exploits here on the Pacific coast. Knowing,
from common report, that the wonders of the Yosemite are more or

less overpowering in their nature, and reasoning that four would offer more resistance than one, it was only fair to suppose that the shock to our sensibilities would be proportionately lessened by being thus distributed over this increased amount of surface. If *one* couldn't stand it, *four* surely could. So we decided to form another league, forgetful of past aggrievances. Organizing as the 'California Mutual Protective Alliance for Resisting the Overpowering Effects of Wild Flourishes of Natural Scenery' we set out prepared for any emergency. Conscious of the newly-created powers with which we had become vested by our corporate name, we bade adieu to the 'City of the Queen of Angels' to which we had but recently returned from the coast, and the Southland to which we had become more or less endeared, and with good courage pushed northward by the Southern Pacific Railway through the cheerful San Fernando valley. Crossing the desolate Mojave desert near the dry lakes, where in the vegetable world, juniper and bunch-grass, dwarf cedar, greecewood and the Yucca palm hold undisputed sway, we entered the Tehachepi mountains in high colors. Swinging around the famous 'Loop' among chaparral-crowned hills and gypsum ridges, and witnessing the most wonderful feats of engineering in the State, we soon reached the great valley of the San Joaquin.

Making short stop-offs at Bakersfield, the capital of Kern county, and Fresno, the center of the raisin-making industry, we gathered some useful information respecting the business interests and mode of life in these places. In our drives into the country we found something worthy of comment in the vast fields of alfalfa and grain, the thousands of sheep grazing on hillsides and 'hog-wallows' and the sleek herds of horses and cattle roving on the plains.

The ubiquitous jack-rabbit, too, is here—more abounding, in fact, than in the south—to the grief of the ranchman and hardly to the joy of the sportsman, since they are really too plenty to make the chase exciting. The inhabitants have resorted to various devices to exterminate this persistent race of mischief-makers, a common method being to steal upon them in an oxcart bearing heavy musketry. While this mode is not according to the golden rule, it is very effectual in weakening the ranks of these deluded lightfoots, who, shy of men, are on familiar terms with roving herds and moving vehicles. Formerly this method was much in vogue, the booty thus secured being shipped to the city markets. Rabbit drives are now more approved. By this plan neighborhoods turn out *en masse* and pursue the pests from all quarters of the horizon into a large corral built to receive them—the pursuers hemming them in and slaughtering them by the hundreds, or perhaps thousands.

Leaving Fresno and vicinity we resumed our northward movements toward the point of departure for the Yosemite. This was an interesting ride through the San Joaquin, presenting, as it did, phases differing in important respects from anything yet seen. Everything seems to be numbered by the thousand here. The ranches contain thousands of acres; sheep and cattle are herded by the thousand; thousands of geese and rabbits and cranes prey upon the crops. But what engaged our interest most were the thousand snow-clad peaks of the Sierras, looking up before us with lordly airs and warning us of the mysteries on exhibition over beyond.

At a small station some one hundred miles from the famous valley we disembarked and secured a livery, having decided upon this means of transit to secure greater freedom in our movements. Besides, the Ohio capitalist's southern real estate having taken a set-back during the past year or two, the rest of the party felt it to be an imperative duty to reprove his customary extravagance and teach him a lesson in economy. To this end we diligently inquired of the German hostler of whom we procured our conveyance, how much this trip would set us back financially. The attending stable boy having interpreted our interrogatories to 'Cousin Michael' the latter responded in true German style:

'Vell, I toldt you all aboudt how it vas. Wie lang bist du in dose Yosemi-tees?'

'O, we want to be gone about ten days.'

'Vell. I vill tell you boudt dot. I make it sheap, genook. Ven you get pack I tole you all about dot price.'

After insisting upon knowing the price before we started, 'Mynheer Closh' finally yields to our demands and says:

'I will make dose oxpenses sheap mit you—I scharge you noor foonf-sick tollars.'

Having about two hundred miles to drive among the hills and mountains we could not go amiss on this price and so without chaffering agreed to pay 'Mynheer' the fifty dollars for his best rig. The latter, pleased that the bargain was consummated, at this point threw in a little free advice with the evident purpose of giving us the full worth of our money.

'I tole you sumdings vot safe you oxpenses undt I vill tole you dot mitoudt scharging nottings' continued clever 'Closh.' 'Dose rates mit dem Yosemite hotels vas four tollar ein day, aber you make him sheaper some ven you dond't put too much shytle on already yet.'

'How's that?'

'Vell, I tole you how it comes aboudt. Dose hotel fellers puts the price vay *oop* to fellers mit shtyle on, undt vay *down* to fellers mitout der shtyle.'

I, for one, being in for economy skirmished around and secured a slouch hat, which, after considerable heated discussion on the part of my comrades, was decided to be a trifle worse than the one I discarded. I tried persistently, but in vain, to induce the rest of the company to follow my example, arguing earnestly and logically that this change in the habiliments of my upper story would save the company at least eight dollars a day on board, and probably not less than one dollar and fifty cents a bushel on oats; and that if they would do as I had done this reduction would be perceptibly larger. I especially insisted that the Ohio real estate operator should, in view of his depreciated city lots, be consistent and lower the standard of his wearing apparel. But all logic was in vain. Each one declared that I had already lowered the standard of dress at least ninety per cent. for the whole party, and that if any reduction of rates were to be had on this basis my slouch hat would secure them. But time was passing, and I succumbed to the decision of the majority, waving my plea for dress reform, conscious of having made enough objections to the course of my opponents to place them on the defensive should anything betide us. After taking these advisable precautions I thus allowed the 'deadlock' which was clogging the wheels of progress, to be broken, having become thoroughly ingratiated into the affections of my bucolic constituency.

We then started off under a favorable sky toward the mountains, all divergences of opinion being either reconciled or tolerated. We were, at least, all harmonious on one point, and that was: to reach the valley. Rain, shine or earthquake, we were bound for the far-famed Yosemite. How we did fly! Over hills, down into the valleys, up the mountains, away into the heart of the Sierras.

Space will not admit of a detailed account of the first two days' drive. In general, however, it may be said that much that was instructive delighted both eye and ear, and equally as much that was entertaining proved highly edifying. Here were sheep and cattle feeding upon a thousand hills. Here were variously colored rocks strewed along the vales and crowning the hill-tops. Here were abandoned shafts and forsaken mining camps. Here, too, was the long flume for rafting lumber, winding like a gargantuan boa around the mountain peaks for many miles. At Grub Gulch (a name dear to the heart of the average prospector since tradition has it that he could make his 'grub' here when he failed everywhere else) there were a number of mines in successful operation. These we duly visited, taking away with us several desirable specimens of gold ore. We also encountered deer en route and several other denizens of the forest to which we found difficulty in affixing the appropriate names. While referring to game it is also worthy to note the profusion of pigeons and quails inhabiting the foot-hills. At least ten thousand of these, started by the sound of our flying wheels, encountered our path within shooting range—enough, properly served up, to have stood the priests of Israel over Sunday in the wilderness, or, if served up according to modern formula, to have made soup for Xenophon and his army of ten thousand during the period of their retreat—one barrel of the emulsion to each soldier. Bagging a few of these tender-loined bipeds, I endeavored to persuade my swell partners to 'rough it' and cook our own game in genuine camp style. But there was no use in trying to force lessons of economy upon my flush attendants. They were opposed to anything which might soil their knee-buckles and so the quails were ordered served up on toast at the tavern.

But without detailing these and similar episodes of the journey, suffice it to say that we were, during this part of the trip, elated, benighted, snowed on, hailed and thundered at by turns. On one occasion Jupiter Pluvius, after smashing up our umbrellas in a violent gale, turned the hose on the whole crowd. But still we sped on like pursued road-runners until after two days of eventful sight-seeing, fusillading and crack driving among the pine-studded heights of the Sierras, we arrived at Big Tree Station, about two-thirds of the distance in the valley. Here we put up for the night, having stopped the first night at Grab Gulch.

Big Tree Station is on the Yosemite Reserve. So now we had to deal with the government and pay government prices. I knew the schedule rates to be four dollars a day, but in view of 'Mynheer's' friendly admonitions in regard to style it was only fair to conclude that I was entitled to 'cut rates'. So, after a good night's rest and an ample breakfast, all feeling in good spirits for another day's drive, I ordered our rig and stepped up to the office to pay the bill. Pulling the slouch hat well down on to my head and twisting my necktie askew over the collar I struck an attitude and enquired, in true western phraseology, as to the amount of tax the government proposed to levy on me and my 'pards.'

'Supper, lodging and breakfast for four—and horse feed, fifteen dollars sir' was the consoling reply.

Being assured that this included tooth-picks and all, I paid the bill like a lord, knowing this to be the regular rate to tourists, and that it was futile to persist in trying to convey the impression of poverty with the Ohio capitalist and his plug hat looming up in our midst. It was equally preposterous to think of posing as local patronage with our names registered from three different states. We were here at about the same altitude as the Yosemite, but must overcome one thousand six hundred feet to reach it. We were good for this, and so boarding our barouche courageously dashed away into the interminable depths of forest before us. I now used all the power of persuasion I could muster to induce my co-travelers to smash in the tops of their stiff hats, arguing that it would save many times the value of their head-gear in the cost of living. But all rhetoric was in vain. The nabobs recklessly persisted in preserving the original shapes of their skull-protectors thus compelling me to unjustly share the loss which must ensue as a logical sequence of their pig-headedness. But never mind, Rome wasn't reformed in a day.

Crack! goes the rattan, and onward we speed through forests of pine, cedar and redwood. Away we fly over dizzy heights, along precipitous banks, down one hill and up two, until we reach the summit. Here we took dinner at a trapper's, there being no hotel between Big Trees and the Yosemite.

During our repast we learned something of the peculiar life of this solitude. Among other interesting incidents of the place, there was once a herd of deer roving about in these mountain wilds, that made it a part of the daily programme to visit the old cabin on the summit. Having here received their usual allowance of salt and regaled their appetites at the festive slop-pail, they returned to their mountain fastnesses, seemingly satisfied with the bill of fare provided by their good-natured host. These, too, were the feelings which we entertained, as we took our leave and sped away down the heights along a precipitous trail toward the valley. After advancing several miles we reached an opening in the almost interminable forest, whence our eyes were greeted by another beautiful panorama of mountain scenery. Beyond the deep, picturesque gorge, on the verge of which the mountain roadway extends for several miles, could be seen hills and mountains rolling away, one above another, far in the distance, and even the Coast Range, at least a hundred miles to the west, standing in dim outline against the sky. But behold! What is this! All at once we reach the height overlooking the valley. A sign-board discloses the fact that we are on the Peak of Inspiration. It is, however, a precipice rather than a peak. But in the matter of inspiration there could be no question, as the Yosemite unfolded its robes of matchless beauty before us.

Here, facing us from the opposite side of the valley, is a huge promontory of granite, having smooth, polished sides, handsomely striped with peculiar tints of light and shade, and rising to the height of fifteen Bunker Hill monuments or seven of Egypt's highest pyramids. This we at once recognized as the El Capitan of which Prof. Whitney wrote: 'It is doubtful if anywhere in the world is presented so squarely cut, so lofty and so imposing a face of rock.' As we stand looking in wonder at this massive pile, a beautiful silvery cloud settles down upon its summit and presents, in the light of the sinking sun, a halo of indescribable beauty crowning the 'great chief of the valley.' Descending along a tortuous trail in the form of a winding stair-case, we soon cross the path of the 'rock avalanche' that recently tore up trees, breaking them into fragments and creating the wildest imaginable scene of destruction. As we reach Pohono bridge, at the foot of the trail, the beautiful Bridal Veil appears in full glory, sifting its waters over a precipice nearly one thousand feet above the valley. In falling, it breaks into a shower of mist that is so deflected by currents of air as to present the appearance of a white silken veil tossed in the wind. On the opposite side of the valley the Ribbon or Virgin Tears Fall plunges, in a slender stream, over the head of El Capitan and breaks into a mist that, to all appearances, loses itself in the air before it has completed a third of its journey. The upper part of this miniature fall being obscured by the nebulous halo resting on El Capitan, the novel spectacle is presented of a delicate cascade falling directly from the clouds.

Three massive monoliths, called the Three Brothers, now rise up before us—the highest six hundred feet above El Capitan. Now Cathedral Rock and its two graceful spires loom into view, reaching heights before which Trinity and St Patrick's would appear like pigmies in the presence of Hercules. Anon 'The Sentinel' appears—a colossal granite obelisk perched upon an eminence two thousand feet above the valley, and rising above this fifteen times the height of Cleopatra's needle. Wonder follows upon wonder, and all at once the Yosemite Falls breaks into full view, facing the giant Sentinel and pouring its restless, roaring waters over a precipice half a mile above our heads or more than sixteen times the height of Niagara. The highest portion of its white, feathery column is soon enveloped in a cumbrous cloud of mist, and again we have the marvelous sight of a cataract falling directly from the heavens.

Reaching the old Yosemite Valley House, shortly before dark we enjoyed from its historic veranda a fine view of the Yosemite falls, pouring over a precipice two thousand five hundred and forty-eight feet above the valley, the precipice being about a thousand feet below the tops of the ledges enclosing it. The valley itself is about four thousand feet above the sea and enclosed by nearly perpendicular walls as much higher.

The Duke of Sutherland, who visited the valley, a few years ago, said: 'The Yosemite spoils one for any other scenery upon earth.' According to this, the writer and his comrades spent several days deliberately and perseveringly spoiling themselves for the average attractions of this earth.

In our perambulations the day following our arrival we passed the old Hutchins cabin with which so many historical events pertaining to the opening of the valley are associated. Here are still to be seen the ancient cooking stove, the dilapidated chairs and broken crockery that did such commendable service' in the days that are gone.' Beyond this, a short distance, we reached the base of the lower Yosemite fall, in approaching which were encountered the wind currents produced by the falling waters. These swept upward under umbrellas and outer garments in the form of a baptismal spray that was most effective. A brief encampment before the cheerful fire-place at the hotel, however, removed any inconveniences we might suffer from this source, and after dinner we were prepared to continue our explorations.

These consisted chiefly of a twenty-mile drive about the valley, including the trip to the cascades, some eight miles down the river. In this direction we were confronted by numberless massive rocks, weighing hundreds of tons, and scattered promiscuously along the banks of the river for several miles. These were perched up in all manner of perilous attitudes, many of them being piled one above another in tumble down positions—here overhanging the roadways and there set up on end some distance above us, freighted with disaster. We know full well that others by thousands had made the tour of the valley unharmed and all reason seemed to indicate that the chances of getting through alive were in our favor. It was, nevertheless, impossible to dispel the conviction that these mountain-sized rocks, so insecurely poised above us, would come tearing down the declivities and put an end to our recreations. Occasionally one of these does actually lose its anchorage and the devastating result is frightful. While nothing could be more fear-inspiring than this journey down the river, few sights could be better calculated to excite wonder than the return trip. In the latter the attention is somewhat withdrawn from those threatening boulders and directed to the imposing wall of masonry, half a mile high, that hems in the valley on both sides, and over the rim or summit of which numerous cascades fall in picturesque beauty.

Here the wildest and most fairy-like scenes break upon the vision. The day we made the trip in this direction nature seemed to have on her high-heeled shoes, and was in all respects dressed as if for some special occasion. The massive granite walls of the valley seemed larger and larger the more minutely they were scanned, and after we had advanced a short distance the very heavens fell in the form of descending clouds, here resting uponthe rocky walls of the valley and in places falling far below into the valley itself. Trees and mountain peaks, three thousand feet above us, appeared through rifts in the clouds, as if standing isolated and alone in the clear sky. Scores of delicate cascades were, for all our senses could discover, falling directly from heaven and everywhere the goddess of enchantment held undisputed sway.

The next day we ordered our rig at an early hour and proceeded to explore the valley in the opposite direction, or up the river. Some two miles above the hotels we found the Merced divided into three branches, which retreat in the form of rocky cañons into the mysterious wilds of the Sierras. To trace these cañons up towards their sources was our purpose.

Beginning at the left branch, called the Tenaya Fork, we drove over a meandering road two miles up the cañon. Of the highway itself little can be said except that it failed to keep the same point of compass or level for any considerable distance. But for all this it faithfully performed its office in bringing us to the small but charming sheet of water that lay so snugly ensconced among the mountains at its terminus. This is the much-talked-of Mirror Lake, in whose silver waters are reflected mountain peaks that rise abruptly from its margin nearly a mile high. We were especially fortunate in the time selected for viewing this phenomenon. The sun, just rising over South Dome, Mount Watkins and other tree-studded peaks, as seen reflected in the smooth surface of the lake, all combined to produce a sublime effect. Just over the lake a curious conformation of outlines and peculiar blending of colors unite to form two novel pictures on the adjacent rocks—the one resembling white garments suspended on a clothes-line, and the other a woman's head. The latter is called the 'Goddess of the Valley.'

Returning to the forks of the river and omitting the ascent of the Illi-louette or southwest fork, whose chief object of interest—the Illilouette Falls—is visible from a point on the main branch, we dismount and proceed on foot up the Nevada trail. This winds along the banks of the main river and affords many charming views *en route* to the more noted points of interest five miles up the trail. A persevering climb of three miles brings us to Register Rock, near which a good view is obtained of Vernal Falls. Continuing the ascent over rocks and crags and amid a galaxy of wondrous sights and sounds, we soon pass through the mists of the falls, climb 'The Ladder' and at last reach the precipice over which the waters of the Merced fall three hundred and fifty feet. Fortune favors the fearless, and here, projecting out from among the rocks above, we espy the hospitable roof of Snow's Hotel, the supplies of which are brought on horseback over a precipitous bridle path five miles in length.

After renewing our drooping energies at this mountain refectory, we proceeded to the precipice overlooking Vernal Falls. Here we find ourselves in one of Nature's grandest temples—hemmed in on all sides by an amphitheatre which has probably no parallel on the continent, if anywhere in the world. A monstrous flat rock, perhaps an eighth of a mile long and half as wide, forms a spacious rostrum over which the observer may wander at pleasure. Another, similar to this, only turned up on end, rises hundreds of feet out of the depths, protruding just far enough above the horizontal one to form a secure breastwork along the edge of the precipice. One is thus enabled to approach to the very brink of the falls without peril. The praises of Yosemite are variously sung as seen from Inspiration and Glacier Point, at the foot of Bridal Veil and the summit of Sentinel Dome and Eagle Peak: but if comparisons are in order amid a host of wonderful sights, all of which seem a consummation of crowning glories, this part of the valley surely deserves the palm as presenting the beau island of true loveliness in nature combined with awful sublimity. The ample collation provided our company by the considerate old gentleman who presides over this sequestered inn, so remote from human habitation, certainly could not account for the favorable impression produced by the environments of the place.

At the right the Merced River glides noiselessly along its unruffled bed and suddenly hurls its full volume of water over the precipice at your feet and far down into the abyss before your eyes. But before it is fairly lodged in these mysterious depths, it throws out a cloud of mist that is borne hundreds of feet into the air by ascending currents, presenting a continual succession of rainbows to the observer standing in the sunlight below. No sooner are these waters marshalled into their channel than they plunge violently down their ragged bed, dashing among rocks and roots, and broken trunks of hemlock and fir, here breaking into feathery shafts and there shooting perpendicularly into the air, boiling, seething and glancing in the sunlight. On either side of this restless flood nearly perpendicular walls of granite rise to the height of three or four thousand feet, and present a beautiful combination of colors. Directly in front, rising over three thousand feet above the valley, is a beautiful triangular glacis crowned with evergreens. In this direction Grizzly Peak and Glacier Point loom up in grand proportions. The waters dash and roar on every side, and a train of other sights and sounds falls upon eye and ear, bewildering sense and leading the mind away from self to a consciousness of higher powers that seem to preside over the place.

Turning to the rear and looking up the river, a view no less enchanting greets the eye. Here the Nevada Falls, also containing the entire volume of the main river, show their white flashing waters as they shoot downward seven hundred feet to the river bed below. Here, gathering themselves within their wonted channel, they dash furiously down among the rocks, forming the beautiful Diamond Cascades. Thence spreading out over the surface of a spacious, flat rock, they flow on as composedly as if nothing had happened, serenely collecting themselves at your side, into a miniature crystal lake. Here, resting a moment, as it were, they make the second mad plunge over the Vernal precipice just described.

From this outlook the more distant view is no less inspiring. South Dome shows his snowy summit a mile above the valley. Mount Broderick lifts heavenward his imperious head, and Starr King triumphantly displays his pine-crowned temples nine thousand feet above the sea. Near by is the Cap of Liberty, standing forth like a guardian of the centuries, raising his mighty granite shaft above us more than ten times the height of the dome of the capitol at Washington.

But here I might as well surrender at discretion. To attempt to convey an adequate conception of these wonderful manifestations, or as some call them 'marvelous freaks' would be presumption. To describe them in detail would be to describe the kaleidoscopic scenes of an ever-shifting panorama. The constant wonder is that the same object of interest impresses the observer so differently at different times. This was especially noticeable on our return from the upper portion of the valley. The three domes, Grizzly and Glacier peaks, Illilouette Falls and the splashing, glistening waters of the Merced all assumed a new garb of glory in the light of the setting sun. Washington Column and North Dome posed in spectral colors, new and strange and the Royal Arches assumed fantastic phases which favored the superstition that we were about to enter the mystic confines of a Druid temple. The summit of the half dome was isolated from its granite pedestal by an ascending cloud, and thus made to appear like the inverted hulk a foundered ship drifting at sea.

The observer at Yosemite is the happy victim of constant surprise. He stands before El Capitan in mute astonishment, contemplating the stupendous proportions of a single granite rock two miles long and two-thirds of a mile high. He sees the great monolithic giants of the earth here resurrected from the sepulchre of the ages, standing mute sentinels before the empyrean heights, guarding, as it were, the gates of Paradise. He hears the deep intonations of surging floods at his feet and the weird music of clashing waters half a mile above his head. He catches the mystic notes, sung by miniature cascades high in the clouds and listens in rapt wonder, as they blend their choral voices with the winds of heaven, chanting wild anthems to the granite hosts, that stand from age to age, unwearied listeners to their ceaseless rhapsodies. But where shall we stop in describing Yosemite? Niagara herself throws up the white flag in attempting to rival it and so must every writer who attempts to describe it.

A Canadian Tour

CHARLES DUDLEY WARNER

The following extract from Charles Dudley Warner's
Studies in the South and West (1890), *chronicles his*
journey across Canada from Montreal to Vancouver.

WE LEFT MONTREAL attached to the regular train, on the evening of September 22nd. The company runs six through trains a week, omitting the despatch of a train on Sunday from each terminus. The time is six days and five nights. We travelled in the private car of Mr T. G. Shaughnessy, the manager, who was on a tour of inspection, and took it leisurely, stopping at points of interest on the way. The weather was bad, rainy and cold, in eastern Canada, as it was all over New England, and as it continued to be through September and October. During our absence there was snow both in Montreal and Quebec. We passed out of the rain into lovely weather north of Lake Superior; encountered rain again at Winnipeg; but a hundred miles west of there, on the prairie, we were blessed with as delightful weather as the globe can furnish, which continued all through the remainder of the trip until our return to Montreal, October 12th. The climate just east of the Rocky Mountains was a little warmer than was needed for comfort (at the time Ontario and Quebec had snow), but the air was always pure and exhilarating; and all through the mountains we had the perfection of lovely days. On the pacific it was still the dry season, though the autumn rains, which continue all winter, with scarcely any snow, were not far off. For mere physical pleasure of living and breathing, I know no atmosphere to that we encountered on the rolling lands east of the Rockies.

Between Ottawa and Winnipeg (from midnight of the 22nd till the morning of the 25th) there is not much to interest the tourist, unless he is engaged in lumbering or mining. What we saw was mainly a monotonous wilderness of rocks and small poplars though the country has agricultural capacities after leaving Rat Portage (north of Lake of the Woods), just before coming upon the Manitoba prairies. There were more new villages and greater crowds of people at the stations than I expected. From Sudbury the company runs a line to the Sault Sainte Marie to connect with lines it controls to Duluth and St Paul. At Port Arthur and Fort William is evidence of great transportation activity, and all along the Lake Superior Division there are signs that the expectations of profitable business in lumber and minerals will be realized. At Port Arthur we strike the Western Division. On the Western, Mountain, and Pacific divisions, the company has adopted the 24 hour system, by which A.M. and P.M. are abolished, and the hours from noon till midnight are counted as from 12 to 24 o'clock. For instance, the train reaches Eagle River at 24.55, Winnipeg at 9.30, and Brandon at 16.10.

At Winnipeg we come into the real North-west, and a condition of soil, climate, and political development as different from eastern Canada as Montana is from New England. This town, at the junction of the Red and Assiniboin rivers, in a valley which is one of the finest wheat-producing sections of the world, is a very important place. Railways, built and projected, radiate from it like spokes from a wheel hub. Its growth has been marvellous. Formerly known as Fort Garry, the chief post of the Hudson's Bay Company, it had in 1871 a population of only one hundred. It is now the capital of the province of Manitoba, contains the chief workshops of the Canadian pacific between Montreal and Vancouver, and has a population of 25,000. It is laid out on a grand scale, with very broad streets—Main Street is 200 feet wide—has many substantial public and business buildings, street-cars, and electric-lights, and abundant facilities for trade. At present it is in a condition of subsided 'boom;' the whole province has not more than 120,000 people, and the city for that number is out of proportion. Winnipeg must wait a little for the development of the country. It seems to the people that the town would start up again if it had more railroads. Among the projects much discussed is a road northward between Lake Winnipeg and Lake Manitoba, turning eastward to York Factory on Hudson's Bay. The idea is to reach a short water route to Europe. From all the testimony I have read as to ice in Hudson's Bay harbors and in the straits, the short period the straits are open, and the uncertainty from year to year as to the months they will be open, this route seems chimerical. But it does not seem so to its advocates, and there is no doubt that a portion of the line between the lakes first named would develop a good country and pay. A more important line—indeed, of the first importance—is built for 200 miles north-west from Portage la Prairie, destined to go to Prince Albert, on the North Saskatchewan. This is the Manitoba and North-west, and it makes its connection from Portage la Prairie with Winnipeg over the Canadian Pacific. An antagonism has grown up in Manitoba towards the Canadian pacific. This arose from the monopoly privileges enjoyed by it as a Dominion road. The province could build no road with extra-territorial connections. This monopoly was surrendered in consideration of the guarantee spoken of from the Government. The people of Winnipeg also say that the company discriminated against them in the matter of rates, and that the province must have a competing outlet. The company says that it did not discriminate, but treated Winnipeg like other towns on the line, having an eye to the development of the whole prairie region, and that the trouble was that it refused to discriminate in favor of Winnipeg, so that it might become the distributing-point of the whole North-west. Whatever the truth may be, the province grew increasingly restless, and determined to build another road. The Canadian Pacific has two lines on either side of the Red River, connecting at Emerson and Gretna with the Red River branches of the St Paul, Minneapolis, and Manitoba. It has also two branches running westward south of its main line penetrating the fertile wheat-fields of Manitoba. The province graded a third road, paralleling the two to the border, and the river, southward from Winnipeg to the border connecting there with a branch of the Northern Pacific, which was eager to reach the rich wheat-fields of the North-west. The provincial Red River Railway also proposed to cross the branches of the Canadian Pacific, and connect at Portage la Prairie with the Manitoba and North-west. The Canadian Pacific, which had offered to sell the province its Emerson branch, saying that there was not business enough for three parallel routes, insisted upon its legal rights and resisted this crossing. Hence the provincial and railroad conflict of the fall of 1888. The province built the new road, but it was alleged that the Northern pacific was the real party, and that Manitoba had so far put itself into the hands of that corporation. There can be no doubt that Manitoba will have its road and connect the Northern Pacific with the Saskatchewan country, and very likely will parallel the main line of the Canadian Pacific. But whether it will get from the Northern Pacific the relief it thought itself refused by the Canadian, many people in Winnipeg begin to doubt; for however eager rival railways may be for new territory, they are apt to come to an understanding in order to keep up profitable rates. They must live.

I went down on the southern branch of the Canadian pacific, which runs west, not far from our border, as far as Boissevain. It is a magnificent wheat country, and already very well settled and sprinkled with villages. The whole prairie was covered with yellow wheat-stacks, and teams loaded with wheat were wending their way from all directions to the elevators on the line. There has been quite an emigration of Russian Mennonites to this region, said to be 9000 of them. We passed near two of their villages—a couple of rows of square unbeautiful houses facing each other, with a street of mud between, as we see them in pictures of Russian communes. These people are a peculiar and some-what mystical sect, separate and unassimilated in habits, customs, and faith from their neighbors, but peaceful, industrious, and thrifty. I shall have occasion to speak of other peculiar immigration, encouraged by the governments and by private companies.

There can be no doubt of the fertility of the prairie region of Manitoba and Assiniboin. Great heat is developed in the summers, but cereals are liable, as in Dakota, to be touched, as in 1888, by early frost. The great drawback from Winnipeg on Westward is the intense cold of winter, regarded not as either agreeable or disagreeable, but as a matter of economy. The region, by reason of extra expense for fuel, clothing, and housing, must always be more expensive to live in than, say, Ontario.

The province of Manitoba is an interesting political and social study.

It is very unlike Ontario or British Columbia. Its development has been, in freedom and self-help, very like one of our Western Territories, and it is like them in its free, independent spirit. It has a spirit to resist any imposed authority. We read of the conflicts between the Hudson's Bay and the North-western Fur companies and the Selkirk settlers, who began to come in in 1812. Gradually the vast territory of the North-west had a large number of 'freemen' independent of any company, and of half-breed Frenchmen. Other free settlers sifted in. The territory was remote from the Government, and had no facilities of communication with the East, even after the union. The rebellion of 1870–71 was repeated in 1885, when Riel was called back from Montana to head the discontented. The settlers could not get patents for their lands, and they had many grievances, which they demanded should be redressed in a 'bill of rights.' There were aspects of the insurrection, not connected with the race question, with which many well-disposed persons sympathized. But the discontent became a violent rebellion, and had to be suppressed. The execution of Riel, which some of the Conservatives thought ill-advised, raised a race storm throughout Canada; the French element was in a tumult, and some of the Liberals made opposition capital out of the event. In the province of Quebec it is still a deep grievance, for party purposes partly, as was shown in the recent election of a federal member of Parliament in Montreal.

Manitoba is Western in its spirit and its sympathies. Before the building of the Canadian pacific its communication was with Minnesota. Its interests now largely lie with its southern neighbors. It has a feeling of irritation with too much federal dictation, and frets under the still somewhat undefined relations of power between the federal and the provincial governments, as was seen in the railway conflict. Besides, the natural exchange of products between south and north—between the lower Mississippi and the Red River of the North and the north-west prairies—is going to increase; the north and south railway lines will have, with the development of industries and exchange of various sorts, a growing importance compared with the great east and west lines. Nothing can stop this exchange and the need of it along our whole border west of Lake Superior. It is already active and growing, even on the Pacific, between Washington Territory and British Columbia.

For these geographical reasons, and especially on account of similarity of social and political development, I was strongly impressed with the notion that if the Canadian pacific Railway had not been built when it was, Manitoba would by this time have gravitated to the United States, and it would only have been a question of time when the remaining North-west should have fallen in. The line of the road is very well settled, and yellow with wheat westward to Regina, but the farms are often off from the line, as the railway sections are for the most part still unoccupied; and there are many thriving villages: Portage la Prairie, from which the Manitoba and North-western Railway starts north-west, with a population of 3000; Brandon, a busy grain mart, standing on a rise of ground 1150 feet above the sea, with a population of 4000 and over; Qu'Appelle, in the rich valley of the river of that name, with 700; Regina, the capital of the North-west Territory, on a vast plain, in 800; Moosejay, a market-town towards the western limit of the settled country, with 600. This is all good land, but the winters are severe.

Naturally, on the rail we saw little game, except ducks and geese on the frequent fresh-water ponds, and occasionally coyotes and prairie-dogs. But plenty of large game still can be found farther north. At Stony Mountain, fifteen miles north of Winnipeg, the site of the Manitoba penitentiary, we saw a team of moose, which Colonel Bedson, the superintendent, drives—fleet animals, going easily fifteen miles an hour. They were captured only thirty-five miles north of the prison, where moose are abundant. Colonel Bedson has the only large herd of the practically extinct buffalo. There are about a hundred of these uncouth and picturesque animals, which have a range of twenty or thirty miles over the plains, and are watched by mounted keepers. They were driven in, bulls, cows, and calves, the day before our arrival—it seemed odd that we could order up a herd of buffaloes by telephone, but we did—and we saw the whole troop lumbering over the prairie, exactly as we were familiar with them in pictures. The colonel is trying the experiment of crossing them with common cattle. The result is a half-breed of large size, with heavier hind-quarters and less hump than the buffalo, and said to be good beef. The penitentiary has taken in all the convicts of the North-west Territory, and there were only sixty-five of them. The institution is a model one in its management. We were shown two separate chapels—one for Catholics and another for Protestants.

All along the line settlers are sifting in, and there are everywhere signs of promoted immigration. Not only is Canada making every effort to fill up its lands, but England is interested in relieving itself of troublesome people. The experiment has been tried of bringing out East-Londoners. These barbarians of civilization are about as unfitted for colonists as can be. Small bodies of them have been aided to make settlements, but the trial is not very encouraging; very few of them take to the new life. The Scotch crofters do better. They are accustomed to labor and thrift, and are not a bad addition to the population. A company under the management of Sir John Lister Kaye is making a larger experiment. It has received sections from the Government and bought contiguous sections from the railway, so as to have large blocks of land on the road. A dozen settlements are projected. The company brings over laborers and farmers, paying their expenses and wages for a year. A large central house is built on each block, tools and cattle are supplied, and the men are to begin the cultivation of the soil. At the end of a year they may, if they choose, take up adjacent free Government land and begin to make homes for themselves, working meantime on the company land, if they will. By this plan they are guaranteed support for a year at least, and chance to set up for themselves. The company secures the breaking up of its land and a crop, and the nucleus of a town. The further plan is to encourage farmers, with a capital of a thousand dollars, to follow and settle in the neighborhood. There will then be three ranks—the large company proprietors, the farmers with some capital, and the laborers who are earning their capital. We saw some of these settlements on the line that looked promising. About 150 settlers, mostly men, arrived last fall, and with them were sent out English tools and English cattle. The plan looks to making model communities, on something of the old-world plan of proprietor, farmer, and laborer. It would not work in the United States.

Another important colonization is that of Icelanders. These are settled to the north-east of Winnipeg and in southern Manitoba. About 10,000 have already come over, and the movement has assumed such large proportions that it threatens to depopulate Iceland. This is good and intelligent material. Climate and soil are so superior to that of Iceland that the emigrants are well content. They make good farmers, but they are not so clannish as the Mennonites; many of them scatter about in the towns as laborers.

Before we reached Medicine Hat, and beyond that place, we passed through considerable alkaline country—little dried-up lakes looking like patches of snow. There was an idea that this land was not fertile. The Canadian Pacific Company have been making several experiments on the line of model farms, which prove the contrary. As soon as the land is broken up and the crust turned under, the soil becomes very fertile, and produces excellent crops of wheat and vegetables.

Medicine Hat, on a branch of the South Saskatchewan, is a thriving town. Here are a station and barracks of the Mounted Police, a picturesque body of civil cavalry in blue pantaloons and red jackets. This body of men, numbering about a thousand, and similar in function to the *Guarda Civil* of Spain, are scattered through the North-west Territory, and are the Dominion police for keeping in order the Indians, and settling disputes between the Indians and whites. The sergeants have powers of police-justices, and the organization is altogether an admirable one for the purpose, and has a fine *esprit de corps*.

Here we saw many Cree Indians, physically a creditable-looking race of men and women, and picturesque in their gay blankets and red and yellow paint daubed on the skin without the least attempt at shading or artistic effect. A fair was going on, an exhibition of horses, cattle, and vegetable and cereal products of the region. The vegetables were large and of good quality. Delicate flowers were still blooming (September 28th) untouched by frost in the gardens. These Crees are not on a reservation. They cultivate the soil a little, but mainly support themselves by gathering and selling buffalo bones, and well set-up and polished horns of cattle, which they swear are buffalo. The women are far from a degraded race and in appearance, have good heads, high foreheads, and are well favored. As to morals, they are reputed not to equal the Blackfeet.

The same day we reached Gleichen, about 2500 feet above the sea. The land is rolling, and all good for grazing and the plough. This region gets the "Chinook" wind. Ploughing is begun in April, sometimes in March; in 1888 they ploughed in January. Flurries of snow may be expected any time after October 1st, but frost is not so early as in eastern Canada. A fine autumn is common, and fine, mild weather may continue up to December. At Dunmore, the station before Medicine hat, we passed a branch railway running west to the great Lethbridge coal-mines, and Dunmore Station is a large coal depot.

The morning at Gleichen was splendid; cool at sunrise, but no frost. Here we had our first view of the Rockies, a long range of snow-peaks on the horizon, 120 miles distant. There is an immense fascination in this rolling country, the exhilarating air, and the magnificent mountains in the distance. Here is the beginning of a reservation of the Blackfeet, near 3000. They live here on the Bow River, and cultivate the soil to a considerable extent, and have the benefit of a mission and two schools.

They are the best-looking race of Indians we have seen, and have most self-respect.

We went over a rolling country to Calgary, at an altitude of 3388 feet, a place of some 3000 inhabitants, and of the most distinction of all between Brandon and Vancouver. On the way we passed two stations where natural gas was used, the boring for which was only about 600 feet. The country is underlaid with coal. Calgary is delightfully situated at the junction of the Bow and Elbow rivers, rapid streams as clear as crystal, with a greenish hue, on a small plateau, surrounded by low hills and overlooked by the still distant snow-peaks. The town has many good shops, several churches, two newspapers, and many fanciful cottages. We drove several miles out on the McCloud trail, up a lovely valley, with good farms, growing wheat and oats, and the splendid mountains in the distance. The day was superb, the thermometer marking 70°. This is, however, a ranch country, wheat being an uncertain crop, owing to summer frost. But some years, like 1888, are good for all grains and vegetables. A few Sarcee Indians were loafing about here, inferior savages. Much better are the Stony Indians, who are settled and work the soil beyond Calgary, and are very well cared for by a protestant mission.

Some of the Indian tribes of Canada are self-supporting. This is true of many of the Siwash and other west coast tribes, who live by fishing. At Lytton, on the upper Fraser, I saw a village of the Siwash civilized enough to live in houses, wear our dress, and earn their living by working on the railway, fishing, etc. The Indians have done a good deal of work on the railway, and many of them are still employed on it. The coast Indians are a different race from the plains Indians, and have a marked resemblance to the Chinese and Japanese. The polished carvings in black slate of the Haida Indians bear a striking resemblance to the archaic Mexican work, and strengthen the theory that the coast Indians crossed the straits from Asia, are related to the early occupiers of Arizona and Mexico, and ought not to be classed with the North American Indian. The Dominion has done very well by its Indians, of whom it has probably a hundred thousand. It has tried to civilize them by means of schools, missions, and farm instructors, and it has been pretty successful in keeping ardent spirits away from them. A large proportion of them are still fed and clothed by the Government. It is doubtful if the plains Indians will ever be industrious. The Indian fund from the sale of their lands has accumulated to $3,000,000. There are 140 teachers and 4000 pupils in school. In 1885 the total expenditure on the Indian population, beyond that provided by the Indian fund, was $1,109,604, of which $478,038 was expended for provisions for destitute Indians.

At Cochrane's we were getting well into the hills. Here is a large horse and sheep ranch and a very extensive range. North and south along the foot-hills is fine grazing and ranging country. We enter the mountains by the Bow River Valley, and plunge at once into splendid scenery, bare mountains rising on both sides in sharp, varied, and fantastic peaks, snow-dusted, and in lateral openings assemblages of giant summits of rock and ice. The change from the rolling prairie was magical. At Mountain House the Three Sisters were very impressive. Late in the afternoon we came to Banff.

Banff will have a unique reputation among the resorts of the world. If a judicious plan is formed and adhered to for the development of its extraordinary beauties and grandeur, it will be second to few in attractions. A considerable tract of wilderness about it is reserved as a National Park, and the whole ought to be developed by some master landscape expert. It is in the power of the Government and the Canadian Pacific Company to so manage its already famous curative hot sulphur springs as to make Banff the resort of invalids as well as pleasure-seekers the year round. This is to be done not simply by established good bathing-places, but by regulations and restrictions such as give to the German baths their virtue.

The Banff Hotel, unsurpassed in situation, amid magnificent mountains, is large, picturesque, many gabled and windowed, and thoroughly comfortable. It looks down upon the meeting of the Bow and the Spray, which spread in a pretty valley closed by a range of snow-peaks. To right and left rise mountains of savage rock ten thousand feet high. The whole scene has all the elements of beauty and grandeur. The place is attractive for its climate, its baths, and excellent hunting and fishing.

For two days, travelling only by day, passing the Rockies, the Selkirks, and the Gold range, we were kept in a state of intense excitement, in a constant exclamation of wonder and delight. I would advise no one to attempt to take it in the time we did. Nobody could sit through Beethoven's nine symphonies played continuously. I have no doubt that when carriage-roads and foot-paths are made into mountain recesses, as they will be, and little hotels are established in the valleys and in the passes and advantageous sites, as in Switzerland, this region will rival the Alpine resorts. I can speak of two or three things only.

The highest point on the line is the station at Mount Stephen, 5296 feet above the sea. The mountain, a bald mass of rock in a rounded cone, rises about 8000 feet above this. As we moved away from it the mountain was hidden by a huge wooded intervening mountain. The train was speeding rapidly on the down grade, carrying us away from the base, and we stood upon the rear platform watching the apparent recession of the great mass, when suddenly, and yet deliberately, the vast white bulk of Mount Stephen began to rise over the intervening summit in the blue sky, lifting itself up by a steady motion while one could count twenty, until its magnificence stood revealed. It was like a transformation in a theatre, only the curtain here was lowered instead of raised. The surprise was almost too much for the nerves; the whole company was awe-stricken. It is too much to say that the mountain 'shot-up;' it rose with conscious grandeur and power. The effect, of course, depends much upon the speed of the train. I have never seen anything to compare with it for awakening the emotion of surprise and wonder.

The station of Field, just beyond Mount Stephen, where there is a charming hotel, is in the midst of wonderful mountain and glacier scenery, and would be a delightful place for rest. From there the descent down the cañon of Kickinghorse River, along the edge of precipices, among the snow-monarchs, is very exciting. At Golden we come to the valley of the Columbia River and in view of the Selkirks. The river is navigable about a hundred miles above Golden, and that is the way to the mining district of the Kootenay Valley. The region abounds in gold and silver. The broad Columbia runs north here until it breaks through the Selkirks, and then turns southward on the west side of that range.

The railway follows down the river, between the splendid ranges of the Selkirks and the Rockies, to the mouth of the Beaver, and then ascends its narrow gorge. I am not sure but that the scenery of the Selkirks is finer than that of the Rockies. One is bewildered by the illimitable noble snow-peaks and great glaciers. At Glacier House is another excellent hotel. In savage grandeur, nobility of maintain-peaks, snow-ranges, and extent of glacier it rivals anything in Switzerland. The glacier, only one arm of which is seen from the road, is, I believe, larger than any in Switzerland. There are some thirteen miles of flowing ice; but the monster lies up in the mountains, like a great octopus, with many giant arms. The branch which we saw, overlooked by the striking snow-cone of Sir Donald, some two and half miles from the hotel, is immense in thickness and breadth, and seems to pour out of the sky. Recent measurements show that it is moving at the rate of twenty inches in twenty-four hours—about the rate of progress of the Mer de Glace. In the midst of the main body, higher up, is an isolated mountain of pure ice three hundred feet high and nearly a quarter of a mile in length. These mountains are the home of the mountain sheep.

From this amphitheatre of giant peaks, snow, and glaciers we drop by marvellous loops—wonderful engineering, four apparently different tracks in sight at one time—down to the valley of the Illicilliweat, the lower part of which is fertile, and blooming with irrigated farms. We pass a cluster of four lovely lakes, and coast around the great Shuswap Lake, which is fifty miles long. But the traveller is not out of excitement. The ride down the Thompson and Fraser cañons is as amazing almost as anything on the line. At Spence's Bridge we come to the old Government road to the Cariboo gold-mines, three hundred miles above. This region has been for a long time a scene of activity in mining and salmon-fishing. It may be said generally of the Coast or Gold range that its riches have yet to be developed. The villages all along these mountain slopes and valleys are waiting for this development.

The city of Vancouver, only two years old since the beginnings of a town were devoured by fire, is already an interesting place of seven to eight thousand inhabitants, fast building up, and with many substantial granite and brick buildings, and spreading over a large area. It lies upon a high point of land between Burrard Inlet on the north and the north arm of the Fraser River. The inner harbor is deep and spacious. Burrard Inlet entrance is narrow but deep, and opens into English Bay, which opens into Georgia Sound, that separates the island of Vancouver, three hundred miles long, from the main-land. The round headland south of the entrance is set apart for a public park, called now Stanley Park, and is being improved with excellent driving-roads, which give charming views. It is a tangled wilderness of nearly one thousand acres. So dense is the undergrowth, in this moist air, of vines, ferns, and small shrubs, that it looks like a tropical thicket. But in the midst of it are gigantic Douglas firs and a few noble cedars. One veteran cedar, partly decayed at the top, measured fifty-six feet in circumference, and another, in full vigour and of gigantic height, over thirty-nine feet. The hotel of the Canadian Pacific Company, a beautiful building in modern style, is, in point of comfort, elegance of appointment, abundant table, and service, not excelled by any in Canada, equalled by few anywhere.

Vancouver would be a very busy and promising city merely as the railway terminus and the shipping-point for Japan and China and the east generally. But is has other resources of growth. There is a very good country back of it, and south of it all the way into Washington Territory. New Westminster, twelve miles south, is a place of importance for fish and lumber. The immensely fertile alluvial bottoms of the Fraser, which now overflows its banks, will some day be diked, and become exceedingly valuable. Its relations to Washington Territory are already close. The very thriving city of Seattle, having a disagreement with the North Pacific and its rival, Tacoma, sends and receives most of its freight and passengers *via* Vancouver, and is already pushing forward a railway to that point. It is also building to Spokane Falls, expecting some time to be met by an extension of the St Paul, Minneapolis, and Manitoba from the Great Falls of the Missouri. I found that many of the emigrants in the loaded trains that we travelled with or that passed us were bound to Washington Territory. It is an acknowledged fact that there is a constant 'leakage' of emigrants, who had apparently promised to tarry in Canada, into United States territories. Some of them, disappointed of the easy wealth expected, no doubt return; but the name of 'republic' seems to have an attraction for Old World people when they are once set adrift.

We took a steamer one afternoon for a five hours' sail to Victoria. A part of the way is among beautiful wooded islands. Once out in the open, we had a view of our 'native land' and prominent in it the dim, cloud-like, gigantic peak of Mount Baker. Before we passed the islands we were entertained by a rare show of right-whales. A school of them a couple of weeks before had come down through Behring Strait, and pursued a shoal of fish into this landlocked bay. There must have been as many as fifty of the monsters in sight, spouting up slender fountains, lifting their huge bulk out of the water, and diving with their bifurcated tails waving in the air. They played about like porpoises, apparently only for our entertainment.

Victoria, so long isolated, is the most English part of Canada. The town itself does not want solidity and wealth, but it is stationary, and, the Canadians elsewhere think, slow. It was the dry and dusty time of the year. The environs are broken with inlets, hilly and picturesque; there are many pretty cottages and country places in the suburbs; and one visits with interest the Eskimalt naval station and the elevated Park, which has a noble coast view. The very mild climate is favorable for grapes and apples. The summer is delightful; the winter damp, and constantly rainy. And this may be said of all this coast. Of the thirteen thousand population six thousand are Chinese, and they form in the city a dense, insoluble, unassimilating mass. Victoria has one railway, that to the prosperous Nanaimo coal-mines. The island has abundance of coal, some copper, and timber. But Vancouver has taken away from Victoria all its importance as a port. The Government and Parliament buildings are detached, but pleasant and commodious edifices. There is a decorous British air about everything. Throughout British Columbia the judges and the lawyers wear the gown and band and the horse-hair wig. In an evening trial for murder which I attended in a dingy upper chamber of the Kamloops court-house, lighted only by kerosene lamps, the wigs and gowns of judge and attorneys lent, I confess, a dignity to the administration of justice which the kerosene lamps could not have given. In one of the Government buildings is a capital museum of natural history and geology. The educational department is vigorous and effective, and I find in the bulky report evidence of most intelligent management of the schools.

It is only by traversing the long distance to this coast, and seeing the activity here, that one can appreciate the importance to Canada and to the British Empire of the Canadian Pacific Railway as a bond of unity, a developer of resources, and a world's highway. The out-going steamers were crowded with passengers and laden with freight. We met on the way two solid trains, of twenty cars each, full of tea. When the new swift steamers are put on, which are already heavily subsidized by both the English and the Canadian governments, the traffic in passengers and goods must increase. What effect the possession of such a certain line of communication with her Oriental domains will have upon the English willingness to surrender Canada either to complete independence or to a union with the United States, any political prophet can estimate.

It must be added that the Canadian Pacific Company are doing everything to make this highway popular as well as profitable. Construction and management show English regard for comfort and safety and order. It is one of the most agreeable lines to travel over I am acquainted with. Most of it is well built, and defects are being energetically removed.

The 'Colonist' cars are clean and convenient. The first class carriages are luxurious. The dining-room cars are uniformly well kept, the company hotels are exceptionally excellent; and from the railway servants one meets with civility and attention.

Quebec and Montmorency

HENRY D. THOREAU

In this extract from A Yankee in Canada (1853), *Henry David Thoreau describes his impressions of Quebec and Montmorency.*

ABOUT SIX O'CLOCK we started for Quebec, one hundred and eighty miles distant by the river; gliding past Longueil and Boucherville on the right, and *Pointe aux Trembles,* 'so called from having been originally covered with aspens,' and *Bout de l'Isle,* or the end of the island, on the left. I repeat these names not merely for want of more substantial facts to record, but because they sounded singularly poetic to my ears. There certainly was no lie in them. They suggested that some simple, and, perchance, heroic human life might have transpired there. There is all the poetry in the world in a name. It is a poem which the mass of men hear and read. What is poetry in the common sense, but a string of such jingling names? I want nothing better than a good word. The name of a thing may easily be more than the thing itself to me. Inexpressibly beautiful appears the recognition by man of the least natural fact, and the allying his life to it. All the world reiterating this slender truth, that aspens once grew there; and the swift inference is, that men were there to see them. And so it would be with the names of our native and neighboring villages, if we had not profaned them.

The daylight now failed us, and we went below; but I endeavored to console myself for being obliged to make this voyage by night, by thinking that I did not lose a great deal, the shores being low and rather unattractive, and that the river itself was much the more interesting object. I heard something in the night about the boat being at William Henry, Three Rivers, and in the Richelieu Rapids, but I was still where I had been when I lost sight of *Pointe aux Trembles*. To hear a man who has been waked up at midnight in the cabin of a steamboat, inquiring, 'Waiter, where are we now?' is, as if at any moment of the earth's revolution round the sun, or of the system round its centre, one were to raise himself up and inquire of one of the deck hands, 'Where are we now?'

I went on deck at daybreak, when we were thirty or forty miles above Quebec. The banks were now higher and more interesting. There was an 'uninterrupted succession of white-washed cottages' on each side of the river. This is what every traveller tells. But it is not to be taken as an evidence of the populousness of the country in general, hardly even of the river banks. They have presented a similar appearance for a hundred years. The Swedish traveller and naturalist, Kalm, who descended this river in 1749, says: 'It could really be called a village, beginning at Montreal and ending at Quebec, which is a distance of more than one hundred and eighty miles; for the farm-houses are never above five arpens, and sometimes but three asunder, a few places excepted'. Even in 1684 Hontan said that the houses were not more than a gunshot apart at most. Erelong we passed Cape Rouge, eight miles above Quebec, the mouth of the Chaudière on the opposite or south side, New Liverpool Cove with its lumber rafts and some shipping; then Sillery and Wolfe's Cove and the Heights of Abraham on the north, with now a view of Cape Diamond, and the citadel in front. The approach to Quebec was very imposing. It was about six o'clock in the morning when we arrived. There is but a single street under the cliff on the south side of the cape, which was made by blasting the rocks and filling up the river. Three-story houses did not rise more than one fifth or one sixth the way up the nearly perpendicular rock, whose summit is three hundred and forty-five feet above the water. We saw, as we glided past, the sign on the side of the precipice, part way up, pointing to the spot where Montgomery was killed in 1775. Formerly it was the custom for those who went to Quebec for the first time to be ducked, or else pay a fine. Not even the Governor General escaped. But we were too many to be ducked, even if the custom had not been abolished.

Here we were, in the harbor of Quebec, still three hundred and sixty miles from the mouth of the St Lawrence, in a basin two miles across, where the greatest depth is twenty-eight fathoms, and though the water is fresh, the tide rises seventeen to twenty-four feet,—a harbor 'large and deep enough', says a British traveller, 'to hold the English navy'. I may as well state that, in 1844, the county of Quebec contained about forty-five thousand inhabitants (the city and suburbs having about forty-three thousand); about twenty-eight thousand being Canadians of French origin; eight thousand British; over seven thousand natives of Ireland; one thousand five hundred natives of England; the rest Scotch and others. Thirty-six thousand belong to the Church of Rome.

Separating ourselves from the crowd, we walked up a narrow street, thence ascended by some wooden steps, called the Break-neck Stairs, into another steep, narrow, and zigzag street, blasted through the rock, which last led through a low massive stone portal, called Prescott Gate, the principal thoroughfare into the Upper Town. This passage was defended by cannon, with a guard-house over it, a sentinel at his post, and other soldiers at hand ready to relieve him. I rubbed my eyes to be sure that I was in the nineteenth century, and was not entering one of those portals which sometimes adorn the frontispieces of new editions of old black-letter volume. I thought it would be a good place to read Foissart's Chronicles. It was such a reminiscence of the Middle Ages as Scott's novels. Men apparently dwelt there for security. Peace be unto them! As if the inhabitants of New York were to go over to Castle William to live! What a place it must be to bring up children! Being safe through the gate we naturally took the street which was steepest, and after a few turns found ourselves on the Durham Terrace, a wooden platform on the site of the old castle of St Louis, still one hundred and fifteen feet below the summit of the citadel, overlooking the Lower Town, the wharf where we had landed, the harbor, the Isle of Orleans, and the river and surrounding country to a great distance. It was literally a splendid view. We could see six or seven miles distant, in the northeast, an indentation in the lofty shore of the northern channel, apparently on one side of the harbor, which marked the mouth of the Montmorenci, whose celebrated fall was only a few rods in the rear.

At a shoe-shop, whither we were directed for this purpose, we got some of our American money changed into English. I found that American hard money would have answered as well, excepting cents, which fell very fast before their pennies, it taking two of the former to make one of the latter, and often the penny, which had cost us two cents, did us the service of one cent only. Moreover, our robust cents were compelled to meet on even terms a crew of vile half-penny tokens, and bung-town coppers, which had more brass in their composition, and so perchance made their way in the world. Wishing to get into the citadel, we were directed to the Jesuits' Barracks,—a good part of the public buildings here are barracks,—to get a pass of the Town Major. We did not heed the sentries at the gate, nor did they us, and what under the sun they were placed there for, unless to hinder a free circulation of the air, was not apparent. There we saw soldiers eating their breakfasts in their mess-room, from bare wooden tables in camp fashion. We were continually meeting with soldiers in the streets, carrying funny little tin pails of all shapes, even semicircular, as if made to pack conveniently. I supposed that they contained their dinners,—so many slices of bread and butter to each, perchance. Sometimes they were carrying some kind of military chest on a sort of bier or hand-barrow, with a springy, undulating, military step, all passengers giving way to them, ever the charette-drivers stopping for them to pass,—as if the battle were being lost from an inadequate supply of powder. There was a regiment of Highlanders, and, as I understood, of Royal Irish, in the city; and by this time there was a regiment of Yankees also. I had already observed, looking up even from the water, the head and shoulders of some General Ponia-towsky, with an enormous cocked hat and gun, peering over the roof of a house, away up where the chimney caps commonly are with us, as it were a caricature of war and military awfulness; but I had not gone far up St Louis Street. Before my riddle was solved, by the appari-tion of a real live Highlander under a cocked hat, and with his knees out, standing and marching sentinel on the ramparts, between St Louis and St John's Gate. (It must be a holy war that is waged there.) We stood close by without fear and looked at him. His legs were somewhat tanned, and the hair had begun to grow on them, as some of our wise men predict that it will in such cases, but I did not think they were remarkable in any respect. Not withstanding all his warlike gear, when I inquired of him the way to the Plains of Abraham, he could not answer me without betraying some bashfulness through his broad Scotch. Soon after, we passed another of these creatures standing sentry at the St Louis Gate, who let us go by without shooting us, or even demanding the countersign. We then began to go through the gate, which was so thick and tunnel-like, as to remind me of those lines in Claudian's Old Man of Verona, about the getting out of the gate being the greater part of a journey;—as you might imagine yourself crawling through an architectural vignette *at the end* of a black-letter volume. We were then reminded that we had been in a fortress, from which we emerged by numerous zigzags in a ditch-like road, going a considerable distance to advance a few rods, where they could have shot us two or three times over, if their minds had been disposed as their guns were. The greatest, or rather the most prominent, part of this city was constructed with the design to offer the deadest resistance to leaden and iron missiles that might be cast against it. But it is a remarkable meteorological and psychological fact, that it is rarely known to rain lead with much violence, except on places so constructed. Keeping on about a mile we came to the Plains of Abraham,—for having got through with the Saints, we come next to the Patriarchs. Here the Highland regiment was being reviewed, while the band stood on one side and played,—methinks it was *La Claire Fontaine*, the national air of the Canadian French. This is the site where a real battle once took place, to commemorate which they have had a sham fight here almost every day since. The Highlanders manoeuvred very well, and if the precision of their movements was less remarkable, they did not appear so stiffly erect as the English or Royal Irish, but had a more elastic and graceful gait, like a herd of their own red deer, or as if accustomed to stepping down the sides of mountains. But they made a sad impression on the whole, for it was obvious that all true manhood was in the process of being drilled out of them. I have no doubt that soldiers well drilled are, as a class, peculiarly destitute of originality and independence. The officers appeared like men dressed above their condition. It is impossible to give the soldier a good education, without making him a deserter. His natural foe is the government that drills him. What would any philanthropist, who felt an interest in these men's welfare, naturally do, but first of all teach them so to respect themselves, that they could not be hired for this work, whatever might be the consequences to this government or that;—not drill a few, but educate all. I observed one older man among them, gray as a wharf-rat, and supple as the Devil, marching lock-step with the rest who would have to pay for that elastic gait.

We returned to the citadel along the heights, plucking such flowers as grew there. There was an abundance of succory still in blossom, broad-leaved goldenrod, buttercups, thorn-bushes, Canada thistles, and ivy, on the very summit of Cape Diamond. I also found the bladder-campion in the neighborhood. We there enjoyed an extensive view, which I will describe in another place. Our pass, which stated that all the rules were 'to be strictly enforced' as if they were determined to keep up the semblance of reality to the last gasp, opened to us the Dalhousie Gate, and we were conducted over the citadel by a bare-legged Highlander in cocked hat and full regimentals. He told us that he had been here about three years, and had formerly been stationed at Gibraltar. As if his regiment, having perchance been nestled amid the rocks of Edinburgh Castle, must flit from rock to rock thenceforth over the earth's surface, like a bald eagle, or other bird of prey, from eyrie to eyrie. As we were going out, we met the Yankees coming in, in a body, headed by a red-coated officer called the commandant, and escorted by many citizens, both English and French Canadian. I therefore immediately fell into the procession, and went round the citadel again with more intelligent guides, carrying, as before, all my effects with me. Seeing that nobody walked with the red-coated commandant, I attached myself to him, and though I was not what is called well-dressed, he did not know whether to repel me or not, for I talked like one who was not aware of any deficiency in that respect. Probably there was not one among all the Yankees who went to Canada this time, who was not more splendidly dressed than I was. It would have been a poor story if I had not enjoyed some distinction. I had on my 'bad-weather clothes' like Olaf Trygesson the Northman, when he went to the Thing in England, where, by the way, he won his bride. As we stood by the thirty-two-pounder on the summit of Cape Diamond, which is fired three times a day, the commandant told me that it would carry to the Isle of Orleans, four miles distant, and that no hostile vessel could come round the island. I now saw the subterranean or, rather, 'casemated barracks' of the soldiers, which I had not noticed before, though I might have walked over them. They had very narrow windows, serving as loop-holes for musketry, and small iron chimneys rising above the ground. There we saw the soldiers at home and in an undress, splitting wood,—I looked to see whether with swords or axes,—and in various ways endeavoring to realize that their nation was now at peace with this part of the world. A part of each regiment, chiefly officers, are allowed to marry. A grandfatherly, would-be witty Englishman could give a Yankee whom he was patronizing no reason for the bare knees of the Highlanders, other than oddity. The rock within the citadel is a little convex, so that shells falling on it would roll toward the circumference, where the barracks of the soldiers and officers are; it has been proposed, therefore, to make it slightly concave, so that they may roll into the centre, where they would be comparatively harmless; and it is estimated that to do this would cost twenty thousand pounds sterling. It may be well to remember this when I build my next house, and have the roof 'all correct' for bombshells.

At mid-afternoon we made haste down *Sault-au-Matelot* street, towards the Falls of Montmorenci, about eight miles down the St Lawrence, on the north side, leaving the further examination of Quebec till our return. On our way, we saw men in the streets sawing logs pit-fashion, and afterward, with a common wood-saw and horse, cutting the planks into squares for paving the streets. This looked very shiftless, especially in a country abounding in water-power, and reminded me that I was no longer in Yankee land. I found, on inquiry, that the excuse for this was, that labor was cheap; and I thought, with some pain, how cheap men are here! I have since learned that the English traveller, Warburton, remarked, soon after landing at Quebec, that everything was cheap there but men. That must be the difference between going thither from New and from Old England. I had already observed the dogs harnessed to their little milk-carts, which contain a single large can, lying asleep in the gutters regardless of the horses, while they rested from their labors, at different stages of the ascent in the Upper Town. I was surprised at the regular and extensive use made of these animals for drawing, not only milk, but groceries, wood, &c. It reminded me that the dog commonly is not put to any use. Cats catch mice; but dogs only worry the cats. Kalm, a hundred years ago, saw sledges here for ladies to ride in, drawn by a pair of dogs. He says, 'A middle-sized dog is sufficient to draw a single person, when the roads are good'; and he was told by old people, that horses were very scarce in their youth, and almost all the land-carriage was then effected by dogs. They made me think of the Esquimaux, who, in fact, are the next people on the north.

Charlevoix says, that the first horses were introduced in 1665.

We crossed Dorchester Bridge, over the St Charles, the little river in which Cartier, the discoverer of the St Lawrence, put his ships, and spent the winter of 1535, and found ourselves on an excellent macadamized road, called *Le Chemin de Beauport*. We had left Concord Wednesday morning, and we endeavored to realize that now, Friday morning, we were taking a walk in Canada, in the Seigniory of Beauport, a foreign country, which a few days before had seemed almost as far off as England and France. Instead of rambling to Flint's Pond or the Sudbury Meadows, we found ourselves, after being a little detained in cars and steamboats,—after spending half a night at Burlington, and half a day at Montreal,—taking a walk down the bank of the St Lawrence to the Falls of Montmorenci and elsewhere. Well, I thought to myself, here I am in a foreign country; let me have my eyes about me, and take it all in. It already looked and felt a good deal colder than it had in New England, as we might have expected it would. I realized fully that I was four degrees nearer the pole, and shuddered at the thought; and I wondered if it were possible that the peaches might not be all gone when I returned. It was an atmosphere that made me think of the fur-trade, which is so interesting a department in Canada, for I had for all head-covering a thin palm-leaf hat without lining, that cost twenty-five cents, and over my coat one of those unspeakably cheap, as well as thin, brown linen sacks of the Oak Hall pattern, which every summer appear all over New England, thick as the leaves upon the trees. It was a thoroughly Yankee costume, which some of my fellow-travellers wore in the cars to save their coats a dusting. I wore mine, at first, because it looked better than the coat it covered, and last, because two coats were warmer than one, though one was thin and dirty. I never wear my best coat on a journey, though perchance I could show a certificate to prove that I have a more costly one, at least, at home, if that were all that a gentleman required. It is not wise for a traveller to go dressed. I should no more think of it than of putting on a clean dicky and blacking my shoes to go a-fishing; as if you were going out to dine, when, in fact, the genuine traveller is going out to work hard, and fare harder,—to eat a crust by the wayside whenever he can get it. Honest travelling is about as dirty work as you can do, and a man needs a pair of overalls for it. As for blacking my shoes in such a case, I should as soon think of blacking my face. I carry a piece of tallow to preserve the leather, and keep out the water; that's all; and many an officious shoe-black, who carried off my shoes when I was slumbering, mistaking me for a gentleman, has had occasion to repent it before he produced a gloss on them.

My pack, in fact, was soon made, for I keep a short list of those articles which, from frequent experience, I have found indispensable to the foot-traveller; and, when I am about to start, I have only to consult that, to be sure that nothing is omitted, and, what is more important, nothing superfluous is inserted. Most of my fellow-travellers carried carpet-bags, or valises. Sometimes one had two or three ponderous yellow valises in his clutch, at each hitch of the cars, as if we were going to have another rush for seats; and when there was a rush in earnest, and there were not a few, I would see my man in the crowd, with two or three affectionate lusty fellows along each side of his arm, between his shoulder and his valises, which last held them tight to his back, like the nut on the end of a screw. I could not help asking in my mind, What so great cause for showing Canada to those valises, when perhaps your very nieces had to stay at home for want of an escort? I should have liked to be present when the custom-house officer came aboard of him, and asked him to declare upon his honor if he had anything but wearing apparel in them. Even the elephant carries but a small trunk on his journeys. The perfection of travelling is to travel without baggage. After considerable reflection and experience, I have concluded that the best bag for the foot-traveller is made with a handkerchief, or, if he study appearances, a piece of stiff brown paper, well tied up, with a fresh piece within to put outside when the first is torn. That is good for both town and country, and none will know but you are carrying home the silk for a new gown for your wife, when it may be a dirty shirt. A bundle which you can carry literally under your arm, and which will shrink and swell with its contents. I never found the carpet-bag of equal capacity, which was not a bundle of itself. We styled ourselves the Knights of the Umbrella and the Bundle; for wherever we went, whether to Notre Dame or mount Royal, or the Champ-de-Mars, to the Town Major's or the Bishop's Palace, to the Citadel, with a bare-legged Highlander for our escort, or to the Plains of Abraham, to dinner or to bed, the umbrella and the bundle went with us; for we wished to be ready to digress at any moment. We made it our home nowhere in particular, but everywhere where our umbrella and bundle were. It would have been an amusing circumstance, if the Mayor of one of those cities had politely asked us where we were staying. We could only have answered, that we were staying with his Honor for the time being. I was amused when, after our return, some green ones inquired if we found it easy to get accommodated; as if we went abroad to get accommodated, when we can get that at home.

We met with many charettes, bringing wood and stone to the city. The most ordinary looking horses travelled faster than ours, or, perhaps they were ordinary looking, because, as I am told, the Canadians do not use the curry-comb. Moreover, it is said, that on the approach of winter their horses acquire an increased quantity of hair to protect them from the cold. If this be true, some of our horses would make you think winter were approaching, even in midsummer. We soon began to see women and girls at work in the fields, digging potatoes alone, or bundling up the grain which the men cut. They appeared in rude health, with a great deal of color in their cheeks, and, if their occupation had made them coarse, it impressed me as better in its effects than making shirts at fourpence apiece, or doing nothing at all; unless it be chewing slate pencils, with still smaller results. They were much more agreeable objects, with their great broad-brimmed hats and flowing dresses, than the men and boys. We afterwards saw them doing various other kinds of work; indeed, I thought that we saw more women at work out of doors than men. On our return, we observed in this town a girl with Indian boots, nearly two feet high, taking the harness off a dog. The puriety and transparency of the atmosphere were wonderful. When we had been walking an hour, we were surprised, on turning round, to see how near the city, with its glittering tin roofs, still looked. A village ten miles off did not appear to be more than three or four. I was convinced that you could see objects distinctly there much farther than here. It is true the villages are of a dazzling white, but the dazzle is to be referred, perhaps, to the transparency of the atmosphere as much as to the white-wash.

We were now fairly in the village of Beauport, though there was still but one road. The houses stood close upon this, without any front-yards, and at any angle with it, as if they had dropped down, being set with more reference to the road which the sun travels. It being about sun-down, and the Falls not far off, we began to look round for a lodging, for we preferred to put up at a private house, that we might see more of the inhabitants. We inquired first at the most promising looking houses, if, indeed, any were promising. When we knocked, they shouted some French word for come in, perhaps *entrez*, and we asked for a lodging in English; but we found, unexpectedly, that they spoke French only. Then we went along and tried another house, being generally saluted by a rush of two or three little curs, which readily distinguished a foreigner, and which we were prepared now to hear bark in French. Our first question would be, *Parlez-vous Anglais?* but the invariable answer was, *Non, monsieur;* and we soon found that the inhabitants were exclusively French Canadians, and nobody spoke English at all, any more than in France; that, in fact, we were in a foreign country, where the inhabitants uttered not one familiar sound to us. Then we tried by turns to talk French with them, in which we succeeded sometimes pretty well, but for the most part, pretty ill. *Pouvez-vous nous donner un lit cette nuit?* we would ask, and then they would answer with French volubility, so that we could catch only a word here and there. We could understand the women and children generally better than the men, and they us; and thus, after a while, we would learn that they had no more beds than they used.

So we were compelled to inquire: *Y a-t-il une maison publique ici? (auberge* we should have said, perhaps, for they seemed never to have heard of the other), and they answered at length that there was no tavern, unless we could get lodgings at the mill, *le moulin*, which we had passed; or they would direct us to a grocery, and almost every house had a small grocery at one end of it. We called on the public notary or village lawyer, but he had no more beds nor English than the rest. At one house there was so good a misunderstanding at once established through the politeness of all parties, that we were encouraged to walk in and sit down, and ask for a glass of water; and having drank their water, we thought it was as good as to have tasted their salt. When our host and his wife spoke of their poor accommodations, meaning for themselves, we assured them that they were good enough, for we thought that they were only apologizing for the poorness of the accommodations they were about to offer us, and we did not discover our mistake till they took us up a ladder into a loft, and showed to our eyes what they had been laboring in vain to communicate to our brains through our ears, that they had but that one apartment with its few beds for the whole family. We made our *a-dieus* forthwith, and with gravity, perceiving the literal signification of that word. We were finally taken in at a sort of public-house, whose master worked for Patterson, the proprietor of the extensive saw-mills driven by a portion of the Montmorenci stolen from the fall, whose roar we now heard. We here talked, or murdered French all the evening, with the master of the house and his family, and probably had a more amusing time than if we had completely understood one another. At length they showed us to a bed in their best chamber, very high to get into, with a low wooden rail to it. It had no cotton sheets, but coarse, home-made, dark colored, linen ones. Afterward, we had to do with sheets still coarser than these, and nearly the color of our blankets. There was a large open buffet loaded with crockery, in one corner of the room, as if to display their wealth to travellers, and pictures of Scripture scenes, French, Italian, and Spanish, hung around. Our hostess came back directly to inquire if we would have brandy for breakfast. The next morning, when I asked their names, she took down the temperance pledges of herself and husband, and children, which were hanging against the wall. They were Jean Baptiste Binet, and his wife, Geneviève Binet. Jean Baptiste is the sobriquet of the French Canadians.

After breakfast we proceeded to the fall, which was within half a mile, and at this distance its rustling sound, like the wind among the leaves, filled all the air. We were disappointed to find that we were in some measure shut out from the west side of the fall by the private grounds and fences of Patterson, who appropriates not only a part of the water for his mill, but a still larger part of the prospect, so that we were obliged to trespass. This gentleman's mansion-house and grounds were formerly occupied by the Duke of Kent, father to Queen Victoria. It appeared to me in bad taste for an individual, though he were the father of Queen Victoria, to obtrude himself with his land titles, or at least his fences, on so remarkable a natural phenomenon, which should, in every sense, belong to mankind. Some falls should even be kept sacred from the intrusion of mills and factories, as water privileges in another than the millwright's sense. This small river falls perpendicularly nearly two hundred and fifty feet at one pitch. The St Lawrence falls only one hundred and sixty-four feet at Niagara. It is a very simple and noble fall, and leaves nothing to be desired; but the most that I could say of it would only have the force of one other testimony to assure the reader that it is there. We looked directly down on it from the point of a projecting rock, and saw far below us, on a low promontory, the grass kept fresh and green by the perpetual drizzle, looking like moss. The rock is a kind of slate, in the crevices of which grew ferns and golden-rods. The prevailing trees on the shores were spruce and arborvitae,—the latter very large and now full of fruit,—also aspens, alders, and the mountain-ash with its berries. Every emigrant who arrives in this country by way of the St Lawrence, as he opens a point of the Isle of Orleans, sees the Montmorenci tumbling into the Great River thus magnificently in a vast white sheet, making its contribution with emphasis. Roberval's pilot, Jean Alphonse, saw this fall thus, and described it, in 1542. It is a splendid introduction to the scenery of Quebec. Instead of an artificial fountain in its square, Quebec has this magnificent natural waterfall to adorn one side of its harbor. Within the mouth of the chasm below, which can be entered only at ebb tide, we had a grand view at once of Quebec and of the fall. Kalm says that the noise of the fall is sometimes heard at Quebec, about eight miles distant, and is a sign of a northeast wind. The side of this chasm, of soft and crumbling slate too steep to climb, was among the memorable features of the scene. In the winter of 1829 the frozen spray of the fall, descending on the ice of the St Lawrence, made a hill one hundred and twenty-six feet high. It is an annual phenomenon which some think may help explain the formation of glaciers.

In the vicinity of the fall we began to notice what looked like our red-fruited thorn bushes, grown to the size of ordinary apple-trees, very common, and full of large red or yellow fruit, which the inhabitants called *pommettes*, but I did not learn that they were put to any use.

Toronto and Belleville

MRS SUSANNA MOODIE

In the following extracts from Life in the Clearings (1853),
*Mrs Susanna Moodie provides an intriguing insight into
her experiences as a settler in Canada.*

THE GLOW OF early day was brightening in the east, as the steamer
approached Toronto. We rounded the point of the interminable, flat,
swampy island, that stretches for several miles in front of the city, and
which is thinly covered with scrubby-looking trees. The land lies so
level with the water, that it has the appearance of being half-submerged,
and from a distance you only see the tops of the trees. I have been
informed that the name of Toronto has been derived from this circumstance, which in Indian literally means, *'Trees in the water'*.

If the island rather takes from, than adds to, the beauty of the place,
it is not without great practical advantages, as to it the city is mainly

indebted for its sheltered and very commodious harbour.

After entering the harbour, Toronto presents a long line of frontage, covered with handsome buildings to the eye. A grey mist still hovered over its many domes and spires; but the new University and the Lunatic Asylum stood out in bold relief, as they caught the broad gleam of the coming day.

It was my first visit to the metropolitan city of the upper province, and with no small degree of interest I examined its general aspect as we approached the wharf. It does not present such an imposing appearance from the water as Kingston, but it strikes you instantly as a place of far greater magnitude and importance. There is a fresh, growing, healthy vitality about this place, that cannot fail to impress a stranger very forcibly the first time he enters it. He feels instinctively that he sees before him the strong throbbing heart of this gigantic young country, and that every powerful vibration from this ever increasing centre of wealth and civilisation, infuses life and vigour through the whole length and breadth of the province.

Toronto exceeded the most sanguine expectations that I had formed of it at a distance, and enabled me to realize distinctly the rising greatness and rapid improvement of the colony. It is only here that you can form any just estimate of what she now is, and what at no very distant period she must be.

The country, for some miles round the city, appears to the eye as flat as a floor; the rise, though very gradual, is, I am told, considerable; and the land is sufficiently elevated above the lake to escape the disagreeable character of being low and swampy. Anything in the shape of a slope or hill is not distinguishable in the present area on which Toronto is built; but the streets are wide and clean, and contain many handsome public buildings; and the beautiful trees which everywhere abound in the neat, well-kept gardens, that surround the dwellings of the wealthier inhabitants, with the broad, bright, blue inland sea that forms the foreground to the picture, give to it such a lively and agreeable character, that it takes from it all appearance of tameness and monotony.

The wharfs, with which our first practical acquaintance with the city commenced, are very narrow and incommodious. They are built on piles of wood, and covered with rotten, black-looking boards. As far as comfort and convenience go, they are far inferior to those of Cobourg and Kingston, or even to those of our own dear little *City of the Bay* as Belleville has not inaptly been christened by the strange madcap, calling himself the *'Great Orator of the West.'*

It is devoutly to be hoped that a few years will sweep all these decayed old wharfs into the Ontario, and that more substantial ones, built of stone, will be erected in their place. Rome, however, was not built in a day; and the magic growth of this city of the West is almost as miraculous as that of Johah's celebrated gourd.

The steamboat had scarcely been secured to her wharf before we were surrounded by a host of cabmen, who rushed on board, fighting and squabbling with each other, in order to secure the first chance of passengers and their luggage. The hubbub in front of the ladies' cabin grew to a perfect uproar; and, as most of the gentlemen were still in the arms of Morpheus, these noisy Mercuries had it all their own way— swearing and shouting at the top of their voices, in a manner that rivalled civilized Europe. I was perfectly astonished at their volubility, and the pertinacity of their attentions, which were poured forth in the true Milesian fashion—an odd mixture of blarney, self-interest, and audacity. At Kingston these gentry are far more civil and less importunate, and we witnessed none of this disgraceful annoyance at any other port on the lake. One of these Paddies, in his hurry to secure the persons and luggage of several ladies, who had been my fellow-passengers in the cabin, nearly backed his crazy old vehicle over the unguarded wooden wharf into the lake.

We got safely stowed at last into one of these machines, which, internally, are not destitute of either comfort or convenience; and driving through some of the principal avenues of the city, were safely deposited at the door of a dear friend, who had come on board to conduct us to his hospitable home; and here I found the rest and quiet so much needed by an invalid after a long and fatiguing journey.

It was some days before I was sufficiently recovered to visit any of the lions of the place. With a minute description of these I shall not trouble my readers. My book is written more with a view to convey general impressions, than to delineate separate features,—to while away the languid heat of a summer day, or the dreary dulness of a wet one. The intending emigrant, who is anxious for commercial calculations and statistical details, will find all that he can require on this head in 'Scobie's Almanack,' and Smith's 'Past, Present, and Future of Canada'—works written expressly for that purpose.

Women make good use of their eyes and ears, and paint scenes that amuse or strike their fancy with tolerable accuracy; but it requires the strong-thinking heart of man to anticipate events, and trace certain results from particular causes. Women are out of their element when they attempt to speculate upon these abstruse matters—are apt to incline too strongly to their own opinions—and jump at conclusions which are either false or unsatisfactory.

My first visit was to King-street, which may be considered as the Regent-street of Toronto. It is the great central avenue of commerce, and contains many fine buildings, and handsome capacious stores, while a number of new ones are in a state of progress. This fine, broad, airy thoroughfare, would be an ornament to any town or city, and the bustle and traffic through it give to strangers a tolerably just idea of the wealth and industry of the community. All the streets terminate at the water's edge, but Front-street, which runs parallel with it, and may be termed the 'west end' of Toronto; for most of the wealthy residents have handsome houses and gardens in this street, which is open through the whole length of it to the lake. The rail-road is upon the edge of the water along this natural terrace. The situation is uncommonly lively, as it commands a fine view of the harbour, and vessels and steamboats are passing to and fro continually.

The St Lawrence market, which is near the bottom of King-street, is a handsome, commodious building, and capitally supplied with all the creature-comforts—fish, flesh, and fowl—besides abundance of excellent fruits and vegetables, which can be procured at very reasonable prices. The town-hall is over the market-place, and I am told—for I did not visit it—that it is a noble room, capable of accommodating a large number of people with ease and comfort.

Toronto is very rich in handsome churches, which form one of its chief attractions. I was greatly struck with the elegant spire of Kox's church, which is perhaps the most graceful in the city. The body of the church, however, seems rather too short, and out of proportion, for the tall slender tower, which would have appeared to much greater advantage attached to a building double the length.

Nothing attracted my attention, or interested me more, than the handsome, well-supplied book stores. Those of Armour, Scobie, and Maclean, are equal to many in London in appearance, and far superior to those that were to be found in Norwich and Ipswich thirty years ago.

This speaks well for the mental improvement of Canada, and is a proof that people have more leisure for acquiring book lore, and more money for the purchase of books, than they had some years ago. The piracies of the Americans have realized the old proverb, 'That 'tis an ill wind that blows nobody any good.' Incalculable are the benefits that Canada derives from her cheap reprints of all the European standard works, which, on good paper and in handsome bindings, can be bought at a quarter the price of the English editions. This circumstance must always make the Canadas a bad market for English publications. Most of these, it is true, can be procured by wealthy individuals at the book stores mentioned above, but the American reprints of the same works abound a hundred-fold.

Sixty years ago, the spot that Belleville now occupies was in wilderness; and its rapid, sparkling river and sunny upland slopes (which during the lapse of ages have formed a succession of banks to the said river), were only known to the Indian hunter and the white trader.

Where you see those substantial stone wharfs, and the masts of those vessels, unloading their valuable cargoes to replenish the stores of the wealthy merchants in the town, a tangled cedar swamp spread its dark, unwholesome vegetation into the bay, completely covering with an impenetrable jungle those smooth verdant plains, now surrounded with neat cottages and gardens.

Of a bright summer evening (and when is a Canadian summer evening otherwise?) those plains swarm with happy, healthy children, who assemble there to pursue their gambols beyond the heat and dust of the town; or to watch with eager eyes the young men of the place engaged in the manly old English game of cricket, with whom it is, in their harmless boasting, 'Belleville against Toronto-Cobourg; Kingston, the whole world.'

The editor of a Kingston paper once had the barbarity to compare these valiant champions of the bat and ball to 'singed cats—ugly to look at, but very devils to go.'

Our lads have never forgiven the insult; and should the said editor ever show his face upon their ground, they would kick him off with as little ceremony as they would a spent ball.

On that high sandy ridge that overlooks the town eastward—where the tinroof of the Court House, a massy, but rather tasteless building, and the spires of four churches catch the rays of the sun—a tangled maze of hazel bushes, and wild plum and cherry, once screened the Indian burying-ground, and the children of the red hunter sought for strawberries among the long grass and wild flowers that flourish profusely in that sandy soil.

Would that you could stand with me on that lofty eminence and look around you! The charming prospect that spreads itself at your feet would richly repay you for toiling up the hill.

We will suppose ourselves standing among the graves in the burying-ground of the English church; the sunny heavens above us the glorious waters of the bay, clasping in their azure belt three-fourths of the land-scape, and the quiet dead sleeping at our feet.

The white man has so completely supplanted his red brother, that he has appropriated the very spot that held his bones; and in a few years their dust will mingle together, although no stone marks the grave where the red man sleeps.

From this churchyard you enjoy the finest view of the town and sur-rounding country; and, turn your eyes which way you will, they cannot fail to rest on some natural object of great interest and beauty.

The church itself is but a homely structure; and has always been to me a great eyesore. It is to be regretted that the first inhabitants of the place selected their best and most healthy building sites for the erec-tion of places of worship. Churches and churchyards occupy the hills from whence they obtain their springs of fresh water,—and such deli-cious water! They do not at present feel any ill-consequences arising from this error of judgement; but the time will come, as population increases, and the dead accumulate, when these burying-grounds, by poisoning the springs that flow through them, will materially injure the health of the living.

The English church was built many years ago, partly of red brick burnt in the neighbourhood, and partly of wood coloured red to make up the deficiency of the costlier material. This seems a shabby saving, as abundance of brick-earth of the best quality abounds in the same hill, and the making of bricks forms a very lucrative and important craft to several persons in the town.

Belleville was but a small settlement on the edge of the forest, scarcely deserving the name of a village, when this church first pointed its ugly tower towards heaven. Doubtless its founders thought they had done wonders when they erected this humble looking place of worship; but now, when their descendants have become rich, and the village of log-huts and frame buildings has grown into a populous, busy, thriving town, and this red, tasteless building is too small to accommodate its congregation, it should no longer hold the height of the hill, but give place to a larger and handsomer edifice.

Behold its Catholic brother on the other side of the road; how much its elegant structure and graceful spire adds to the beauty of the scene. Yet the funds for rearing that handsome building, which is such an ornament to the town, were chiefly derived from small subscriptions, drawn from the earnings of mechanics, day-labourers, and female servants. If the Church of England were supported throughout the colony, on the voluntary principle, we should soon see fine stone churches, like St Michael, replacing these decaying edifices of wood, and the outcry about the ever-vexed question of the Clergy Reserves, would be merged in her increased influence and prosperity.

The deep-toned, sonorous bell, that fills the steeple of the Catholic church, which cost, I have been told, seven hundred pounds, and was brought all the way from Spain, was purchased by the voluntary donations of the congregation. This bell is remarkable for its fine tone, which can be heard eight miles into the country, and as far as the village of Northport, eleven miles distant, on the other side of the bay. There is a solemn grandeur in the solitary voice of the magnificent bell, as it booms across the valley in which the town lies, and reverberates among the distant woods and hills, which has a very imposing effect.

A few years ago the mechanics in the town entered into an agreement that they would only work from six to six during the summer months, and from seven till five in the winter, and they offered to pay a certain sum to the Catholic church for tolling the bell at the said hours. The Catholic workmen who reside in or near the town, adhere strictly to this rule, and, if the season is ever so pressing, they obstinately refuse to work before or after the stated time. I have seen, on our own little farm, the mower fling down his scythe in the swathe, and the harvest-man his sickle in the ridge, the moment the bell tolled for six.

In fact, the bell in this respect is looked upon as a great nuisance; and the farmers in the country refuse to be guided by it in the hours allotted for field labour; as they justly remark that the best time for hard work in a hot country is before six in the morning, and after the heat of the day in the evening.

When the bell commences to toll there is a long pause between each of the first four strokes. This is to allow the pious Catholic time for crossing himself and saying a short prayer.

The Arctic Prairies

ERNEST THOMPSON SETON

In these passages from The Arctic Prairies *(1912), Ernest
Thompson Seton describes his expedition into the far
northern territories of Canada in search of the caribou.*

CAMP MUSK-OX PROVIDED many other items of interest beside the Great
River, the big Musk-ox, and the Arctic Fox. Here Preble secured a
Groundsquirrel with its cheek-pouches full of mushrooms and shot a
cock Ptarmigan whose crop was crammed with leaves of willow and
birch, though the ground was bright with berries of many kinds. The
last evening we were there a White Wolf followed Billy into camp, keeping just beyond reach of his shotgun; and, of course, we saw Caribou
every hour or two.

'All aboard' was the cry on the morning of August 19, and once more
we set out. We reached the north arm of the lake, then turned north-

eastward. In the evening I got photos of a Polar Hare, the third we had seen. The following day (August 20), at noon, we camped in Sandhill Bay, the north point of Aylmer Lake and the northernmost point of our travels by canoe. It seems that we were the fourth party of white men to camp on this spot.

> Captain George Back, 1833–34.
> Stewart and Anderson, 1855.
> Warburton Pike, 1890.
> E. T. Seton, 1907.

All day long we had seen small bands of Caribou. A score now appeared on a sandhill half a mile away; another and another lone specimen trotted past our camp. One of these stopped and gave us an extraordinary exhibition of agility in a sort of St Vitus's jig, jumping, kicking, and shaking its head; I suspect the nose-worms were annoying it. While we lunched, a fawn came and gazed curiously from a distance of 100 yards. In the afternoon Preble returned from a walk to say that the caribou were visible in all directions, but not in great bands.

Next morning I was awakened by a Caribou clattering through camp within 30 ft of my tent.

After breakfast we set off on foot northward to seek for Musk-ox, keeping to the eastward of the great Fish River. The country is rolling, with occasional rocky ridges and long, level meadows in the lowlands, practically all of it would be considered horse country; and nearly every meadow had two or three grazing Caribou.

About noon, when six or seven miles north of Aylmer, we halted for rest and lunch on the top of the long ridge of glacial dump that lies to the east of Great Fish River. And now we had a most complete and spectacular view of the immense open country that we had come so far to see. It was spread before us like a huge, minute, and wonderful chart, and plainly marked with the processes of its shaping-time.

Imagine a region of low archaean hills, extending one thousand miles each way, subjected for thousands of years to a continual succession of glaciers, crushing, grinding, planing, smoothing, ripping up and smoothing again, carrying off whole ranges of broken hills, in fragments, to dump them at some other point, grind them again while there, and then push and hustle them out of that region into some other a few hundred miles farther; there again to tumble and grind them together, pack them into the hollows, and dump them in pyramidal piles on plains and uplands. Imagine this going on for thousands of years, and we shall have the hills lowered and polished, the valleys more or less filled with broken rocks.

Now the glacial action is succeeded by a time of flood. For another age all is below water, dammed by the northern ice, and icebergs breaking from the parent sheet carry bedded in them countless boulders, with which they go travelling south on the open waters. As they melt the boulders are dropped; hill and hollow share equally in this age-long shower of erratics. Nor does it cease till the progress of the warmer day removes the northern ice-dam, sets free the flood, and the region of archaean rocks stands bare and dry.

It must have been a dreary spectacle at that time, low, bare hills of gneiss, granite, etc.; low valleys half-filled with broken rock and over everything a sprinkling of erratic boulders; no living thing in sight, nothing green, nothing growing, nothing but evidence of mighty power used only to destroy. A waste of shattered granite spotted with hundreds of lakes, thousands of lakelets, millions of ponds that are marvellously blue, clear and lifeless.

But a new force is born on the scene; it attacks not this hill or rock, or that loose stone, but on every point of every stone and rock in the vast domain, it appears—the lowest form of lichen, a mere stain of gray. This spreads and by its own corrosive power eats foothold on the granite; it fructifies in little black velvet spots. Then one of lilac flecks the pink tones of the granite, to help the effect. Soon another kind follows—a pale olive-green lichen that fruits in bumps of rich brown velvet; then another branching like a tiny tree—there is a ghostly kind like white chalk rubbed lightly on, and yet another of small green blots, and one like a sprinkling of scarlet snow; each, in turn, of a higher and larger type, which in due time prepares the way for mosses higher still.

In the less exposed places these come forth, seeking the shade, searching for moisture, they form like small sponges on a coral reef; but growing, spread and change to meet the changing contours of the land they win, and with every victory or upward move, adopt some new refined intensive tint that is the outward and visible sign of their diverse inner excellences and their triumph. Ever evolving they spread, until there are great living rugs of strange textures and oriental tones; broad carpets there are of gray and green; long luxurious lanes, with lilac mufflers under foot, great beds of a moss so yellow chrome, so spangled with intense red sprigs, that they might, in clumsy hands, look raw. There are knee-deep breadths of polytrichum, which blends in the denser shade into a moss of delicate crimson plush that baffles description.

Down between the broader masses are bronze-green growths that run over each slight dip and follow down the rock crannies like streams of molten brass. Thus the whole land is overlaid with a living, corrosive mantle of activities as varied as its hues.

For ages these toil on, improving themselves, and improving the country by filing down the granite and strewing the dust around each rock.

The frost, too, is at work, breaking up the granite lumps; on every ridge there is evidence of that—low, rounded piles of stone which plainly are the remnants of a boulder, shattered by the cold. Thus, lichen, moss, and frost are toiling to grind the granite surfaces to dust.

Much of this powdered rock is washed by rain into the lakes and ponds; in time these cut their exits down, and drain, leaving each a broad mud-flat. The climate mildens and the south winds cease not, so that wind-borne grasses soon make green meadows of the broad lake-bottom flats.

The process climbs the hill-slopes; every little earthy foothold for a plant is claimed by some new settler, until each low hill is covered to the top with vegetation graded to its soil, and where the flowering kinds cannot establish themselves, the lichen pioneers still maintain their hold. Rarely, in the landscape, now, is any of the primitive colour of the rocks; even the tall, straight cliffs of Aylmer are painted and frescoed with lichens that flame and glitter with purple and orange, silver and gold. How precious and fertile the ground is made to seem, when every square foot of it is an exquisite elfin garden made by the little people, at infinite cost, filled with dainty flowers and still later embellished with delicate fruit.

One of the wonderful things about these children of the Barrens is the great size of fruit and flower compared with the plant. The cranberry, the crowberry, the cloudberry, etc., produce fruit any one of which might outweigh the herb itself.

Nowhere does one get the impression that these are weeds, as often happens among the rank growths farther south. The flowers in the wildest profusion are generally low, always delicate and mostly in beds of a single species. The Lalique jewelry was the sensation of the Paris Exposition of 1899. Yet here is Lalique renewed and changed for every week in the season and lavished on every square foot of a region that is a million square miles in extent.

Not a cranny in a rock but is seized on at once by the eager little gardeners in charge and made a bed of bloom, as though every inch of room were priceless. And yet Nature here exemplifies the law that our human gardeners are only learning; 'Mass your bloom, to gain effect.'

As I stood on that hill, the foreground was a broad stretch of old gold—the shining sandy yellow of drying grass—but it was patched with large scarlet mats of arctous that would put red maple to its reddest blush. There was no Highland heather here, but here were whole hillsides of purple red vaccinium, whose leaves were but a shade less red than its luscious grape-hued fruit.

Here were white ledums in roods and acre beds; purple mairanias by the hundred acres, and, framed in lilac rocks, were rich, rank meadows of golden-green by the mile.

There were leagues and leagues of caribou moss, pale green or lilac, and a hundred others in clumps, that, seeing here the glory of the painted mosses, were simulating their ways, though they themselves were not truly mosses at all.

I never before saw such a realm of exquisite flowers so exquisitely displayed, and the effect at every turn throughout the land was colour, colour, colour, to as far outdo the finest autumn tints of New England as the Colorado Canyon outdoes the Hoosac Gorge. What Nature can do only in October, elsewhere, she does here all season through, as though when she set out to paint the world she began on the Barrens with a full palette and when she reached the Tropics had nothing left but green.

Thus at every step one is wading through lush grass or crushing prairie blossoms and fruits. It is so on and on; in every part of the scene, there are but few square feet that do not bloom with flowers and throb with life; yet this is the region called the *Barren Lands of the North*.

And the colour is an index of its higher living forms, for this is the chosen home of the Ducks, the Ptarmigan, the Laplongspur and Snowbunting. The blue lakes echo with the wailing of the Gulls and the eerie magic calling of the Loons. Colonies of Lemmings, Voles, or Groundsquirrels are found on every sunny slope; the Wolverine and the White Wolf find this a land of plenty, for on every side, as I stood on that high hill, were to be seen small groups of Caribou.

This was the land and these the creatures I had come to see. This was my Farthest North and this was the culmination of years of dreaming. How very good it seemed at the time, but how different and how infinitely more delicate and satisfying was the realisation than any of the day-dreams founded on my vision through the eyes of other men.

On the morning of August 1 we launched on Artillery Lake, feeling, for the tenth time, that now we really were on the crowning stretch of our journey, that at last we were entering the land of the Caribou.

Over the deep, tranquil waters of the lake we went, scanning the painted shores with their dwindling remnants of forest. There is something inspiring about the profundity of transparency in these lakes, where they are 15 ft deep their bottoms are no more obscured than in an ordinary eastern brook at 6 in. On looking down into the far-below world, one gets the sensation of flight as one skims overhead in the swift canoe. And how swift that elegant canoe was in a clear run I was only now finding out. All my previous estimates had been too low. Here I had the absolute gauge of Tyrrell's maps and found that we four paddling could send her, not 3½, but 4½ or 5 miles an hour, with a possibility of 6 when we made an effort. As we spun along the southeast coast of the lake, the country grew less rugged; the continuous steep granite hills were replaced by lower buttes with long grassy plains between; and as I took them in, I marvelled at their name—*the Barrens*; bare of trees, yes, but the plains were covered with rich, rank grass, more like New England meadows. There were stretches where the herbage was rank as on the Indiana prairies, and the average pasture of the bleaker parts was better than the best of central Wyoming. A cattleman of the West would think himself made if he could be sure of such pastures on his range, yet these are the *Barren Grounds*.

At 3 we passed the splendid landmark of Beaver Lodge Mountain. Its rosy-red granite cliffs contrast wonderfully with its emerald cap of verdant grass and mosses, that cover it in tropical luxuriance, and the rippling lake about it was of Mediterranean hues.

We covered the last 9 miles in 1 hour and 53 minutes, passed the deserted Indian village, and landed at Last Woods by 8.30 p.m.

The edge of the timber is now the dividing line between the Hudsonian and the Arctic zones. It is the beginning of the country we had come to see; we were now in the land of the Caribou.

At this point we were prepared to spend several days, leave a cache, gather a bundle of choice firewood, then enter on the treeless plains.

That night it stormed; all were tired; there was no reason to bestir ourselves; it was 10 when we arose. Half an hour later Billy came to my tent and said, 'Mr Seton, here's some deer.' I rushed to the door, and there, with my own eyes, I saw on a ridge a mile away our great Caribou standing against the sky.

We made for a near hill and met Preble returning; he also had seen them. From a higher view-point the 4 proved part of a band of 20.

Then other bands came into view, 16, 61, 3, 200 and so on; each valley had a scattering few, all travelling slowly southward or standing to enjoy the cool breeze that ended the torment of the flies. About 1,000 were in sight. These were my first Caribou, the first fruits of 3,000 miles of travel.

Weeso got greatly excited; these were the forerunners of the vast herd. He said, 'Plenty Caribou now' and grinned like a happy child.

I went in one direction, taking only my camera. At least 20 Caribou trotted within 50 ft of me.

Billy and Weeso took their rifles intent on venison, but the Caribou avoided them, and 6 or 8 shots were heard before they got a young buck.

All that day I revelled in Caribou, no enormous herds but always a few in sight.

The next day Weeso and I went to the top ridge eastward. He with rifle, I with camera. He has a vague idea of the camera's use, but told Billy privately that 'the rifle was much better for Caribou.' He could not understand why I should restrain him from blazing away as long as the ammunition held out. 'Didn't we come to shoot?' But he was amenable to discipline, and did as I wished when he understood.

Now on the top of that windy ridge I sat with this copper-coloured child of the spruce woods, to watch these cattle of the plains.

The Caribou is a travelsome beast, always in a hurry, going against the wind. When the wind is west, all travel west; when it veers, they veer. Now the wind was northerly, and all were going north, not walking, not galloping—the Caribou rarely gallops, and then only for a moment or two; his fast gait is a steady trot a 10-mile gait, making with stops about 6 miles an hour. But they are ever on the move; when you see a Caribou that does not move, you know at once it is not a Caribou; it's a rock.

We sat down on the hill at 3. In a few minutes a cow Caribou came trotting from the south, caught the wind at 50 yards, and dashed away.

In 5 minutes another, in 20 minutes a young buck, in 20 minutes more a big buck, in 10 minutes a great herd of about 500 appeared in the south. They came along at full trot, lined to pass us on the south-east. At half a mile they struck our scent and all recoiled as though we were among them. They scattered in alarm, rushed south again, then, gathered in solid body, came on as before, again to spring back and scatter as they caught the taint of man. After much and various running, scattering, and massing, they once more charged the fearsome odour and went right through it. Now they passed at 500 yards and gave the chance for a far camera shot.

The sound of their trampling was heard a long way off—half a mile—but at 300 yards I could not distinguish the clicking of the feet, whereas this clicking was very plainly to be heard from the band that passed within 50 yards of me in the morning.

They snort a good deal and grunt a little, and notwithstanding their continual haste, I noticed that from time to time one or two would lie down, but at once jump up and rush on when they found they were being left behind. Many more single deer came that day, but no more large herds.

About 4.30 a fawn of this year (2½ or 3 months) came rushing up from the north, all alone. It charged up a hill for 200 yards, then changed its mind and charged down again, then raced to a bunch of tempting herbage, cropped it hastily, dashed to a knoll, left at an angle, darted toward us till within 40 yards, then dropped into a thick bed of grass, where it lay as though it had unlimited time.

I took one photograph, and as I crawled to get one nearer, a shot passed over my head, and the merry cackle told me that Weeso had yielded to temptation and had 'collected' that fawn.

A young buck now came trotting and grunting towards us till within 16 paces, which proved too much for Weeso, who then and there, in spite of repeated recent orders, started him on the first step toward my museum collection.

I scolded him angrily, and he looked glum and unhappy, like a naughty little boy caught in some indiscretion which he cannot understand. He said nothing to me then, but later complained to Billy, asking, 'What *did* we come for?'

Next morning at dawn I dreamed I was back in New York and that a couple of cats were wailing under my bedroom window. Their noise increased so that I awoke, and then I heard unaccountable caterwauls. They were very loud and near, at least one of the creatures was. At length I got up to see. Here on the lake a few yards from the tent was a loon swimming about, minutely inspecting the tent and uttering at intervals deep cat-like mews in expression of his curiosity.

The south wind had blown for some days before we arrived, and the result was to fill the country with Caribou coming from the north. The day after we came, the north wind set in, and continued for three days, so that soon there was not a Caribou to be found in the region.

In the afternoon I went up the hill to where Weeso left the offal of his deer. A large yellowish animal was there feeding. It disappeared over a rock and I could get no second view of it. It may have been a wolf, as I saw a fresh wolf trail near; I did not, however, see the animal's tail.

In the evening Preble and I went again, and again the creature was there, but disappeared as mysteriously as before when we were 200 yards away. Where it went we could not guess. The country was open and we scoured it with eye and glass, but saw nothing more of the prowler. It seemed to be a young Arctic wolf, yellowish white in colour, but tailless.

Next day at noon Preble and Billy returned bearing the illusive visitor; it was a large Lynx. It was very thin and yet, after bleeding, weighed 22 pounds. But why was it so far from the forest, 20 miles or more, and a couple of miles from this little grove that formed the last woods?

This is another evidence of the straits the Lynxes are put to for food, in this year of famine.

The Yukon

M.H. HAYNE AND H. WEST TAYLOR

The severity and desolation of winter in the Yukon Territory as experienced by early settlers, is captured in this vivid account from The Pioneers of the Klondike *(1897)*

WINTER WAS NOW upon us—the long dreary Arctic winter, during which the Yukon and its adjacent country is as a sealed book, as entirely shut off from the outside world as though it were on another planet. There are no roads, the river itself is the one and only highway; and for more than six months the river is blocked with ice—not smooth glassy ice such as one is accustomed to in Europe, but gigantic blocks of jagged ice rising from an equally rough solid base. Winter in those regions is really a most serious matter, far more serious both for those there already and for those just entering the country, than the thousands of irresponsible folk who have crowded thoughtlessly in, in spite of repeated emphatic warnings, have any notion. Whatever it may be in the future, when possibly some means of constant communication with the outside world may have been established, there is no denying the fact that for those who spent the winter of '95 and '96 in the district—those immediately preceding the present boom—the question of food supplies was a terribly serious one, and a source of grave anxiety for all whose greed for gold had not blinded them to all sense of responsibility.

Of course we were better off than most, for we had taken with us a complete year's supplies; and as we were travelling officially, and could therefore carry Government freight, the amount of baggage per man was in our case much larger than that which a miner can possibly hope to get in. But even we were on reduced rations of flour during last winter—and flour is the cheapest thing to be had up there—and this in spite of the fact that the Companies had contracted to keep us supplied, which they had not done for the miners. The whole winter's provisions must be laid in beforehand, for there is seldom anything in reserve in the stores; the cargoes brought upon the steamers during the few months that the river is open being all 'bespoke' before they have started, and snapped up immediately upon arrival.

I dwell purposely upon this aspect of the question, for no account of these regions, tempting as they are, would be, in any sense of the word, complete that did not emphasize the criminal folly of attempting to enter them without a full and sufficient amount of money to lay in at the outset a supply of food and other necessaries, at least enough to *subsist on* for a year. It is to be feared that the worst of the many reports which come pouring in every day now that winter is again setting in are not one whit exaggerated. It is, unhappily, as difficult to exaggerate the suffering and privation that awaits the man who takes nothing but a pick and a blanket, trusting to luck to supply the rest, as it is to overstate the fabulous amount of wealth lying within a few inches of the surface of practically the whole of that large area.

Undoubtedly 'the Yukon is no place for "tenderfeet."' The conditions of existence are so entirely different from those that marked most of the other great historical mining 'rushes'—a difference due, of course, to the locality of the fields. California, Africa, and Australia are totally different places to the Yukon, the reason, of course, being that they are—and have been from the first—so much more easy of access, and so much more in touch with the rest of the world. A man might be alone or lost on the veldt or in the bush, but somehow, by hook or by crook, he could generally contrive to struggle through to some place where he could beg, borrow, steal, or purchase food when his own stock had run out. Egress was never actually blocked, even if he had not the strength to fight his way out. But here it is not so. Once there, always there—until the long winter is past. There is no place to procure food, and even supposing there were, a man could not reach it. Travelling over any distance is a physical impossibility.

It is just this difference of locality and local characteristics, in connection with the whole business which, it seems to me, the enthusiast has not paused to consider. He has gone through, or heard and read the accounts of, the first rushes to the world's other great gold-mining districts, and he concludes he has only to do likewise. He imagines he has merely to purchase a pick and a gold-pan, deck himself out in a picturesque red shirt and slouch hat—and get there. When once there (he fondly dreams) he has only to dig up a few shovelfuls of earth to be at once a millionaire, and live at ease. I am not saying that this was by any means the general impression, but I am afraid that some such ideas as these have been at the bottom of the frantic rush that nothing has been able to check; and, after all, the loss of one life as the result of such folly would be sufficiently deplorable and entire justification for insisting on the point. When it comes to tens and hundreds of lives being similarly thrown away, it will be readily seen that it has become a very serious matter indeed. It is not that there is not sufficient gold, for there is gold to spare for one and all who can live to take it out. It is entirely that man can no more live by gold alone—when there is no food for gold to buy—than he can live by the Tempter's 'stone.'

Strong men with enough money *to begin with* to lay in a year or more's provisions before starting from the coast will succeed: a 'tender-foot' will go under, be he as rich as Croesus to start with. At no time should any man start with less than $1,000. The lowest sum on which a man can purchase his necessaries and reach the fields from Montreal is $100; so clearly the 'dismal failures' and the 'might-have-beens' who are desperately resolved to have 'one more last try' will fail ignominiously unless they can procure at least that sum. Those starting from England will want considerably more.

The only difficulty we had facing us after we were established in our new quarters was that of fuel. We had been too much occupied in collecting sufficient wood to build a roof to cover us, to have had any spare time for laying in any supply for burning. This was a serious matter, and the consequence was we had to go out and 'rustle' (collect and bring in) wood for fires practically every day, and every day we had naturally to go further afield. Luckily there is a good supply of small spruce on the banks of the river, but even so this daily 'rustling' involved a very considerable labour, and kept us fully occupied all the time. We burnt from two to four cords every day, all of which had to be cut, collected, hauled in on sledges over the rough ground, and then cut up into stove-lengths. It was accordingly just as well for us that the people were orderly and law-abiding, and gave us no serious or prolonged trouble. Making due allowance for the free and easy mode of life and somewhat irregular manners and customs which always prevail in such communities, we allowed them as large an amount of licence as was at all compatible with decency and the maintenance of law and order; but when a man over-stepped this limit, we lost no time in 'dropping on him' and so the people—naturally inclined to be peaceful and law-abiding: another difference, by the way, from some other mining settlements!—came to have a very wholesome respect for us. And not only were we shown respect, but we were always treated with very great civility on all sides, and this helped to make our task an easy one, much easier, in fact, than we had expected, or than it might very well have been.

The freezing-up of the river is a notable sight, though less so than the break-up in the spring. The first sign of it which we had was when the small streams started 'throwing ice'—*i.e.* ice started running down them in blocks into the main stream. The appearance of this as seen from some distance is very similar to that of a 'choppy' sea in the Channel: it is not until one gets nearer that one can distinguish the blocks of ice. These blocks rise from the bottom of the rivers, and are evidently the remains of the last winter's ice which had not all run out in the spring. It must have been frozen hard on to the bottom; released by the gradual rising of the temperature of the water, which of course reaches the highest point in the 'fall' after the atmosphere has begun to turn chilly; and have then risen to form the first beginnings of the succeeding winter's block-up.This state of things goes on for a time, the progress getting rapidly slower and the ice thicker, until it almost ceases to move altogether. The river then presents an appearance not unlike that of a fleet of fishing-boats riding at anchor close together. The blocks of ice are still separate and move up and down, but their onward movement is for the most part checked by the river being too full to allow space for it. The tributaries are continuing to pour in their quota, and occasionally the whole mass will shift a few yards further down until the whole river becomes a hopeless and inextricable 'jam' which speedily 'freezes up rough' into one huge solid mass—a river of motionless ice.

So tremendous has been the pressure of fresh ice crowding down upon that already stationary, that huge blocks are forced upwards above the surface of the rest, and so freeze in, forming little mountain-tops of ice above the surrounding plain. Many of these blocks were as large as big houses. Sometimes great fissures will open up as they do on glaciers in the Alps, whilst in other places there may be considerable expanses of moderately level ice. Later on the whole is covered with six or eight feet of snow, which freezes as fast as it falls, and this gives the river a fallaciously smooth appearance in the photographs, the biggest blocks alone showing up to any remarkable height.

Speaking of photographs reminds me of some more peculiar experiences I had in the preparation of my views, some of which have been included in this volume. My outfitter unfortunately neglected to provide me with a colour-screen, and therefore many of my photos of snow effects lose much of the startling brilliancy of the originals owing to the snow appearing so dead-white in the prints. Isochromatic plates are useful, but they will not entirely do away with this defect. 'Snow-scapes' as I see they are now called, are in some ways the hardest branch of out-door photography, and some contrivance for neutralizing this dead whiteness and monotony is indispensable. Then the water of the Yukon (when it is possible to get any) is normally of the colour of white mud, which is not exactly the most suitable for washing plates or prints. In winter water had to be got by going out on to the middle of the river and digging ice-holes, or by bringing in frozen snow and melting it. This was again a drawback to successful photography, inasmuch as one's supply of water was very limited, and not of the cleanest, and most of my plates show signs of insufficient washing, because I could not command sufficient water to 'eliminate all the Hypo' as the manuals say. I used eikonogen entirely for developing, and borax for toning, and always used all solutions at a temperature of at least 70° Fahr.

However, in spite of all these difficulties and drawbacks, I succeeded in bringing safely home close on one hundred negatives, many of them, I think I may say, very good ones. The prints in my scrap-book have an interest which is probably so far unique. They were all toned with a solution made of nitro-hydrochloric acid and pure Yukon gold, dug straight out of the drift. This, mixed with water and a small lump of borax, was the only toning agent I had, and a remarkably good one it was. The prints are all of a rich purple-black, and fairly free from stains, especially when one takes into consideration the state of the water-supply, and the fact that many of them were made on paper, which I had had fifteen months in stock, and which had 'roughed' it considerably on sea and land. It may interest amateur photographers to know that in addition to a supply of 'aristotype P.O.P.,' supplied by a firm in New York, I had several packets of the Eastman Co.'s 'solio,' which stood the test—no light one for a sensitive substance like that— exceedingly well.

It was on October 17, 1895, that the Yukon finally froze up. After that date there was no perceptible movement in the ice till the following spring. The head-waters were probably closed before this date, for the river freezes right up to its source, and the long line of lakes at the head are also icebound all through the winter. On October 28 the highest temperature was 17°, and the lowest 15.5°, and after that date it was freezing every night. On one or two occasions the thermometer was above freezing-point during the warmest hour or so of the day, but it speedily fell again. On the 29th, for instance, a maximum temperature of 36.5° was registered, but it was only for a very short time.

The last occasion that winter during which the thermometer rose above freezing-point was on October 21, *from November 1 until the following spring it never once thawed*. The first sign of anything of a thaw was on March 14, 1896, when the thermometer rose for half-an-hour to 39°. After November 10 the thermometer was below zero every night, and it was then that the cold weather started in earnest. During December and January it never once rose above zero by day or night. In January especially we had very steady cold weather. The average temperature for that month worked out very close to 48° below zero—or 80° of frost. On the 26th of that month the thermometer fell to 73° below zero.

It was a common sight to see a good-sized encampment of Indians with fires burning merrily, pitched right in what had once been mid-stream, and there they would stay during the winter, even erecting such comparatively permanent things as 'caches'—small store-huts raised on long supports above the level of their dwelling-huts, not at all unlike the lake-dwellings in Switzerland.

In spite of the fact that considerably more than three-quarters of the whole mining is and only can be done in winter, the miners mostly stay in their shacks during the days of very excessive cold. A miner has means of his own of measuring the intensity of the cold, for he does not usually find room for a 'Negretti and Zambra' in his pack. But his method is equally effective. He merely hangs out a bottle of mercury, which he knows freezes at 40° below zero. When he sees that frozen he usually stays within-doors. Some hardier spirits take no notice of the mercury, and impose a severer test upon their endurance. These hang out a bottle of somebody's patent 'pain-killer'—a mixture which contains a large percentage of pure alcohol. Now Ogilvie, the lexicographer, states in his 1882 edition, that alcohol has 'never been frozen.' The person responsible for that statement had obviously never visited the Yukon, for it is common knowledge among miners there that pure alcohol freezes at 72° below zero. On the rare occasions when a man has found his 'pain-killer' thermometer—'gelumeter' would be a more appropriate name—frozen, he has invariably decided that it is too cold to do any digging that day, be he never so hardy.

Our life during the first winter was more or less regular. We had no definite area to look after, and no fixed system of supervision. We made occasional patrols round the principal creeks at which mining was going on, but whether it was that the men were really a peaceable, orderly lot, or whether the mere knowledge of our presence and the fact that we held supreme power acted as a healthy restraint, I do not know. Probably there was a little of both. But be that as it may, we had very little difficulty with them all through the winter, and no serious case to deal with at all. At first the question of the Boundary was still unsettled, and we had to proceed somewhat cautiously. When there was any little trouble we were quickly on the spot, and our arrival was usually sufficient to bring it to an end. As soon as the Boundary question was definitely decided, we patrolled round Glacier and Miller Creeks, and collected the mining dues from the various claims. There was no Gold Commissioner there, and all this sort of work devolved upon us. This meant a journey up Forty Mile river, and then a long march of twenty-six miles across hilly country to Sixty Mile. It was very rough travelling with dogs and sleighs.

Practically the whole of the rest of our time was spent in 'rustling' wood. It took us all our time to get sufficient to keep the (very necessary) fires going.

In travelling with dogs—of which I shall have more to say in the next chapter—you generally have four or five, which you harness to a low, narrow sledge. Occasionally when you come to a stretch of smooth frozen snow in travelling on the river, and your sledge is not too heavily laden, you may be able to take a short ride on it yourself, for they run very easily on smooth ground, and the dogs are strong and wiry animals and capable of pulling a heavy weight even over rough ground. But more often you have to run alongside, or even go on ahead on your snow-shoes to clear a track for the dogs and sleigh. In addition to your own provisions you have to carry all your dog's food on the sledge. The best 'brand' of this is dry salmon. But you cannot always depend on being able to get this, and an effective substitute is bacon and flour boiled up together.

At that time flour was the cheapest commodity up there, selling at $8 a hundred. It has gone up since, and we were ourselves, as I have already said, on short rations during the following winter. When a steamer bearing provisions arrives during the summer there is an immediate rush to secure them, and the two or three old log huts that constitute the stores, are not able to keep pace with the demand. They take good care, however, that no man shall get more than he requires for his own personal use, and so prevent a 'corner' in any line of goods. All supplies are, therefore, on arrival divided up as nearly equally as possible. Each Company had their own steamers, and these were the only ones coming up the river in those days.

Our staple food during the winter, and practically during the whole two years we were there, was bacon and dry brown beans, of which we took up a large supply. We mostly drank tea with occasional bursts of execrably bad whisky—which was not, however, included in the rations supplied by Government. The only variation to bacon and beans that we had was when we were able to get fresh meat or fish from the Indians, and this—the latter especially—was only very seldom. Some of us took up condensed milk, but the majority went without milk altogether. We were our own bakers, and also manufactured our own yeast.

There are two ways of doing this. If you have hops to use, you are a Sybarite and can make proper hop-yeast; but the miners mostly adopt the second alternative, which is known as sour-dough yeast. This is very simply made. All that has to be done is to mix a little flour and water and leave it till it turns sour, when it acquires all the leavening qualities of proper yeast. It has become such an institution up there, that one of the islands in Forty Mile river has been christened 'Sour-dough Island.'

The miners also principally subsisted on bacon and beans, with some caribou and moose when they can get any. These men generally have a little portable tin stove and a frying-pan in their shacks. With a frying-pan and a pot you can cook almost anything if you set about it the right way. Some men used to cook in their gold-pans.

There was a continual stream of miners passing in and out of Forty Mile all the winter. The result was that the population was entirely a floating one, but the numbers remained stationary on the whole. There was abundant variety of all kinds, both of men and amusements. Several saloons were kept busily going day and night, and did a roaring trade. There was also a variety entertainment started by an enterprising manager with a troop of music-hall girls from San Francisco. The enter-tainment was really excellent, especially the dancing of one or two of the girls. Some of the scenery was quite elaborate: one of the favourite turns—a drama in two chapters—in which, by the way, not a soul appeared on the stage from first to last, had for its setting a richly-furnished and upholstered room with table, Chippendale chairs, heavy curtains, and richly-carved buffet with pier-glass complete! And this was in an almost uninhabited country within a few miles of the Arctic Circle. After the performance, audience and performers would adjourn to the nearest saloon, and generally contrived to make things 'a bit lively' in the course of the night. But although they were noisy—often boisterously so—and there was a rough and ready unconventionality about some of the subsequent proceedings, I never saw anything the least objectionable take place when I was on duty, and we had very little difficulty arising from the presence of the saloons. I think this says a good deal for the general 'tone' of the pioneers on the Yukon, and certainly contrasts well with tales that have filtered through of doings in some of the other mining centres.

When he is at work the miner drinks little but tea and a small quantity of coffee, but when he 'comes to town' he generally indulges in a 'fling' for a day or two, until he is tired of it, or his 'sack' of gold is emptied. Gold-dust is the currency there, and absolute honesty is the order of the day. When a miner goes into a saloon or a store to buy anything, he flings down his sack on to the bar or counter, and turns his back whilst the dealer weighs out the amount in his scales. The latter would be grossly insulted were he to see you watching him, and the man who was seen to be keeping his eye on his sack or the weights whilst the amount was being weighed out would be considered 'no gentleman.' Such a thing as cheating is unknown in these transactions. One man was once detected at it, and it was evidently held that it would not be good either for the community or for his own moral welfare that he should be allowed to try it on a second time, for within a very short time of detection a bullet had placed him beyond the reach of further temptation. This was before our arrival!

Drinks and cigars in these saloons cost four 'bits' (50 cents, or about 2s.) apiece. As the supply of whisky was very limited, and the throats down which it was poured were innumerable, it was found necessary to create some sort of a supply to meet the demand. This concoction was known as 'hooch'; and disgusting as it is, it is doubtful if it is much more poisonous than the whisky itself. This latter goes by the name of 'Forty rod whisky'—a facetious allusion to its supposed power of killing at that distance!

The manufacture of 'hooch' which is undertaken by the saloon-keepers themselves, is weirdly horrible. It is as follows:

Take of sugar of molasses an unlimited quantity; add a small percentage of dried fruit or, in summer, of berries; ferment with sour dough; flavour to taste with anything handy—the 'higher' flavoured the better—such as old boots, discarded (and unwashed) foot-rags, and other delicacies of a similar nature. After fermentation, place in a rough sort of sill, for preference an empty coal-oil (kerosene) tin, and serve hot according to taste.

A very small quantity of this filth produces an immediate effect. The price for this is also four 'bits' a drink. Dropping in for a drink is an expensive matter—if you get off with the expenditure of $100 you may consider yourself lucky—for by the unwritten etiquette of the country, you must call in every one within sight to have a drink at your expense at the same time. To refuse a proffered glass is an unpardonable insult—the only loophole of escape left is to take a cigar instead, and it is a toss-up which is the least deadly!